Naked Germany

Naked Germany

Health, Race and the Nation

Chad Ross

Oxford • New York

English edition
First published in 2005 by
Berg
Editorial offices:
First Floor, Angel Court, 81 St Clements Street, Oxford OX4 1AW, UK
175 Fifth Avenue, New York, NY 10010, USA

© Chad Ross 2005

All rights reserved.
No part of this publication may be reproduced in any form
or by any means without the written permission of Berg.

Berg is the imprint of Oxford International Publishers Ltd.

Library of Congress Cataloging-in-Publication Data
Ross, Chad.
 Naked Germany : health, race and the nation / Chad Ross.
  p. cm
 Includes bibliographical references and index.
 ISBN 1-85973-861-3—ISBN 1-85973-866-4 (pbk.)
1. Nudism—Germany—History—20th century. 2. Nudism—Social aspects—Germany. I. Title
GV451.3.G3R67 2005
613'.194'09430904—dc22   2004023160

British Library Cataloguing-in-Publication Data
A catalogue record for this book is available from the British Library.

ISBN 978-1-85973-866-5

Typeset by Avocet Typeset, Chilton, Aylesbury, Bucks
Printed in the United Kingdom by Biddles Ltd, King's Lynn.

www.bergpublishers.com

Contents

List of Figures		vii
Acknowledgments		ix
Introduction: The Decline of the Germans		1
1	Nudism and Nudists	15
2	Pastors, Priests, Nazis and Police: The Moral and Political Campaigns against *Nacktkultur*	35
3	Nudism and Medicine	67
4	The Healthy Body	83
5	The Beautiful Body	101
6	The Nudist Woman	119
7	Sex, Race and Nudism	135
Epilogue		161
Notes		169
Select Bibliography		211
Index		229

List of Figures

1.1	Richard Ungewitter, one of the most important and earliest of nudist ideologues.	17
1.2	Here park grounds are improved by nudists.	21
2.1	Club life. Swimming in Frankfurt.	37
3.1	A woman ascends a mountain peak.	70
3.2	Nudists often traveled to Germany's waterways to practice nudism.	71
4.1	The sun held enormous power and appeal for nudists.	87
4.2	Three nudists play in the snow.	91
4.3	Nudists working in a quarry.	92
4.4	Three women having a snack.	95
4.5	Having fun with friends in the snow.	96
5.1	'Does housework exhaust? Not us.'	102
5.2	An idealized communion with nature.	107
5.2	Nudists sought to recreate themselves in the image of their Greco-Germanic ancestors.	108
5.4	A healthy, well-built body was the ideal.	115
6.1	Song and companionship at the nudist club.	120
6.2	Nudist girls return from swimming.	125
7.1	Body training or having fun?	152
7.2	German nudists sunning themselves.	159

Acknowledgments

The genesis for this book comes from reading Hans Fallada's novel *Kleiner man, was nun?* In the story, Pinneberg, the hero, unexpectedly finds himself participating in a night of naked swimming with his friend, Heilbutt, while his wife is in hospital delivering their child. Pinneberg's response to the whole idea of being publicly naked intrigued me, and as I explored the topic more, both in literature and in conversations with friends, in particular David Wakefield and Joel Brereton, the idea intrigued me too. Greatly encouraged by my advisor's enthusiasm and support, I explored it further. For the completion of this book I owe thanks to a number of individuals and institutions without whose help, guidance, support and friendship neither research nor writing and finishing would have been possible.

Early research for this dissertation was conducted on the grounds of the American Nudist Research Library (ANRL) located in Kissimmee, Florida. The ANRL is now the home of the Johnson Archive of Nudism, an impressive and large collection of nudist thought and publications spanning a number of decades and a number of languages. I would like to thank in particular the staff of the library, Dott, Mr and Mrs Carl Sturm, and President Helen Fischer for their hospitality and generosity in allowing me to visit and to work.

The bulk of the research for this book was conducted at the International Nudist Library located in Baunatal, near Kassel, Germany. Founded by Karwilli Damm and now operated by his son Jörg Damm, the International Nudist Library has a very large and important collection of works that span a number of fields, all related to the human body, sexuality and, of course, nudism. It is an invaluable resource for anyone interested in *Nacktkultur*. The magnanimity of the Damm family was exceeded only by its friendliness, especially that of Gisela and Hilde, who during my seven month visit there always had time for a friendly chat or musical interlude.

I would like to thank the Friedrich-Ebert-Stiftung and Maria Holona for the generous grant that enabled me to spend a year in various archives throughout Germany and the International Nudist Library in Baunatal. The Department of History at the University of Missouri also funded a good portion of my research, both in Florida and in the Federal Republic, for which I am grateful.

In Germany, a number of people deserve special thanks for their help with my research. I wish to thank Herr Prof. Dr Christoph Dipper of the Universität

Darmstadt for agreeing to be my *Betreuer*; his help was repeated and much appreciated. My research took me to a number of archives, and I am deeply indebted to the staffs of them, who with only the slightest, occasional giggle would bring me my requested files on *Nacktkultur*.

Professionally, vast sections of this work have been improved by the comments of a number of people at various conferences. I would like to thank in particular the German Historical Institute, Richard Wetzells, Andy Daum, Roger Chickering, Adelheid von Saldern, Ulrich Hebert and all the participants of the GHI's Trans Atlantic Doctoral Seminar in 2001. The comments of Frank Biess, David Sabean and Julia Bruggemann at the German Studies Association Conference and at the American Historical Association's annual meeting in Chicago were critical and helpful in straightening out a number of ideas about the nudists. The criticisms and comments of Karin Schutjer, Linda Reeder, Richard Bienvenu, Cathryn Rymph, and of course, my *Doktorvater* Jonathan Sperber greatly aided the revising of the book. My many thanks to all of you.

At Berg Publishers I would like to thank Kathleen May and Ken Bruce and the anonymous reader for their guidance, support and, above all, patience and encouragement.

A year abroad can be a long, lonely time. For us, this was not the case, and we were befriended by a number of Germans, whose kindness, friendship, love and concern for our well-being were always forthcoming, and very much appreciated. In Kassel, Inge and Dieter Hoffmann opened their hearts and their home to us; American Mary Dylewski was a friend with whom we could always commiserate and just talk. In Kiel, the Hoffmann family, Sigrid-Ursula, Gerd and Matthias, once again helped this wayward Texan, this time with wife and family, adjust to living in Germany. In Stuttgart, the Ibald family kindly opened its doors to the (now) three of us, as in Berlin-Friedrichshain Jochen Pridat did. In Buxtehude, old friends Ingrid, Bernhard and Michael Will once again made their home my home. In Munich, Julia Hoffmann probably got more than she bargained for when we showed up at her apartment, but she enthusiastically showed us her city, for which we are still thankful. It is no exaggeration that without the generosity of the Kassel Hoffmanns, the Kiel Hoffmanns, the Damms, the Ibalds, the Wills, Jochen Pridat, Gesa O., Anita Jensch of AOK, *Hebamme* Birke Thie, the staff of Klinik Dr Koch, Meike Dallmann of Lübeck and so many others, much valuable research would not have been done. All together they made Germany a *Heimat* for us.

Both during the research and writing and rewriting of this book, Vikki Vickers, Hillery and Alex Oberle, Kristi Keuhn, Lorie Vanchena, Cassandra Rogers, Lisa Higgins, Rebecca, Eric, and Ian Thompson made important, intangible contributions. Without their friendship and help, this book would be much less than it is. My thanks to Barbara Phillips for teaching me German, lo these many years.

Our year in Germany was made still more fun and exciting – and less distant –

by a number of people who visited and lightened our hearts. Among these I wish to thank Greta Dowling, Cathleen Waters, Susan and David Weingärtner, Nancy and Frank Claunts, Becky, Ron and E. Scott Ross. Midway through the year, Aruna Isabel decided to arrive, and she continues to lighten our hearts. To Aruna, whose whole life has thus existed alongside that of this project, I am happy to say: Daddy can play now.

I dedicate this book to my mother, who gave me roots and wings, strength and will; my father, who taught me to question, to write, to imagine and to achieve, and as a great storyteller gave me a sense of history; finally to my wife, Symbra, the bravest and most intrepid traveler I know, for all the joy, love and happiness she has brought me.

Chad Ross

Introduction: The Decline of the Germans

Emerging at the end of the nineteenth century out of dissatisfaction with Germany and disgust at Germans was the ideology of *Nacktkulktur*, or nudism. German nudism was one of a number of loosely confederated reform movements known collectively as *Lebensreform* that sought to change Germans and Germany. The ideology of nudism revolved around the idea of first healing and then beautifying the physical body as part of the larger effort of reforming and regenerating the national or racial body to create a vigorous and racially pure Germanic nation. In nudism, reforming the *Volk* began with reforming the individual. From its earliest appearance, nudism established its goal as nothing less than the transformation of the German nation into a harmonious, strong, racially pure *Volk* by first transforming Germans into healthy and beautiful bearers of the racial seed.

Unlike other utopian ideologies, the ideology of nudism was not a revolutionary movement that sought to transform from above first Germany and then Germans. In *Nacktkultur* there would be no nudist 'seizure of power.' Rather, in German nudism personal and national regeneration were intimately connected; to reform the individual body was to reform the national or racial body. In its very structure, proponents argued, *Nacktkultur* was designed to benefit the individual first and the *Volk* second.[1] From its earliest days, nudism was conceived and practiced as a means by which Germans could regenerate their nation by first regenerating themselves into healthy and beautiful bearers of the race, who, while breeding a racially pure *Volk*, would also establish a nature-based utopia and a conflict-free society more akin to that of their ancient Germanic ancestors.

The Curse of the Nineteenth Century

Germany at the dawn of the twentieth century was a nation poised to assume a dominant role in world affairs. Wilhelm II's celebrated declaration that Germany needed to obtain a 'place in the sun' conveyed the image of Germany as a vigorous and robust nation, one literally bursting at its borders, ready to expand into the world, as indeed in many respects it was. The years after national unification had seen Germany grow from a patchwork collection of semi-agricultural states to one of the world's industrial powerhouses in steel manufacturing as well as in the newer chemical and electrical industries. German industry grew at a steady rate in

1

the last third of the nineteenth century, despite the economic depression of those same years, bringing with it prosperity, population growth and urbanization. By 1900, at the latest, industrialization had transformed Germany into a fully modern society, complete with a burgeoning population crammed into crowded cities and an industrial economy. In all outward appearances, Germany seemed the very model of a dynamic nation.

Nationhood, industrialization, rapid population growth and the development of large cities at the end of the nineteenth century effected a fundamental transformation of German society, which brought with it unparalleled anxiety and alarm for many Germans. Disappointingly, national unification had not brought unity along with it, but rather had magnified and intensified social tensions, many of which were preexisting in German society before 1871. Centuries-old religious differences not only persisted, but also were exacerbated by Bismarck's attack on the Catholic minority during his Kulturkampf. Industrialization created vast inequalities of wealth and power, as well as a class consciousness that found expression in the organization of Europe's largest and most disciplined socialist party, the German Social Democrats (SPD). Politically, Bismarck's divisive political system and rule retarded democratic initiative and process, especially among the middle classes, and prevented the creation of an effective forum for debate or even a national consensus. His system did not, however, discourage political party growth, even among the repressed or outlawed parties, which further heightened notions of factionalism. Separated by religion, class and politics Germans had precious little that contributed to a sense of national belonging. In short, Germany was in peril.

The sense of dislocation wrought by such processes found expression in a number of reactionary intellectual and social movements.[2] Many of the movements and ideologies that sought to overcome the divisions separating Germans from each other focused increasingly on German culture or on Germans themselves in order to unite the fractured *Volk*, and made extensive use of national images and symbols, whether from modern or ancient eras.[3] Foreign influences, too, were purged from German culture and thought. Attempts, for example, were made to Germanize Christianity both in its Protestant and Catholic varieties.[4]

The nineteenth century was a dangerous one not only for the German nation, which despite all of its apparent progress and modernity was nonetheless perceived as being in a state of advanced decay by nudists and other cultural critics. Germans, too, suffered because of the nineteenth century. The prosperity brought by capitalism and industry changed Germans' priorities, pushing them more towards 'unGerman' pursuits such as dogmatic materialism, Philistinism (*Spießbürgertum*) or the superficial pursuit of fashion.[5] 'The desire for money and the pleasures it could purchase, the reckless pursuit of economic or political power, the estrangement from nature and the *Heimat*,' wrote the pastor turned painter

Magnus Weidemann, had left the German *Volk*, 'degenerate, fallen into decay from fashion-fever, pleasure madness [*Lustwahn*], nervous derangement and lowered morals.'[6]

To nudists it was obvious that Germans had degenerated over the course of the nineteenth century. Observing his contemporaries, one nudist commented that 'men walk about with reddened, fixed, glassy eyes, bald heads, breathing only in gasps, with a sagging gut and spongy, flabby muscles, behind whom women, first as corseted marionettes, later in the greatest corpulence, waddle.'[7] Another announced that 'instead of a generation founded on an ideal way of looking at life that possessed strong, resistant bodies, healthy, natural [*unbefangen*] intellects, and whose souls were noble,' pre-1914 German society 'raised a weak and nervous generation, ignoble in its thoughts and actions, oriented not to affirming life, but to negating it.'[8] Still another believed the 'system of personal and economic freedom and development of sciences and technology' that took root in the nineteenth century had slowly eaten away at the German character until, as a nation of paunchy beer-swillers or effete thinkers, the race's continued existence had become doubtful.[9]

As a whole, the *Lebensreform* movement aimed to reform the Germans and Germany. Viewed in its component parts, the various Life-Reform groups offer their suggestion as to what was Germany's root problem. Educational reformers believed new schooling philosophies were needed; environmentalists wanted to lessen the blow dealt to nature by industry and cities; the temperance campaign sought to sober Germans; the list could go on. Life-Reform was broad and complex.[10] The ideology of nudism understood that the root of all decay and degeneration stemmed from the denigration of the body. To be sure, nudism shared a number of philosophical points with other Life-reformers, including environmentalism, education reform, temperance, food reform, sex reform and others. However, in nudism, the declining German nation could only be repaired by first building better Germans, and Germans could only be regenerated by transforming their bodies. The body, of course, needed to be returned to its natural, naked state so that it could effect change upwards: first Germans, then the race and nation.

In the nineteenth century, nudists argued, the body, which for centuries found itself under the domination and control of the Christian worldview and which had been denigrated in favor of the spirit, was forced to retreat still further in importance behind the mind as well. By the turn of the twentieth century, the body had become so neglected and unimportant that social and national degeneration were the only possible outcomes, and indeed, along with racial decline, appeared to be spreading apace. Regardless which element of the classical trinity was being promoted or neglected, the imbalance would exact a destructive toll on the individual and adversely affect social institutions as well.

The Shattered Trinity

The fundamental problem with the modern body, as the nudists understood it, was that it was not internally whole. Modern Europeans, Germans especially, had lost the harmonious, internal balance of body, mind and spirit that nudists alleged had prevailed at the dawn of humanity and that had been the foundation of Western, specifically Greek and Germanic, culture. Worse still, few had any concept of the 'racial unity of mind and body.'[11] The German body had clearly decayed. Its internal unity fractured; a decline that presaged and likely caused the national decay that seemed so evident to so many contemporary observers.

Any imbalance in the trinity could produce harmful results for one or both of the other components of the body. For example, since the body was the 'mirror of the soul,' any corruption of one's physical form would eventually cause equally negative effects on the soul or intellect.[12] Emphasizing the value or superiority of the body at the expense of the soul would only result in significant damage to the soul. 'Generally speaking,' noted author K. Besser, 'a disharmonious physical constitution leads to a disharmonious tension of the soul.'[13] Degeneration of the body, warned another, would eventually cause spiritual degeneration.[14] Finally, noted one author, the struggle to revive Germans' souls was a great struggle, one 'that might be greater than the struggle for the health of our bodies.'[15]

Rehabilitating the body was key to creating new Germans and a new Germany. The body was understood as the 'foundation and expressive form of the soul and the mind.'[16] 'The body,' realized one author, 'was the bearer of the intellectual-spiritual, which gained its expression from the body, and which together constructed a whole.'[17] Nudist activity made the body once again a healthy place for the soul to reside, and indeed fostered a unity of body and soul not seen since the arrival of Christianity so many centuries before.[18]

Neglect of the body, while possibly beneficial in the short term, to promote, for example, the development of one's intellect or spiritual needs, could not long continue before it began to exert a negative effect on individuals, society or the race. Only in a healthy body could a powerful intellect or a 'glowing spirit' expect to reside.[19] Denigration of the body only created other problems, often affecting the mind or the soul, not to mention creating a disparity that eventually expressed itself in a sunken culture.

Generally speaking, nudist authors agreed that it was the intellect that had lately come to dominate the trinity of body-mind-soul. Germany, bluntly put, had become too intellectual. The domination of the intellect at the expense of both soul and body generated a society that destroyed bodies and culture. 'One sensed quite suddenly that our seemingly so scientifically and technically advanced era possessed only a civilization, that is to say, a stop-gap settlement of external contradictions, but absolutely no culture, no inner configuration,' argued one nudist.[20]

Human intellectual growth, it seemed, occurred at a high price, namely the atrophying and wasting of the body. 'Human development encouraged mental capabilities far too much, and did so using the body's nourishment for itself, the consequence of which was necessarily the degeneration of the body, and finally that of the mind, which must follow.'[21] Intellectual ascendancy was dangerous for the soul as well as the body. Intellect, reason, knowledge were considered cold, and forced the human soul further into darkness, where it suffered.[22] Nature, nudists maintained, could help restore the soul and begin the process of reintegrating the person.[23] *Nacktkultur* repaired the soul by repairing the body.[24]

Some nudists suggested that it was simply civilization that was to blame for the imbalance, as it damaged the human body.[25] One author believed the origin of the disunited German Self occurred, almost ironically, because of the unique character and duty of the German as a bearer of culture, bringer of civilization and historical beacon of advancement to unenlightened peoples across the globe. It was the instinctive drive of all 'civilized peoples' (*Kulturvölker*) to pursue their intellectual needs, inadvertently allowing the body to wither, and over time to devolve into the weak, ugly, sickened, disproportionate forms that dominated Germany.[26]

Others located the schism of the body-mind-soul trinity more recently in the society and social environment of the nineteenth century that placed more importance on one's intellect to the conscious denigration of the body. Nudist Hans Vahle said of the nineteenth-century disparity between the mind and body that, 'the importance of intellectual performances led to an exaggeration of the mind with the consequence that everything relating to the body was valued less and less, [the body] was pushed further away.'[27]

In part, this criticism of the ascendancy of the mind over the body was part of the larger Life-Reform and nudist condemnation of the educational system of the day. The German educational system of the nineteenth century focused disproportionately on classicism and idealism, ignored the body and prevented a deeper understanding of it from developing.[28] Schools, complained nudist Adolf Weide, promoted ill health because their instruction only taught and developed the mind. The body was disregarded entirely, as either a subject worthy of teaching or as a form to be developed.[29]

The means by which the imbalance of body-mind-soul occurred was first through the disappearance of the naked body through clothing, and second through the denigration of the idea of both nakedness and the body through a variety of religiously derived social mores carefully reinforced by the needs of bourgeois capitalism, which left the body with little positive meaning. In modern society, it seemed to nudists, the naked man was considered with suspicion and was grossly misunderstood, in part, because civilization had stolen the purity of nakedness. Germans living in civilized society, according to one nudist author, feared the 'self-understood chastity' of nakedness.[30] The way to return Germans to the harmony of body, mind and soul was to correct the imbalance by returning the body to its full position in the trinity.

In the ideology of *Nacktkultur*, the body was the opposite of 'the ideological world of body enmity that has been passed over to us.'[31] Only through intense nudist activity and attention to the body would Germans learn 'that the body is not the enemy of the intellect.'[32] The history of nudism is at once the history of Germany in the twentieth century and the history of the body.

The Body as History

In many ways, the history of the twentieth century itself is the history of the body. Efforts – violent struggles really – to create, to improve, to purify, to regulate, to protect or to eliminate political bodies, national bodies, social bodies, racial bodies, women's bodies, fetal bodies, men's bodies are all characteristic of twentieth-century European history. The desire to transform either the collective body or the individual body or both was far more than a matter of state interest and state policy, however. Individuals were similarly transfixed with the idea of improving their own bodies, and were often equally obsessed with the vision of improving the collective national or racial body. Indeed, in the first half of the twentieth century the effort to transform the German race and nation, an effort that centered foremost on the body, made everybody a soldier, every body a battlefield. The fate of the modern nation was intimately tied to the body, and the nation would rise or fall with the body.

The body is a constant form. It can be altered in a number of different ways, for example through surgery, by weight gain or weight loss; it can be scarred, deformed, and mutilated (intentionally or otherwise), but as a form the body's mutability is limited, it cannot go beyond its basic construction except and until decomposition occurs.[33] The body, however, is far more than the sum of its parts; it exists in a symbolic as well as a physical realm. Human societies have always assigned meaning to the body, subjected it to interpretations, bestowed it with special religious, magical or curative powers, burdened it with metaphors, suffused it with meaning, respected, feared, loved and loathed it.[34]

Unlike the physical body, the symbolic body shifts, changes and mutates in meaning, reflects social and cultural attitudes or in some cases drives them.[35] Over the course of time, the body has transmitted different messages to its many interpreters, shed old connotations and acquired new ones. It has been the site of restless struggle between individuals and various political, religious and scientific authorities.[36] The body has literally embodied the values, prejudices, beliefs and ideologies of whole cultures, races and nations.[37]

As an object of historical inquiry, the body is enormously complex, and unlike categories of gender, sex, race or class, the body seems to deny any effort to construct an adequate theoretical apparatus for use as a tool of historical investigation.[38] There are multiple bodies, each with multiple meanings, often shifting, and all further tempered by the equally shifting and even contradictory perspective of the observer. For individuals, the body is an endless source of mystery, familiarity, delight, disappointment, discovery, pain, pleasure, contradiction, constancy and change – it is overburdened with meaning. For nations and ideologically motivated regimes, the body is at once a threat and a hope, something to protect, to fear, to nurture and to destroy.

The development of the modern body has had a long history. It dates from the Renaissance and especially the sixteenth century, when scientific dissections and anatomical observation of cadavers began to contradict the venerated theories of the body and its construction postulated by ancient physicians, especially Aristotle and Galen. Historians have argued that the distant origins of the modern conception of the body can be located in the eighteenth century, when Enlightenment philosophers, doctors and scientists began to liberate it from the twin tyrannies of the Ancients' postulates and Christian theology, only to subordinate it to their own authority and control over the course of the nineteenth century.

During that same industrious century, the rising middle classes seized the body and subjugated it to a new, more rigorous moral code that strengthened traditional prejudice against the body by combining Christian teachings that eroticized it and anathematized its nakedness with bourgeois notions of productivity, restraint and modesty. The bourgeoisie, armed with its new moral code, sought, insofar as possible, to govern and regulate the body, and to limit and minimize its passions, its sexual impact and overall expression.[39] The body was the focus of vast attention, though at the same time, an unwelcome sight.

By the dawn of the twentieth century, the body had become a source of amazement and pride, a symbol of human strength, ability and endurance. Culminating with the invention of the Modern Olympics in the 1890s, the growth of sport culture in the nineteenth century made the body the main attraction in the great age of athletic competition and exhibitions, a position it continues to hold.[40] A proud symbol of human achievement, of national power and prestige, the body was also a source of popular wonderment and scientific curiosity. Scientific investigations and public exhibitions, such as those at Dresden's Hygiene Museum in 1911 and again in the Weimar Republic at the *Gesolei*, provided important information on the latest research and understanding of the body, health and biology.[41]

Another effect of the cumulative efforts of various medical professionals, bourgeois moralists, state and religious officials was the successful production of an understanding of the body as complex and sinful, mysterious and vulgar and, importantly, as the source of a barely controllable, potentially explosive, dangerous sensuality. If unleashed this threatened the individual with madness, the social order with chaos, and the race with degeneration.[42] Increasingly after the turn of the century, racists and racial theorists located the intellectual and moral attributes of whole races directly on the body, making them just as immutable, just as permanent as the physical characteristics.

The same scientific and popular milieu that informed about the biology of the body, improved its physical form and made it such an important symbol of health, vitality and beauty also introduced a parallel meaning of the body as a threat to personal well-being and national survival. People knew more about the physical body and its functions than ever before, but the implications of such knowledge both for the body itself as well as for society, the race and nation were still largely unknown, if not vexingly ambiguous.[43] Over the course of centuries, familiar or straightforward understandings of the body had been steadily dismantled and replaced with a multitude of meanings that intertwined the physical and the symbolic bodies more closely. The body was both a symbol and, through its sexual and reproductive functions, a transmitter of races, political ideologies, even nations.

Nudism and the Whole Body

The ideological center of nudism was the desire to transform the body, both physically, so that it was healthy and beautiful, and in its meaning, so that it symbolized virtue and Germanness.[44] In nudist ideology the body was the vehicle of national transformation, but the body could itself only be transformed in the naked experience. The body appeared as both a beacon in the chaos and an organizational starting point for a new personal, national and cultural beginning.

Nudists believed themselves to be in revolt against the previous age, whether that of the nineteenth century or the present modern era. 'The current generation,' explained one enthusiastic nudist, 'is fighting for the freedom of the individual from all manner of hindrances and compulsions.'[45] Nudism was 'nothing more than a religiosity that derived predominately from the body, and that overcame the previous imprisonment, devaluation and desecration, and that stormed across the devastated world of the cult of the intellectual,' proclaimed one.[46] Historian George Mosse attributes the turn-of-the-century desire to revolt against the prevailing social norms and conventions as one of the most important impulses behind nudism, and more generally what helped fuel the rediscovery of the human body.[47]

Ridding the body and society at large of the intellectual, ideological vestiges of the non-nudist society and social system that prevailed, or had for centuries prevailed, was crucial to the development of the new German. 'It was not possible and also not conceivable that we could, through the lies around the body, raise ourselves to truth and purity,' commented another nudist author.[48] Liberation of the body from its past constraints, both tangible and intangible, was necessary to develop the new German being, someone whose internal qualities would carry over to rebuild the national consciousness.

Nudism promoted wholeness of body and wholeness of nation and *Volk*; it was a means 'to free people from the excess of harmful, individual sensations.'[49] The body, open and free, was the standard-bearer of this new era. 'Only when one places the body in its proper place, frees it from lies and secretiveness, can one reach the path to intellectual honesty and arrive at a true culture.'[50] To be naked was to build the new body and, more distantly, a superior culture.

Nakedness would set Germans free from the moral order imposed on their bodies by civilization and misdirected moral concepts. Proponents and ideologues of *Nacktkultur* wanted 'to free the body from the presuppositions placed upon it by such a different morality,' and return to it its 'holy naturalness,' in the nude experience. The first step in this process was 'to make the naked body in its movements into an expression of the happy, healthy power of life.'[51] To do so, noted one author, 'we must therefore give our bodies more light, air and sun, specifically, we must provide it with the opportunity to expose itself, unclothed, without covering of any sort, to the air and sunlight, in order to make it stronger and healthier.'[52] Nakedness and attention to the body were singular in their ability to create a person unified of body, mind and spirit. 'Alone from the body-oriented way of living,' explained one author, 'arises internal independence, intellectual and physical efficiency as well as joy of life, all of the highest measure.'[53]

Once naked, the return of Germans to the coveted ideal of internal balance and harmony could begin. Nakedness and devotion to the culture of the body 'can lead to a whole culture, to a cultivation of a complete or whole humanity, to a style of living that will complete itself in later generations, the seeds for which grow in the life of light.'[54] Possessing a healthy and beautiful body provided for the 'highest intellectual accomplishments, the deepest scientific realizations,' and the 'strengthening of morality and character.'[55]

Focusing attention on the body would repair the hidden damage to the soul. 'A person,' declared J.M. Seitz, 'will only become completely beautiful and noble when he or she has a completely beautiful body and an equally beautiful soul.'[56] Reestablishing the body-mind-soul balance meant above all returning the body to its place in the trinity, but not placing too much importance on it, thus inadvertently causing the scales to tip too far towards the body. Body culture, which promised to restore the body to the trinity, also ensured that the perfect balance could be struck and maintained. 'We believe, that it is exactly here that the essence, the sense and the responsibility of *Körperkultur* lies: to connect powerful physicality with deeper intellectualism.'[57]

The intangible effects of nudism on the body and the nudist were among its most important. 'For the future,' observed one nudist visionary, *Nacktkultur* would help create a 'morally pure, internally and externally healthy, powerful, joyous generation [that lived] in harmony with nature.'[58] *Nacktkultur*, argued one author, was best regarded 'as a self-understood and important means to demand the attainment of a renewal of life, outwardly and inwardly.'[59] The new German forged in the nudist experience would possess noble qualities and personality traits that clearly set him or her apart from all previous types.

The new German man, for example, born in the nudist experience would reject the boorish behavior of his predecessors, avoiding student fraternities or the debauchery of long nights spent at the tavern.[60] The person who practiced *Nacktkultur* would emerge as a unified, calm, sexually chaste naked person possessing inner peace, in stark contrast to both the pre-World War and immediate post-World War types, who, drenched in sexual over-stimulation, nervousness, ill health, and bound by a negative, Christian-inspired view of the body, could not expect to ever attain inner peace or unity.[61] The foundation for this new German and the new Germany was the body, which through interaction between its naked self, the sun, air, light and nature would be made healthy and beautiful. Once naked, healthy and beautiful, the transformation of the body would be completed by creating a new meaning for it in nature and under the watchful eyes of fellow Germans.

Nakedness and naked activity would build a unified person, and constitute ultimately a liberation of humanity.[62] Nudism and the naked experience promoted unity of the individual and of the *Volk* and nation. The nudist experience and the ideology of *Nacktkultur* corrected the fragmenting and divisive tendency of the modern world that left people isolated in social classes and artificial environments and instead encouraged an awareness that one belonged to a larger community, whether nation or race, or both. Nakedness itself 'meant a neglect, a disdain for rank, title and purse.'[63] One could only come to 'a proper life when he or she bound all parts and values of the body,' in particular the body with the mind and soul.[64] Nudism would reverse the atomizing effects of centuries of history, and unify bodies, souls, minds, as well as religions, classes and genders into an organically whole, unified nation.

Nudism in Germany

Nudist ideology underwent little change in the first half of the twentieth century. As a movement, nudism grew steadily throughout the repressive Kaiserreich and the democratic Weimar Republic. The experience and loss of the First World War, in fact, imparted a sense of urgency to the apparent national and racial degeneration, and nudist groups multiplied in the 1920s. Initially banned by the Nazis in 1933, nudism was soon recognized as an important social movement with an ideology and goals similar to the Nazis' own. Nudism became Nazified as Deutsche Leibeszucht (German Body Cultivation) and continued to flourish under a regime that itself attempted to create a racial utopia. The idea of constructing healthy and beautiful bodies in the context of nature with the long-term goal of creating a racially pure society found high levels of support in the NS state.

Previous works on German nudism have presented nudism as a kind of back-to-nature movement, a prototype of the 1960s counterculture.[65] Other German-language studies portray nudism as an aspect of outdoor sports, similar to the famed *Turnvereine*, however, these too fail to consider its racism or utopianism,[66] or have been overly concerned with identifying its main figures without questioning their nudism itself.[67] More recently, Karl Toepfer and others have understood nudism as part of a larger culture of the body, which it undoubtedly was, but also as a critical expression of the 'crisis of modernity,' which overlooks its racism, eugenics and longevity.[68] Michael Hau's recent work is an important contribution to the history of the body, health and beauty in the twentieth-century German context.

A final group attempts less of an analysis of nudism, of its ideology and its practice, but focuses more on reproducing the photographs from the era, in a way highlighting its inherent voyeurism and sexuality, but not in a way that nudists themselves understood it.[69] The historiography of nudism is not extensive, and a number of important issues such as nudism's politically amorphous nature are not adequately addressed in it. Other works, such as Oliver König's *Nacktheit*, are useful sociological studies of the idea of nakedness, often with overlap with the nudist movement in the twentieth century. König's important work is far more concerned with nakedness rather than social nudism, however.[70]

There is also a substantial body of work, including Professor Toepfer's, that has at its center the study of dance, including nudist dance. Naked dance is in its own right deeply important to the transformation of bodies and the nation. Its ideas were not always related to those of the *Nacktkultur* movement. Nudist theorists and writers may have been personally influenced by the naked dance movement, but this influence is rarely expressed in their work. Certainly other independent movements and influences, such as the youth movement or the beauty movement, made much deeper impressions on nudists. I have not included a discussion of naked dance.

Nudists believed deeply in the power of the body, itself healed and beautified in nature, to regenerate and to heal the nation. Nudism was not an anti-modern reaction to Wilhelmine industrialization and urbanization or even the expansion of democracy in the Weimar Republic. Rather, nudism was a way to reconcile and harmonize the deep divisions in the German nation, often exacerbated by industry, politics and religion. A central tenet of nudist ideology was that nudism was not an end in itself, but rather the means to halt present degeneration in order to achieve the larger goal of creating a classless, nudist racial utopia. Nudism was a movement to create a racially better Germany by first building a better personal body.

The focus of this study is the period from roughly 1900 to 1950, when nudism first became practiced and published about and as it moved from fringe phenomenon among a few *völkisch* nationalists in the Kaiserreich to a mass popular movement of the 1920s and finally to its promotion by the National Socialist state in the 1930s. The nudist ideology of health, beauty and race receives particular attention because of what it reveals of German nationalism and the discourse of national or racial regeneration, which loom so large in Germany's twentieth century.

The chapters are organized thematically beginning with discussions of nudism's relationships with German society and various political and religious regimes. The relationship between nudism and the state was never as difficult nor as hostile as ideologues imagined it would be. At worst German society and politicians were indifferent to nudism; more often than not they openly supported local nudists. There was something about nudism that appealed to Germans, regardless of whether they practiced it. The characteristically ambiguous relationship between nudism and the state crystallized with the rise of the Nazis. They found in it an ideology remarkably like their own in a number of ways; whilst they initially banned nudism, then accepted it, they never stopped suspecting it of dangerous political tendencies.

Later chapters focus more heavily on nudism's ideology, exploring its conception of the body in an age of increasing scientization and medicalization. Nudist ideology envisioned a bright, harmonious future for Germany, one that was distinctly different from the present, where the experiences of the twentieth century seemed only to confirm nudists' bleak view of their contemporaries, their bodies and their future. This future would form as a result of nudists transforming their bodies through the natural elements, light, air and sun, mass social nakedness and mutual visual inspection of that nakedness.

Though ultimately all failures, the period 1900–45 featured a number of efforts by Germany to reshape itself, its people and all of Europe. During this time German doctors, politicians and nationalists exercised little restraint in their pursuit of creating a better version of their race. Often the focus of these men centered on altering or destroying others' bodies to effect an improved racial body; rarely did they focus on themselves. German nudism underscores the ways in which the personal body relates to the national or racial body and the ways in which they can both be formed and reformed. In nudism the path to a superior racial, national and social body began with healing and beautifying one's own body using only sunshine, fresh air and its unadorned self.

A Note on Terms

There are a number of different spellings and terms for nudism, including *Nacktkultur*, *Freikörperkultur* and, more recently, *Naturismus*. There are a variety of reasons for nudism's name changes. In some cases the change was a reaction to the popular conception of nudists as a sexually wild, orgiastic bunch. For example, the term *Nacktkultur* became so saturated with negative connotation attached to it because of confusion in the popular mind with what occurred in the seedy nightclubs and racy dance revues that dotted urban Germany's streetscape in the 1920s 'that it threatened to become an expression for the worst outgrowths of our morally empty civilization,' explained Hans Surén.[71] Eventually, it was discarded in favor of the term *Freikörperkultur*, or 'free-body culture,' often abbreviated simply as FKK.

By 1930, at the latest, the use of the term FKK had become common both among nudists as well as non-nudists; however, lamented one author, few understood what was really meant by it, suggesting that despite the name change some confusing of nudism with eroticism by the non-nudist population nevertheless persisted.[72] The accepted terminology of nudism would remain FKK roughly until the middle of the 1930s, when it would again undergo a change, becoming officially known in the Nazi canon as Deutsche Leibeszucht, or 'German Body Cultivation'; this was most likely in order to project more directly Nazi ideological and racial tenets. After the Second World War, much as Germans attempted to forget and to distance themselves from the Hitler regime's excesses and ideology, so too did nudists endeavor, more or less successfully, to rid their ideology of all that suggested or reminded of Nazism or racial ideology, which was also the occasion for nudism to undergo another name change, reverting back to FKK.

In the post Second World War era, nudists and non-nudists alike would again use the term FKK, in rotation with the word 'nudism' (*der Nudismus*) to designate nudism. Both terms suggested little or no association with Nazism, or more distantly with the racists and racial hygienists of the Weimar and Wilhelmine eras. In more recent years, however, in a move that spans linguistic borders, true believers have begun calling themselves 'naturists,' both because of a creeping association of the term FKK with lewdness or even 'swinging,' mildly reminiscent of nudists' experiences of the 1920s, and to reflect more accurately what they believe the purpose of nudism is, namely to be natural and in a natural environment.[73]

Throughout the text, I have elected to use *Nacktkultur* (literally 'naked culture') as a synonym for nudism, as it was the first term devised by nudists, and, I think, one that best captures the ideas of the early ideology.

–1–

Nudism and Nudists

In December 1918, the German League for the Encouragement of Naked and Free-Swimming petitioned local police officials for permission to swim naked and for a general repeal of prohibitions against nakedness.[1] The naked body, seeming to appear at the moment just before the birth of the Weimar Republic, just as Germany descended into political, social and economic chaos, would in many ways come to be the characteristic symbol of the roaring twenties. Then as now, the naked body and the Weimar Republic have been linked in the popular imagination, and rightly so. In many ways, the 1920s was the decade of wild nights of booze and sex, of erotic nightclub dancing, of risqué cabarets, of Josephine Baker and others stripping, of nakedness.[2]

Though no less famous, the nakedness advocated and petitioned for by the German League for the Encouragement of Naked and Free-Swimming, however, was altogether different from the nakedness of Weimar's celebrated cabarets and kicklines. The German League for the Encouragement of Naked and Free-Swimming and the hundreds of nudist leagues like it throughout Germany differed from the naked dancers and eroticized audiences of nightclubs in certain key regards. By 1918, when the rest of Germany seemed to discover the appeal of the naked, albeit erotic, body, German nudism was already a well-established ideology and practice. In the twentieth century, nudism grew quickly, reaching the level of a mass cultural phenomenon by the 1920s, which it has remained ever since. This is quite unlike the nakedness of cabarets, which have come and gone with Germany's many different political regimes.

The Spread of Nudism

The general trajectory of nudism's growth over the past century is one of increased popularity and participation, in the face of very little resistance by either state or church officials. Aside from two brief episodes in the early 1930s, one initiated by the Prussian government in 1932 and the other an outright (but quickly rescinded) prohibition by the Nazis in 1933, the major impediment to the growth of organized nudism were the nudists themselves, especially during the very earliest years of nudists practicing the ideology.

Speaking in the broadest terms, the history of German nudism in the twentieth century has two distinct phases, pre- and post-1945. The post-1945 era is largely beyond the scope of this study; however, its characteristics can be sketched. Nudism since the Second World War has been very much the free-time activity, widely spread throughout the population that early nudist proponents dreamed it someday would be. Chiefly, post-1945 German nudism is notable for its lack of ideology, though it still retains its fundamental belief in the benefits, superiority and naturalness of the naked body and the public demonstration of that nakedness.

The nudism of the pre-1945 era, that which is the focus of this study, is, unlike its postwar counterpart. It is a deeply ideological, often racist, eugenics-oriented, utopian belief in the power of nakedness to transform the body and in the power of the naked body to transform Germans and Germany, physically, spiritually, metaphorically and racially, into better individuals, a better race and a better nation.

Ideally, *Nacktkultur* belonged among the people, as a custom or national practice, not closed off among exclusivist organizations. Some nudists viewed *Nacktkultur* as a civil duty that needed to be recognized as such by national leaders.[3] The ultimate goal of *Nacktkultur* was for it to become so widespread and so prevalent among Germans that even the many nudist clubs and leagues would eventually become superfluous and dissolve.[4] This moment would be reached when, 'a naked *Volk* frolicked on every river, at every lake, on every ocean's beach, when naked youth stepped onto athletic fields for competition, and when the sun glowed, one could lay with languor in green fields or warm hammocks.'[5] *Nacktkultur* was to pervade and transform German society at a popular level, which would then influence other aspects of society.

As is true of so many aspects of nudism, the reality of nudist practice often fell far short of what the ideology prescribed. Nudists, then as now, organized themselves into clubs, leagues and unions for the purposes of practicing public nakedness among the like-minded. Ideologically and structurally, nudism existed on a kind of continuum from its murky nineteenth-century origins to its de-ideologization after the Second World War. Nevertheless, three periods of growth can be discerned in pre-1945 nudism: the Independent Phase lasting from its likely origins in the 1890s to 1918, the Popular Phase from 1919 to 1933, and the State Phase from 1933 to 1945. (Nudism in the post-1945 era might best be termed the Normal Phase, when it is an accepted, widely practiced leisure-time activity.)

The Independent Phase of nudist growth is characterized on the one hand primarily by individuals, usually men, making the decision to become nudists for health reasons, and then celebrating and propagating their ideas in heavily illustrated, self-published books, and on the other hand by small groups of individuals collecting together as an organization, and just as quickly splintering. Thus Heinrich Pudor of Leipzig and Richard Ungewitter of Stuttgart each appear independently of one another to have struck upon the idea of becoming nudists. Each published heavily; and of the two men Ungewitter was far more successful, both in commercial terms and in terms of spreading nudism across Germany.

In the very early years of *Nacktkultur*, there arose in southern Germany an important publishing and organizing force around Ungewitter (see Figure 1.1). His books began appearing at nearly the same time as Heinrich Pudor's, which caused the latter to accuse the former of plagiarism. It is a dubious claim at best.[6] Richard Ungewitter founded his Lodge of Rising Life (Loge des aufsteigenden Lebens), later the Loyalty Club for Rising Life (Treubund f.a.L), in 1907, and it would remain an important presence in the nudist world for years, possibly becoming the first organization to achieve a nationwide presence.[7] A separate nudist club may have been founded in Stuttgart at the same time; Ungewitter is himself unclear on this.[8] J.M. Seitz alludes to a club that met on the outskirts of Munich, though he gives no date for its activity.[9]

Figure 1.1 Richard Ungewitter, one of the most important and earliest of nudist ideologues. Original caption: 'At play' From Richard Ungewitter, *Die Nacktheit in entwicklungsgeschichtlicher, gesundheitlicher, moralischer und künstlicher Beleuchtung.* Courtesy of ANRL.

In a prime example of the sectarian nature of nudism, it was from Ungewitter's organization the Treubund that a new organization sprang at the end of the First World War. Headed by J M Seitz, the Bund der Lichtfreunde (League of Lightfriends) spread rapidly among the branches of Ungewitter's organization, and within a short time had expanded to Aachen, Berlin, Bremen, Cassel, Danzig, Elberfeld, Erfurt, Gießen, Glogau, Hamburg, Hildesheim, Kösen, Liegnitz, Ludenscheid, Munich, Münster, Nuremburg, Quedlinberg, Rees and Stuttgart.

However important for the growth of *Nacktkultur* Ungewitter's efforts were, it was Berlin, not Stuttgart, that was the uncontested center of nudist activity and organization, both in the early period as well as in the Weimar era. Moreover, the second characteristic of early nudism, of groups forming and quickly splintering, is typical of those clubs located in Berlin. Their experience is worth exploring, as the sectarian nature of nudism remains a characteristic feature of the movement.

Nudism, despite its ideology of wholeness, social and political unity, was a spectacularly sectarian movement, with splinter organizations forming almost as quickly as a group registered with police. Reconstructing the early development of organized nudism can only be done impressionistically, as it is fraught with incomplete sources often written by contemporaries who themselves seemed to lack any awareness of the larger nudist picture. Generally, the earliest nudist clubs tended to be quite short-lived, often fracturing for the most banal though also most understandable of reasons, namely sex.

According to one author, in 1904 Dr Schwarz founded the Hellas-Loge (Hellas Lodge). Another claims that in 1906 or 1907, Dr Zumbusch founded a nudist group called Hellas-Loge. Both sources agree on numbers, Hellas Lodge had about twenty-nine members, two or three of whom were women. The Hellas-Loge met in a female artist's apartment. The Lodge quickly fell apart, however, as male members bickered about individual male members spending time alone with one or two of the few female members, rather than with the entire group. Years later, the chronicler of this early history suspected that those men and women who kept retreating to be alone among themselves had not joined the club strictly out of a sense of idealism, but for, other prurient reasons.[10]

After the Hellas group drifted apart, the more serious nudists along with Dr Zumbusch then founded a new nudist club called the Walhalla Lodge. Reportedly, the Walhalla was characterized by very strict rules, a lesson likely learned from recent experience. Initially, the Walhalla met in some of Berlin's 'nearly 2000 vacant apartments' (a strange statement, as one usually hears of housing shortages, not surpluses). Although total membership numbers are unavailable, the chronicler suggests that there were three to four men for every woman in the Walhalla nudist club.[11] Walhalla soon went bankrupt and folded due to high rents and low membership, however.[12]

At about the same time, a Professor H. created the Nudo-Natio, an aristocratically minded group that met in the Lichterfeld section of Berlin in 1906.[13] Nearby, the Freya-Bund, led by Dr Konrad Küster and actively supported by Wilhelm Kästner, was founded in 1909, in an effort to bring unity to the sectarian world of nudist clubs.[14] Membership figures seem to have been higher, though still unknown, in the Freya-Bund, as they were able to lease an orchard for their activities.[15] Brünner, a member of the Freya-Bund, angrily left the group after Kästner published an unauthorized naked photo of him in the group's organ, *Der Lichtfreund* (Friend of the Light).[16] Brünner then refounded yet a different Walhalla nudist organization and on alternate days used the same orchard as the Freya-Bund for its nudist activities. Yet another member of Freya-Bund, for reasons he or she chooses not to explain, also splintered from the group to found a different organization.[17] Soon, both groups fell apart for unknown reasons, and many members drifted to the nearby Neusonnlandbund.

Another important group from the early era of nudism, aside, of course from Richard Ungewitter's LdaL, which mysteriously seems to have escaped mention by many authors despite its presence in nearly every state of the German Empire, was the Monboddobund. Named after an eighteenth-century Scottish scientist, who was allegedly observed bathing nude with his daughters by the German natural philosopher Lichtenberg, the Monboddobund, was founded, depending on one's contemporary source, on either February 6, 1913 or in 1911.[18] Seitz suggested that the Monboddobund was formed from remnants of the old Nudo-Natio. Examples of the blizzard of clubs' founding and dissolving from this early era could be multiplied, but what is more important than determining when which club was founded and by whom is understanding what tore these small groups apart.

The story of these early groups reveals one of the major fault lines in *Nacktkultur*, namely, women and sex. Brünner, for example, complained that in all of the organizations of which he was a member, there were too few women. For the Freya-Bund and the reconstituted Walhalla, for example, there was a combined total of six women. Low membership numbers among women clearly frustrated male nudists, something that suggests their own motives for becoming nudists may have had more to do with sexual curiosity and desire than with ideological commitment, a suspicion intimated by nudists themselves.

Convincing women to participate in nudism and to join a nudist organization was a major focus of many of the male nudist organizers, and one is forced to wonder to what extent the possibility of sex or voyeurism motivated men to join nudist leagues, despite nudism's ideology that preached the moral purity of the nudist experience. Related to this is the problem of sex. Brünner makes no secret that the Hellas-Loge fell apart because one or more of the women were spending time exclusively with one of the male members while naked, thus giving rise, at the very least, to suspicions, resentment and even jealousy by the other males in the group. It is not clear what the two members were doing alone naked together, but whatever it was, it was sufficient to cause the group to dissolve acrimoniously. Sex, whether as an act or as an educational principle within the movement, was not the only fault line, but it was the most important, and hints of it sowing discord appear again and again in nudist history.

The Popular Phase (1919–33)

Though some important growth occurred prior to the First World War, it was primarily ideological and not structural. Without question, nakedness and nudism became more common in German society and culture in the years after the First World War.[19] In the 1920s, organizations and publications – often working in tandem – that advocated nudism proliferated at a fantastic rate. As befits the first great age of mass culture, during the Weimar Republic nudism became a mass cultural phenomenon in which millions of Germans participated, whether as members of nudist leagues or more simply (and far more likely) as weekend beachgoers. Furthermore, nudist ideologues and proponents made use of the latest technology of the day – photographs, cinema – to further their movement.

Nudists were themselves unable to explain the rapid growth of the nudist movement that occurred in the years after the First World War.[20] Some nudist ideologues suggested that it was because of the experience of the war itself, especially of soldiers in the field, who lacking swimsuits would bathe and swim naked during periods of rest.[21] Nudist author Richard Ungewitter claimed he received dozens of letters from soldiers from the front who said that it became customary for whole companies to have a naked airbath, and he concludes, somewhat dramatically, that a majority of the millions of soldiers who fought during the war spent time naked in an airbath.[22]

It is possible, even likely, that German soldiers who swam and bathed naked during lulls in the fighting were not acting as nudists, and that they were merely taking advantage of an opportunity, or were bringing to the front such customs as may have been familiar – even common – to the prewar countryside. In any event, fellow nudist J.M. Seitz suggested that the custom of being naked took root in the soldiers' minds and they brought it home with them, so to speak, and introduced it back to their families and continued to do it in the postwar era.

Whatever the actual cause, and it may not be possible to determine with any precision, the 1920s were a period of marked growth for *Nacktkultur*. Hints of nudism's growth and popularity in the Weimar Republic can be gleaned from comments made by Germany's clergy, who took an interest in *Nacktkultur* after 1925. Religious authorities turned their attention to nudism with an eye to end it as an apparently obvious example of the declining moral health of Germany. Though their findings about nudism's moral character surprised them, Germany's religious

Nudism and Nudists • 21

Figure 1.2 Here park grounds are improved by nudists. From Richard Ungewitter, *Nacktheit und Kultur: Neue Forderungen*. Courtesy of ANRL.

leaders also learned that nudist practice was widespread throughout the nation.

For example, near Cannstatt (today a rather urbanized section of Stuttgart), naked swimmers were a constant sight along the Neckar river, much to the chagrin and offense of Bishop Keppler. He noted that families in his congregation complained to him that they could no longer engage in family walks through the forest without fear of 'coming across half-naked persons or couples.' Moreover, he continued, on nearly every river in the region, the Neckar, the Danube and others, mixed gender, naked swimmers could be found everywhere.[23]

In east Prussia, the pastors of a number of small towns complained that they had been deluged with nudists and naked swimmers since the First World War. So large were the numbers of nudists that it was far beyond anyone's capacity to stem the tide. In Haffstrom, a village of 352 inhabitants,[24] nudists came in alarming numbers, reaching 5,000 or more on days such as Whitsun or Ascension Day. 'Naked people flooded the church lands and disturbed religious celebrations,' one pastor complained. He explained to his superiors in the Lutheran church hierarchy that soldiers who had been stationed in nearby Königsberg during the war introduced the idea of naked swimming to the area. Years later, it still occurred. This pastor, and undoubtedly others like him, were simply overwhelmed and had no means to halt the mass nakedness about him. Other villages reported smaller numbers of nude bathers, but found them no less annoying.[25]

Reports from all parts of Germany by Lutheran pastors give the impression that nudism and naked activity were national phenomena, even if overall numbers were not large. Witnessing public displays of nakedness leaves a strong impression, however. Lutheran pastors in Opladen near Düsseldorf in western Germany complained about nudist activity, as did those in Silesia in eastern Germany, who also noted that nudists tended to remain within their fences.[26] In the north-eastern German city of Stettin, Pastor Küßner informed that no organized nudists were present, but numerous naked individuals were. He especially objected to a communist youth group that swam naked in the waters around Baltic Sea island of Wollin, which compelled other swimmers to leave the area.[27] Near Magdeburg, at Torgau in central-eastern Germany, 'members of nudist clubs had made themselves regrettably noticeable'; further south in Naumburg, an instance of naked dancing in the forest had been reported in the press, and it was well known that a nudist club from Leipzig occasionally made its way to nearby Eulau.[28]

Naked swimmers walked upstream and swam downstream near the village of Artern. Much further east, near the town of Merseburg, while there was no nudism, daily dancing by swimmers in their swimsuits pushed ecclesiastical patience to the limit. Near Gera, a freethinker had established a home school where he, his family and the twenty-five students all practiced nudism.[29] In the western German city of Münster, nudists who liked to use the Emskanal were known to enter villages while naked.[30] In the nearby Lüneburger Heath, nudists were a well-known sight, just as they were in and around Hamburg.

Clearly, the area of Germany where nudism was most prevalent and nudists were most visible was Berlin, a city surrounded by small lakes. Pastors from all over the city complained about growing incidents of naked youth who harassed passersby either by yelling at them or by just being visibly naked.[31] Nudism only ended in Breslau after being officially banned by the government in the early 1930s.[32]

In the Weimar Republic, nudism became a popular phenomenon and was closely linked to the expansion of free-time recreation opportunities. Nudist Magnus Weidemann declared that in the mid 1920s the movement was so large that no one who wanted to practice it would need to do so alone.[33] Municipalities began allowing for some nudist swimming at swim facilities, at least for those nudists who were organized into clubs; this practice continued until the early 1930s.[34] Walter Heitsch noted with satisfaction that nudism had spread to other countries, and that foreign clubs modeled themselves on the German example.[35]

In Germany, more and more nudist organizations were founded and registered with authorities, including a branch of Seitz's Bund der Lichtfreunde, the Licht-Luft-Gesellschaft (Light-Air Society) in Munich. In Hamburg, the Freiluftbund under Hugo Hillig began holding slide-show presentations around Germany.[36] Although initially conceived as a nudist colonization society, the Neusonnland (New Sun Land) in Berlin, known also as the Freisonnlandbund (League of the

Free Sun), headed by the lawyer A.F. Fuchs, attracted Berliners looking for an opportunity to relax naked in the sun and refresh themselves in a *Luftbad*, and could accommodate nearly three hundred at a time.[37]

In addition to the increasing numbers of nudist clubs that formed, a second way to measure the popularity of and interest in nudism during the Weimar years is to consider nudist efforts to spread their message. Judging by the popular media of the day, especially print but also film, nudism was a topic of great interest. Nudist works by Richard Ungewitter went through dozens of editions, selling well into the hundreds of thousands. In 1924, Hans Surén wrote nothing less than a nudist best seller titled *Der Mensch und die Sonne* (*People and the Sun*). It went through no fewer than seventy-three editions *that year*. Scores of book-length nudist works appeared throughout the 1920s, most with impressive publication figures.

As impressive as nudist book sales were, the real growth in the interest of nudism is most observable in the quantity of periodicals dedicated to *Nacktkultur* that appeared, undoubtedly aided by Weimar's absence of police censorship of the press.[38] Though numbers for the sake of comparison are difficult to find, the nudist magazine *Lachendes Leben* had a usual press run of about 25,000 in the late 1920s.[39] *Figaro*, another leading nudist publication, had a smaller press run of somewhere between 15,000 and 17,500 at that time.[40]

Nudist magazines published on a wide range of topics. Ethics, dance, the new generation, relaxation techniques, happiness, education, freedom, the eye as well as Life-Reform oriented topics were common in *Die Freude* (Joy). *Deutsch Hellas* (German Hellas) printed fiction, poetry alongside calls to Life-Reform and nudism, as did *Das Freibad* (The Freebath). *Urania* and its nudist supplement *Der Leib Urania* achieved the highest levels of topical diversity, with features on blood tests to determine paternity, digestion, evolution, genetics, coincidences, science, Buddhism, fossils, Brazilian nature, sex reform and Viennese sex reformer and socialist Viktor Adler.

Often a magazine was explicitly linked to one particular nudist organization and acted as that group's organ. Such was the case, for example, of Ungewitter's magazine and the Treubund, *Lachendes Leben* and the Liga für freie Lebensgestaltung, and briefly *Figaro* and the nudist Pelagianer-Bund established in 1927.[41] Here too, examples could be easily multiplied, though by no means was every nudist organization linked directly to a publication, nor was every nudist periodical an organ of a nudist league. Magazines devoted to *Nacktkultur* were primarily important for spreading the ideas and images of nudism to a wider public, even if that did not necessarily result in larger membership numbers for that magazine's particular group.

In addition to the many magazines that appeared, the ideas of nudism, health and healing under the sun with naked skin were undoubtedly advanced by the movies *Wege zur Kraft und Schönheit* (*Ways to Strength and Beauty*) and to a lesser extent *Sonnenkinder-Sonnenmenschen* in 1924 (*Children of the Sun-People of the Sun*). Of the two, *Ways* was and is the more well known, though frankly it is hardly a strong call to nudism. *Ways* shows little actual nudism (even very little nudity) and provides almost no information about nudist ideology. It does further ideas about proper care of the body and about the need to recreate the beauty of ancient Greeks and Romans under the sun.[42] *Ways* was produced by the major film studio, Ufa, whereas *Children* was produced by nudists, which may explain its smaller audience and lesser reputation.[43]

The popularity of *Nacktkultur* during the Weimar Republic can be said to have climaxed with the convoking of an international congress of nudism in the German village of Dornzhausen in 1930. Even in this moment of apparent success, however, the sectarian nature of nudism expressed itself. At the meeting, unspecified problems arose immediately from the French delegation. The editors of *Das Freibad* were angered by the translations of the proceedings.[44] The event must be considered at best a partial success, and other attempts do not appear to have been made.

Continued Sectarianism

At the meeting in Dornzhausen, nudists were subjected to another dose of reality about their movement when the results of Fred Look's informal survey of passersby on the street suggested ambivalent attitudes among the general population, with about equal numbers supporting, rejecting and not having any idea what *Nacktkultur* even was.[45]

Whatever the failures of nudism's international impulses, organizational unity did not accompany nudism's popular growth within Germany either, and repeated efforts to confederate Germany's many nudist leagues all ultimately failed. J.M. Seitz, along with others, realized that no single nudist organization would ever be formed, and they began to work towards the creation of a super-organization to which independent clubs could attach themselves. Seitz and others originally imagined a kind of umbrella organization to offer protection and assistance but no interference in internal matters to all member groups.[46]

There were practical as well as ideological reasons behind the idea of creating such an umbrella organization. Unity and cohesion, it was generally agreed, would offer a degree of security against pressures to prohibit or to restrict *Nacktkultur*.[47] Ideologically, it was important, Seitz noted, 'that the believers in the movement joined together in a movement, through whose large membership figures an impression can be made on the public, and which is financially in a position to increase enlightenment to wider circles through publications and presentations.'[48]

Accordingly, the Arbeitsgemeinschaft der Bünde deutscher Lichtkämpfer (Confederation of the Leagues of German Fighters for Light) was eventually formed in July 1924, to subdued publicity, as nudism was experiencing general bad press from the recent scandal involving Adolf Koch and his efforts to introduce nudism to his public schoolchildren in Berlin-Moabit in 1924. The Arbeitsgemeinschaft had a difficult start, due in part to the hyperinflation of 1923 that destroyed the German economy and to the sudden death of its intended first leader, Hugo Hillig. Hillig had planned for the Arbeitsgemeinschaft to include all nudist organizations and for its organ to be called *Licht-Luft-Leben*.[49] For reasons that are not clear the Arbeitsgemeinschaft did not long endure, though personality and various groups' positions on other non-nudist, *Lebensreform* issues, such as sex reform, may have played a major role.[50]

In the early 1930s renewed calls for the creation of an umbrella organization were made, though this time with an air of urgency, not idealism.[51] In one such call, a self-described '*alte Kämpfer*' (old fighter), a term later employed by the Nazis to describe those Germans who joined the Nazi Party very early on and remained members through thick and thin, was inspired by an article of Therese Mühlhause-Vogeler's, to once again promote nudism actively. Having joined originally in 1911 with an Ungewitter TfaL (Treubund f.a.L) branch, he now asked his fellow Munich-based nudist groups to form a local umbrella organization, in order to promote intra-nudist understanding and harmony as well as for their mutual good in the face of intensifying pressure from opposition groups. Little seems to have come of his call, and nudists remained divided in Munich and elsewhere until 1934.[52]

Unlike the experience of nudist groups prior to the First World War, Weimar nudists were able to establish a viable nudist club and maintain it, but they could not align themselves successfully into larger, national alliances. As we have seen, early nudist leagues were fractured by sexual activity or innuendo, and their group dynamic was greatly aggravated by low numbers of women nudists. In the Weimar Republic this was not the case, rather, personality further aggravated by questions of sex education fueled the acrimony between Germany's nudist leagues.

Seitz himself noted that the peculiarities of nudism and especially that groups formed around personalities often contributed to their volatile nature.[53] The chronicler Brünner comments that Ungewitter had the most restrictive application process to join his group, which involved personal recommendation by a current member, three months' probation and Ungewitter's personal approval, as well as a non-Semitic family background.[54] Especially annoying to many were Ungewitter's views on temperance of alcohol and nicotine, something more than one contemporary commented on.[55] Though difficult to imagine given his own virulent racial anti-Semitism, Seitz complained that Ungewitter's racial fanaticism kept numbers small.[56]

Fanaticism was a charge leveled at many nudists and their groups, though it is not always clear just what is meant by the claim. Most likely, 'fanaticism' was used to insult another group, or to create distance between one's own version of nudism and others whose version was slightly different. Charly Sträßer, for example, disagreed vehemently with Seitz's effort to create financial support for elderly nudists, opposed Seitz's ideas on the use of naked photos in publications, and generally thought the nudist preoccupation with rooting out the impure, the old-fashioned, and the incurably degenerate city folk was a waste of time, as was the tendency of so many nudists to seal themselves off from society in tightly knit, exclusivist clubs.[57] Labeled 'pathological fanatics,' Charly Sträßer's organization, the Birkenheide, was removed from the nudist confederation created during the Weimar Republic.[58]

The meaning of 'fanaticism' as a grounds for excluding one nudist organization from the mainstream or for breaking away from one and forming a new group altogether seems to apply to a group's attitude about members' lives beyond the nudist grounds. Walter Heitsch, for example, noted that a nudist league ought to allow a member to live his or her life as she might wish once away from the nudist park. Heitsch hints that this means letting people eat meat, smoke and consume alcohol, if they so wished in their private lives.[59] Clearly, some Germans participated in nudism as a free-time activity and were less driven, though it is impossible to say how much less, by the ideology of national and racial regeneration through personal healing, beautification and breeding. At the nudist park, they behaved as nudists should: they were naked and eschewed such poisons as tobacco, alcohol and meat. In clothed society, however, they wished to behave as they were accustomed and if they wanted a beer, a cigarette or a steak, they would consume one.

During the Weimar Republic, the most divisive issue in nudism's early history combined elements that had been present in a number of earlier, minor rifts – namely sex, personality differences and even charges of fanaticism – into a major, deeply bitter struggle between two large factions of nudists: those behind Robert Laurer and those arranged around the magazine *Figaro*. The affair lasted throughout much of the second half of the 1920s, and showed no signs of dissipating when the Nazis banned nudism in 1933.

Robert Laurer was born as a Czech-German in 1899 to a good bourgeois family. He fought in the First World War, and afterwards, his mini-biographer, Therese Mühlhause-Vogeler, would have us believe, he sort of stumbled onto the idea of publishing. It is unclear how he became a nudist, though she does mention that his wife had been the local leader (*Gauführerin*) of Ungewitter's TfaL organization in the Rhineland.[60]

Laurer's role in the business world of nudism during the 1920s is important, and he was one of the most active publishers of nudist material, both periodicals and books. In 1923, he acquired Magnus Weidemann's financially imperiled *Die Freude*, and moved it to his enclave Egestorff in the Lüneburger Heath, about an hour south of Hamburg. Weidemann, in his departing words as founder, owner and editor, noted that personality differences, presumably between himself and Laurer, prompted his own departure after Laurer's purchase of the magazine. In the new format, there would be few changes other than the abandonment of discussion of sexual matters, such as sex education for youth.[61] Later, Laurer founded his own magazine, *Lachendes Leben* (Laughing Life), which became a successful competitor to other publications, notably *Figaro*.

Abandoning discussions of sex, sexuality and especially sex education, something that publications associated with Laurer did almost universally, appears to have been a point of major contention in the unfolding dislike of Laurer by other nudists and nudist publications.[62] Gröttrup, the editor of *Figaro*, and others maintained that Laurer increased his own sales and his own popularity by attacking other nudists and their magazines.[63]

As the 1920s wore on, the antagonism between Gröttrup's *Figaro* and Laurer's publishing house in Egestorff intensified. Laurer was accused of abandoning the true ideals of *Nacktkultur*, especially after the editors of *Figaro* made the decision to align more closely with sex reform, and Laurer's groups chose a less sex reform minded path. Laurer charged that precisely because of its devotion to sex reform, *Figaro* had little to do with true nudism.[64] Anton Putz zum Adlersthum later made the claim that Laurer had lost his belief in true nudism, and that *Lachendes Leben* was only a mouthpiece for his own business interests. In his race for profit, Adlersthum maintained, Laurer threatened to turn his followers into Helots, and nudism was headed for a fratricidal conflict.[65] Laurer had exchanged his naked idealism for profit, violating and angering many who remained true believers in the naked ideal.[66] Nudism, despite the internecine conflict among its publishers and leaders, nevertheless appealed to large numbers of Germans, and grew steadily.

Germany's many nudist clubs and leagues were of course eventually transformed into a single, nationwide organization. Ironically, this single nudist organization, known eventually as the Bund für Leibeszucht, was created by the state, not as protection from it. The ascension of the Nazis to power in 1933 marked a new phase for Germany's nudists, one of official recognition and integration into the nation's leisure-time activities. The integration into the Nazi state was not without its tribulations, however.

The period of state support of nudism (1933–45) was a mixed blessing. It is not possible to determine if the level of nudist participation by Germans increased, stagnated or declined during the Nazi era. After an initial ban on nudism that lasted from March 1933 to January 1934, nudism was recognized by leading National Socialists as an important, racially aware ideology, quite similar in many respects to National Socialism itself. The ideology and its practice were wholeheartedly supported by the regime. Nudists, however, experienced no small amount of investigation and harassment at the hands of the Nazi regime. The scrutiny placed on the nudists during the Third Reich was motivated above all else by the regime's paranoia that *Nacktkultur* was a refuge for Marxists.

The relationship between nudism and the Nazi state is unlike the relationship between nudism and the state under the Kaiser or during the Weimar Republic. The fate of nudism and the experience of nudists under the Nazi regime raise the question of nudism's own political orientation, a question that will be addressed in Chapter 2, as part of a broader discussion of nudism and its relationship to the church and state. At this point, I would like to turn to the question of who participated in nudism.

Nudist Demographics

Reconstructing the demographics of a social movement from archival sources is fraught with problems. Nevertheless, the data can suggest certain important points. For the period under study in this book, 1900–50, membership lists mostly from the 1930s and 1940s for some clubs do exist in various archives. In Schleswig there is the membership list from 1933 for the Deutscher Lichtfreunde (German Friends of the Light) located in Lübeck with forty-five members.[67] From Leipzig, there is the membership list for the Bund der Sonnenfreunde zu Leipzig (Leipzig League of Friends of the Sun) from 1930 with eighteen members, and a list of the members of the Nazi nudist organizations, the Bund für Leibeszucht (BfL), dating from 1943 with 301 members.[68] Finally, from Hamburg is a list of members from the reconstituted Liga für freie Lebensgestaltung from 1950 with 226 members.[69] Each list offers different information, all include name and address. Some lists include occupation or age. The Hamburg list for Liga für freie Lebensgestaltung (LffL) includes only the name of the member. (See Tables 1.1, 1.2, 1.3.)

Table 1.1 Total Nudist Membership by Gender and Family of Select Organizations

Nudist Organizations	Individual Male	Individual Female	Total Individual Members	Family Memberships
Deutscher Lichtfreunde-Lübeck, 1933	24	21	45	13
Bund der Sonnenfreunde zu Leipzig, 1930	14	4	18	4
Bund für Leibeszucht-Leipzig, 1943	159	142	301	86
Liga für freie Lebensgestaltung-Hamburg, 1950	145	82	227	47
Total	342	249	591	150

Table 1.2 Male Membership in Select Nudist Organizations

Nudist Organizations	Family Men	Single Men	Boys
Deutscher Lichtfreunde-Lübeck, 1933	12	6	6
Bund der Sonnenfreunde zu Leipzig, 1930	4	10	0
Bund für Leibeszucht-Leipzig, 1943	83	30	46
Liga für freie Lebensgestaltung-Hamburg, 1950	47	98	?
Total	146	144	52

Table 1.3 Female Membership in Select Nudist Organizations

Nudist Organizations	Family Women	Single Women	Girls
Deutscher Lichtfreunde-Lübeck, 1933	13	1	7
Bund der Sonnenfreunde zu Leipzig, 1930	4	0	0
Bund für Leibeszucht-Leipzig, 1943	86	22	34
Liga für freie Lebensgestaltung-Hamburg, 1950	46	35	?
Total	149	58	41

From the information available in these lists, it is possible to assemble a rough gender and social composition of nudist organizations, and therefore gain an idea of *Nacktkultur*'s appeal among Germans. Easiest to determine is the sex of a nudist member, as it is identifiable by first name. In some cases, a member's occupation is listed, and for women these are often 'mother' or 'housewife.' In those cases where a woman has a paid occupation outside the home, the nature of the German language indicates her sex through its noun endings. From these membership lists it is also easy to determine relationships among nudists, as children are often listed as 'son' or 'daughter,' or birthdates are included. In those cases where no birthdate is provided it is assumed that the individual sharing the last name with others is not running his or her own household (often listed third of fourth, below a man and a woman, suggesting lower rank in a hierarchy). These people are called here a boy or girl. Finally, individuals over eighteen are not considered children, even if clearly listed with parents. In determining family status, married couples are considered families; the level of family participation is both high and noteworthy. Finally, some idea of social class of nudists can be ascertained, but with important caveats.

Men, Women and Families

In the city of Lübeck, home of the Deutscher Lichtfreunde, a total of forty-five members belonged. Of this number there were twenty-four men (53%) and twenty-one women (46%). The sex of one member cannot be readily determined, as only the initial 'M' is given under the name; however, 'M' is most likely a man. Of the twenty-four male members, there were five single men and six boys, as suggested by their birthdates. Of the remaining thirteen men, twelve are identifiably married, thus suggesting that the fourteenth was a single man bringing the total of single men to six. The numbers for women also suggest that 'M' was a man. There were twenty-one female members, one single woman, and seven were young girls. This leaves twelve married women, thus matching the number of married men, suggesting that 'M' was a male and bringing the total number of single men to six. Interestingly, the Deutscher Lichtfreunde was overwhelmingly populated by families.

In the data, thirteen families with a total membership number of thirty-nine people, including thirteen children, can be identified. One family did not indicate a husband, but appeared to be headed by a woman with two small children, making the family total higher (13) than the married men and women totals (12 each). Families constituted 86 per cent of the league's membership. Unfortunately, social class cannot be determined from this membership list.

In the relatively small group Bund der Sonnenfreunde zu Leipzig, numbering only eighteen members in 1930, there were fourteen men (77%) and four women (22%). Four couples can be identified, leaving ten single men in the group. Here, the membership information includes only first and last names as well as addresses. In the case of this nudist club, single men composed roughly half of the overall total membership (55%), with no single women. The Bund der Sonnenfreunde zu Leipzig group is dominated by families and single men with an imbalanced single male to single female ratio (10:0). This club did not long endure, and was largely defunct by the arrival to power of the Nazis. Though a definitive cause for the Bund's demise cannot be found in the data, one is reminded of the early nudist groups fracturing and dissolving due to similar imbalanced sex ratios.

In the much more detailed list of BfL members dating from 1943 it is possible to learn a great deal about nudist membership, at least during the Nazi era, including social class, as this list includes not only members' names and addresses but also occupations. In the 1943 BfL, there were 301 members. Dividing the members according to sex reveals that including those whose occupation is listed as 'son,' there were 159 male members (52.8% of total membership). Including those whose occupation is listed as 'married woman' and 'daughter' as well as those single women who had occupations, there were 142 female members (47.1%). There were thirty (9%) single men and twenty-two (7%) single women. This suggests that roughly equal numbers of men and women, single or married, participated in the BfL.

As in the case of the organization from Lübeck, the BfL was dominated by families. Again a family is any group of two or more individuals who share a last name and the same address. Easing the identification of families, as has been mentioned, is the fact that this list includes occupation of members. Women were listed as 'married woman' or 'daughter.' There is a total of eighty-six families, consisting of eighty-three men and eighty-six women (three women were members with children but with no obvious husband member). In all, eighty children (26.5% of all members), forty-six sons and thirty-four daughters, can be discerned giving a total membership figure of 249 (82%) for families. Married men thus totaled eighty-three of the 113 men (73%), and married women eighty-six of the 108 women (79%). Single men comprise thirty members and single women number twenty-two, for a total of forty-two members. Single, unmarried members constituted a relatively small number (17.2%) of total members in the Bund für Leibeszucht.

Finally, the membership file from the reconstituted Hamburg-based Liga für freie Lebensgestaltung (LffL) drawn in 1950 provides some further indication that families were an important unit of nudist clubs. This list only provides members' first and last names. Couples, however, can be inferred by the fact that they are often listed together, for example, 'Heinrich und Gertrud Scheffer.' There remains the possibility that the Scheffers and others listed like them are brother and sister, and in at least one case it would appear that two brothers joined; however, this would still make them family. The membership information available for the Hamburg group presents striking disparities between men and women, with the former outnumbering the latter by nearly two to one, something that is not readily explainable. Total membership for the LffL was 227, of whom 145 were men (64%) and eighty-two were women (36%). There were forty-seven families, and it is not possible to determine to what extent children were present, if any were, from the file. The total number of nudist members who belonged to a family was ninety-three (41% of all members), or just under half of the total membership. This leaves ninety-eight single men (67.5% of all male members) and thirty-five single women (42.6% of all female members).

Taken all together, the presence of a family in the various nudist organizations is quite high. Total membership of all nudist organizations from these membership lists is 591; of these 342 (57.8%) members were men, including boys, and 249 (42%) were women, including girls. Of the total men, 144 (42%) are single and of the total women fifty-eight (23%) are single or never before married, independent women, suggesting, too, that nudism was more popular among men than women, generally speaking. Nonetheless, the family was an important part of a nudist club's organization and membership. Of groups available here for study, there are a total of 150 families, with a total membership of 389 (65.8% of all members) people, including a total children's membership of ninety-three (15% of all members). (This is a number that does not include any children who may have belonged to the reconstituted LffL in 1950, as that list does not make such identification possible.) This membership information roughly corresponds to that gathered by Ulrich Linse in his history of nudism in Lower Saxony during the time of the Nazis.[70]

Families and families with children constitute an important part of any nudist organization, about two-thirds (65.9%) of the total. Single men represent a lower figure (42%) and single women indicate a much lower figure still (22.9%).

Social Class

Reconstructing class from memberships is an extremely difficult exercise. Knowing only the occupation of someone does little to tell of their status. (Does he own the shop or just work in it?) Nevertheless, the membership from the Bund für Leibeszucht-Leipzig 1943 provides an interesting look into the backgrounds of members. Of all the membership data available, it is the most thorough, although also the most fraught with problems. With information from the Nazi era, one must exercise caution. Just after coming to power in 1933, the Nazis ruthlessly 'synchronized' (*gleichgeschaltet*) German society, as part of an effort to efface social distinctions and class hostility. If we ask only what social groups were attracted to nudism, as opposed to whether all social groups were represented in a particular nudist club, then the data from the BfL list is instructive.

The occupations for the 1943 Bund für Leibeszucht-Leipzig cover a wide range of middle- and working-class fields, including businessman, lawyer, architect, teacher, university lecturer, student and government official, including postal employee (*Beamten*) as well as machinist, stenographer, tailor, paperhanger, technician and mechanic. There are over seventy different occupations listed in the membership roll. The claim of nudists that their ideology attracted all classes would seem to be supported by this list.[71]

Finally, it is possible to determine the social origins of many of the leading nudist writers and ideologues. Richard Ungewitter was born into a working-class family in Thuringia and was originally trained to be a gardner.[72] Wilhelm Kästner was a ladies' tailor. Heinrich Pudor originated from a very wealthy and established family in Leipzig. Indeed, his father had been a musician to the King of Saxony.[73] Additionally, Hans Surén came from a well-established military family; one that could trace its service in the officer corps back to Frederick the Great.[74] Therese Mühlhause-Vogeler, Magnus Weidemann and Robert Laurer were all members of Germany's celebrated *Bürgertum*.

Conclusion

The reality of nudism, especially how nudists behaved, organized and regarded each other was very different from what the ideology of nudism predicted. Preaching unity and social harmony of all Germans as they disrobed and marched forward under the sun to a bright future, ideologues were often unable to unite even among themselves to build a successful, viable nudist organization to bring about the nudist racial utopia or even to propagate the ideas of nudism among Germans. German nudism was marked by bitter, internecine conflict among its leading figures and publicists.

The idea of nudism was generally accepted by German society, however. The practice of nudism seems to have fascinated and even to have been accepted by Germans, and though vast numbers do not appear to have actively belonged to any nudist organization, there is some evidence to suggest that public nakedness was something of a popular phenomenon in the 1920s and beyond. In the Weimar years, German society experienced a major shift in its attitudes towards nakedness and the naked body by the 1920s at the latest. This is something that is hinted at in the works of such contemporary German authors as Thomas Mann, especially Hans Fallada, and even in the works of the somewhat later Günter Grass, though such observations were not recounted by foreign authors.[75]

There is the temptation to suggest that nudism grew in this period of social and political freedom (and upheaval) as a result of a general breakdown of the moral order following the armistice and revolution of 1918. Certainly, the so-called dance wave that swept Germany was attributed to the breakdown of the moral order that governed German society under the Kaiser, as were the rises in prostitution, venereal disease, erotic dance revues and crime. It is unlikely that nudism belongs to this same milieu of immediate postwar social chaos and immorality, however. Nudism was dominated in the 1920s and beyond by married couples and by families with small children, not by lusty, sexually excited men and women looking for a weekend romp. Nudism's longevity and appeal rests in its accessibility as a leisure-time pursuit and in its practice within and by family groups.

The history of the nudist movement drawn from police and other official reports offers a different view of the movement, and one that not only casts the nudists in a different light, but that also challenges some notions about German society and its relationship to public nakedness in the period from the turn of the century to the end of the Second World War. Campaigns against nudism, the focus of the next chapter, were both infrequent and anemic, and ultimately quickly abandoned.

–2–

Pastors, Priests, Nazis and Police: The Moral and Political Campaigns against *Nacktkultur*

The practice of nudism is startling to behold and its appeal can be difficult to comprehend. Nudist ideology was often anti-Christian, and vehemently anti-Catholic. It explicitly called for a reversal of the negative view of the body (*Körperfeindlichkeit*), the elimination of shame and of the 'governing 2000 year old religious-ethical moral order.'[1] In its practice, nudism directly threatened any number of traditional mechanisms for maintaining social control and public morality, in particular through its elimination of feelings of bodily shame. Freeing the body of the moral chains that shamed, bound and clothed it was part of the larger nudist effort to recast German society and to regenerate the German race.

To opponents, groups of naked men and women together seemed nothing more than a temptation to sexual misbehavior, and indeed this was a suspicion long held in the popular mind. On moral grounds, the practice of *Nacktkultur* would seem to invite a stiff response from church or state officials, or both, yet such a response was slow to materialize and largely ineffective when it did. Germans were long able to practice nudism without interference from any kind of police, municipal, state or church official. Serious attention by state or religious authorities to nudism only emerged in the second half of the 1920s, and was motivated by a moral concern for the nation. The Weimar moral campaign against nudism that climaxed in 1932 was briefly continued by the Nazis a year later. However, under Nazism official opinion about *Nacktkultur* quickly shifted from prohibiting it to promoting it. The Nazi state exhibited far more concern over nudism's possible political composition than its moral nature.

Nacktkultur and Weimar Municipalities

Generally speaking, nudists maintained healthy if not comfortable relationships with church and state authorities. In one remarkable example, the city of Danzig, disconnected from the rest of Germany by the Treaty of Versailles, appears to have been quite enthusiastic about nudism and actively supported a local *Nacktkultur* league. Adolf Weide was the leading nudist of Danzig, and in his book *Verjüngung absolut* (Absolute Rejuvenesence) he thanked the authorities of the city for neither preventing nor prohibiting his movement over the course of the 1920s.[2]

The level of support for nudism extended by the Free City of Danzig was unparalleled. The city senate donated land for Weide's club to use during its big nudist exposition and day of sport competitions, for which Weide was still more grateful. 'The pictures reproduced here,' he noted in his book, 'are largely from the bountiful nature reserve, which the senate of the Free City of Danzig placed at the disposal of the nudist movement.'[3] Another nudist group known as Finus also received fourteen acres (twenty *Morgen*) of land at the city's edge, about fifteen minutes from downtown.[4]

In 1921 Adolf Weide and his organizations held a day of sporting competition for youth up to age twelve. Everyone who participated did so nude, and the contest was to determine who had the best body. Judges looked for proportion, healthy musculature as well as proper physical development. There were some running and other gymnastics competitions. Judges were doctors and artists. The competition was open for anyone, and anyone who wished could observe, though in the case of the older girls some viewing restrictions did apply. Interestingly, city officials were present at the competition, and found what they saw so pleasing that they chose on the spot to transform the naked competition into a yearly event.[5]

The cooperation of the city of Danzig must be considered one end of the spectrum of the relationship of government officials to public nudism, and does not appear to have been the case throughout Germany. Typically though, few municipalities strove to eliminate the nudists in their midst, and appear to have been largely indifferent to, if not accepting of, nudist practice.

During the 1920s, attitudes towards nudists and nudism at the municipal level were quite accommodating, and nudists seldom faced harassment from police or other county officials. Local police action against a nudist organization is almost impossible to find in archives, suggesting that either there was no police action against nudism or that those particular files have been destroyed. It seems likeliest that police and municipal officials in the Weimar Republic simply left the nudists to themselves. Indeed, the most significant headache for local gendarmes with regard to nudist activity may have been crowd control around the nudist parks. A particularly illustrative example of municipal as well as public attitudes towards *Nacktkultur* comes from a series of police and county investigations that occurred near the city Darmstadt in Hesse in the mid 1920s.

Near Darmstadt were the grounds of the nudist organization Orplid, a member of the Reichsverband für Körperkultur, and headed by Dr Hans Fuchs, already a prominent nudist and one who would continue to be so under the Nazis.[6] On two separate occasions Orplid was investigated by officials to determine exactly what transpired on its grounds, who and how many belonged to the organization. In one investigation the mayoral deputy from Arheilgen, the nearest town, and the county

Pastors, Priests, Nazis and Police • 37

commissioner, Laroche, traveled to the nudist park to learn what they could.

The park was located about thirty minutes away from Arheilgen on the edge of a forest. The unforested side was protected by a simple chain-link fence stuffed with a layer of straw, in some places two layers. The fence's door was easily penetrated, and it was easy to see over the fence, which was about four and a half feet tall. On the day of the visit by the mayor's deputy and Commissioner Laroche the weather was 'cold and rainy.' Nevertheless on the park grounds were two men, 'one of whom was completely disrobed.' The visiting party, upon interviewing the nudists learned that only members were allowed in the park, and all were required to be naked. Alcohol and nicotine were forbidden.[7]

While on the park grounds, members were not separated by sex, and men and women of all ages were encouraged to frolic together. Some of the land had been purchased from the city of Arheilgen itself, and Orplid was the sole owner of the land. On Fridays the group Socialist Workers' Youth used the park. Of the members, the mayor's deputy learned that two or three unmarried citizens of Arheilgen belonged, as did one married couple. In what would eventually reveal itself to be a commonplace occurrence, there were a number of fully clothed, non-nudist locals gathered alongside the outside of the fence carefully watching the naked people on the other side.[8]

Figure 2.1 Club life. Swimming in Frankfurt. From *Freikörperkultur und Lebensreform* (November 1929). Photo by G. Menz. Courtesy of ANRL.

Not shying from its task, the investigative committee stopped to interview a number of the Peeping Toms, after first noting that to get to the straw fence was itself an impressive feat, requiring one either to traverse a meadow or to go through the forest and over a barbed wire fence. The mayor's deputy and Commissioner Laroche asked a number of onlookers if they found the nudists offensive or were disturbed by them. In every case the answer they received was negative. Apparently, far from finding nudism offensive, people enjoyed what they saw. The party then moved its investigation to the local gendarmerie to determine whether and to what degree the nudists caused a public disturbance.[9]

As it turns out, there were a number of complaints generated by the presence of the nudist park. On Sundays, especially, complaints from surrounding farmers were high, due to the crop damage caused by the throngs of locals who gathered at the fence's edge to spy on the nudists. When the weather was nice, large numbers of Peeping Toms collected around the fence and crop damage was significant, the gendarme reported. On 'some Sundays,' the officer informed the investigators, 'the number of onlookers was large. They gather around the fence and peer through the straw to see the users of the park. It is estimated that 500 to 600 people collect in this manner to watch.' In their official report, the mayor's deputy and Commissioner Laroche recommended only that signs stating 'Forbidden Way' and 'Entrance Forbidden' be strategically placed to deter the voyeurs.[10] Nudism was a public nuisance, but not because the nudists were a wild, ribald bunch, but because they attracted a crowd. Interestingly, no citations seem to have been passed out to the significant numbers of onlookers for trespassing on the farmers' fields.

The problem of nudism and the public comes into sharper focus from the results of a prior investigation, also involving Orplid, that occurred just months before the visit from Arheilgen's officials. A police captain named Jungmann from the criminal division of Groß-Gerau, the county seat, was inadvertently drawn to the nudist park one Wednesday afternoon as he was passing by. His attention was first caught by the sight of a number of individuals who had collected along a fence. Captain Jungmann's report is particularly useful in understanding one level of the relationship between nudism and German society. It is also revealing of nudist behavior.

At the south-east corner of the area, Jungmann observed a number of holes in the straw fence. A 45-five-year-old man was peering through one of the holes. As Captain Jungmann approached on the east side of the park, he further noted several individuals, whose names he did not take, who informed him of the nudists on the other side. From the other side of the fence he heard laughing and screaming. When the officer looked through the fence he saw two approximately 20-year-old women, one naked, one wearing underwear and shirt, and two fully naked men, about twenty-five to thirty years old, engaged in conversation. All at once, one woman suggested to the other that they wrestle, which they began to do. When the ladies were stretched out on the ground wrestling, one of the men, Jungmann reports, nominated himself to be the referee, announcing that he would like to determine whose shoulders were forced to the ground and thus who lost the wrestling contest.

To Captain Jungmann's surprise and barely concealed disgust, the self-appointed referee placed himself at the wrestling women's feet, rather than at their heads, where he would be in a better position to determine whose shoulders were pinned down. The contest continued for some minutes, until, in Jungmann's rather delicate words, 'the man ran away visibly morally excited.'[11] At the same time, while still on top of her fellow nudist, one woman exclaimed 'that this was so wonderful, she could lay thusly for hours.' A bit later still, Jungmann could observe that the man physically relaxed, though he did not return to the wrestlers. Jungmann concluded his report with some obvious satisfaction that some nudists did not join the nudist organization purely motivated by health concerns.

Responding to both the Arheilgen investigation and to Jungmann's report, as well as to a number of recent newspaper articles, police officials at the county seat in Groß-Gerau in December ordered the police in Darmstadt to open an investigation into Orplid and other possible nudist organizations in the area. Their report largely mirrors that of the Arheilgen deputies. Orplid's park is described as 120 feet by about 500 feet with a six-foot tall wicker fence. Meadows bordered the park on the south and east sides, and the north side had a path that led to Arheilgen.[12]

The park was mostly used on Wednesdays, Saturdays and Sundays, when about twenty people of all ages and sexes met to play ball and other games while naked. There was a shelter for disrobing and a water pump on the grounds. About forty-five families from Darmstadt and three from Arheilgen belonged to Orplid, and fourteen individuals from Darmstadt were members. In nearby Offenbach there were ninety-five active nudist families. There were no members from outside Hesse.[13] The officials declined to take any action against the Arheilgen nudists, and the groups appear to have remained unmolested by any police or other authorities at either the city or county level until the arrival of the Nazis to power in 1933.

Nacktkultur and the Weimar State and Church

Nudists were left largely to themselves by local officials in the Weimar Republic. At the state level, however, concerns for the protection of public morality, whether raised by the state itself or more often by a morality league or church official, often forced some kind of investigation into *Nacktkultur*. State and church actions against nudists or nudism belong primarily to the second half of the Weimar Republic, and were especially vigorous in 1932. State and church opposition were often based on the blind assumption that *Nacktkultur* was immoral and that it promoted public immorality. When evidence to the contrary was discovered – and it nearly always was – that particular campaign against nudism ceased. Efforts by church and state officials to restrict or to prohibit nudism assumed two forms, and both were grounded in concerns for the moral health of the nation. One level of attack focused on nudism itself, the other, far more successful effort targeted nudist publications.

Generally speaking the strongest moral campaigns against nudism as a movement came from the Catholic Church. If official reaction to nudism during the good years of the Weimar Republic was casual or even indifferent, the attitude of the Catholic Church, not surprisingly, was not. Generally suspicious of the naked body, Catholic officials in Germany condemned *Nacktkultur* on theological as well as moral grounds.[14] Of Germany's two major confessions, the Catholic Church acted far more vigorously against nudism than did the Lutheran, hosting two conferences to deal with and to condemn it.

The first Catholic conference occurred in 1924, and in one of its points denounced nudism as a threat to chastity, morality and shame, the last of which in particular was believed responsible for maintaining order. Nudism placed youths' souls in jeopardy. From the Church's point of view, separation of the sexes in physical activity was necessary for morality, an idea nudists allegedly actively worked to destroy.[15]

At the 1931 bishops' conference in Fulda, in Hesse, a condemnation of *Nacktkultur* was again pronounced. At the conference, Cardinal Faulhaber inveighed against women's fashion, housing shortages, the modern world and nudism. The conference called for an end to so-called wild bathing in Germany's waterways, recommended wearing of swimsuits, strict observance of public bathing areas, a prohibition on appearing naked on Germany's beaches and, of course, the separation of the sexes.[16] Breslau's princebishop joined the chorus and condemned nudism.[17] Catholics could also force the state to act against nudism, though not often successfully.

In 1925, the Prussian State Parliament was forced to consider the issue of *Nacktkultur* when a deputy from the Catholic Center Party demanded to know whether the minister of the state was aware that 'in theatre, cinema, and in every exhibition there exists a *Nacktkultur* movement that in no way represents art, but instead lasciviousness?'[18] The question was motivated by the fear that shame, keeper of the public order, was on the verge of disappearing.[19] The Prussian government dutifully explored the problem and Oberregierungsrat Bandmann presented his report in early October.

Bandmann reported that the nudist movement had existed for some decades. The movement, Minister Bandmann explained, promoted hygiene, sports and aesthetics, and exhibited a number of ethical points, especially regarding sexual ethics, that in no way satisfied lasciviousness or other base instincts. Nudism, he continued, encouraged morality and respect for one's own and others' bodies. It also promoted the effort to keep oneself pure.[20] Minister Bandmann's report was accepted, and no further government efforts against nudism as a movement or a practice occurred in Prussia for the next few years.

By the early 1930s, public attitudes began to shift away from nudism. Nudist ideologue Walter Heitsch noted with regret that people were once again putting their clothes back on. 'The observable general desire towards free bodiliness (if not outright total clotheslessness) in the years right after the war was undoubtedly reversing!'[21] Women, he complained further, were again wearing more clothes. Where there had once been nakedness, now one could see swimsuits, capes, skirts, coats, hats, everywhere.[22] Police efforts against nudists in the eastern sections of Berlin, especially near the city's many lakes, were intensified in 1929.[23] The trend away from nakedness and clotheslessness that Heitsch and other nudists detected was part of a broader campaign to restore decency to society by restricting nudism and other public nakedness.

Adolf Koch, for example, the former schoolteacher devoted to bringing nudism to the children and to the working class, suffered several setbacks in 1928 and 1929, as two of his naked schools, one in Mannheim and one in Ludwigshafen, were closed.[24] Dr von Winterfeld, a member of the Deutsch Nationaler Volkspartei complained in the *Große Anfrage* in June 1932 about a performance by Adolf Koch and his students that had recently occurred in Berlin. It featured naked girls and women aged from childhood through their mid twenties who did rhythmic exercises. There were also naked males who appeared to be commanded by the women. Whatever the performers' pretensions about furthering health and body culture 'reliable witnesses' reported that the exhibition 'made the impression of a most nauseating sexual orgy.'[25]

Eventually, campaigns to improve public morality from its excesses of the 1920s would compel the Prussian Minister of Culture, Dr Bracht, in 1932 to issue a clothing edict, derided by many as the *Zwickerlaß* or Spandrel Edict, that essentially required full-length body swimsuits, such as one might have seen at the turn of the century, for all swimmers and bathers in Germany's waterways.[26] One nudist author complained, in obvious exaggeration, that during an enforcement of the *Zwickel* the enforcing officer required him to do a handstand to demonstrate that no gaps in his swimsuit could be observed.[27]

Other legal efforts to roll back the nakedness of the 1920s were also underway, and, for example, the once felicitous relationship between nudism and Danzig was under fire.[28] Dr Melcher, Berlin's chief of police, began placing restrictions on the nudist group Fichte, specifically forbidding it to invite guests to its nudist evenings.[29] Though nudism would be briefly banned by the Nazis, the Bracht, or *Zwickerlaß*, remains the most important official pronouncement against nudism as such by any of the many governments of the period 1900–50, as unlike in the case of the Nazis' prohibition it was not reversed.

Finally, and though it hardly qualifies as organized opposition to the nudist movement, in the Weimar Republic's courts participation in nudism could be grounds for a divorce. In the late 1920s, a man successfully sued for and was granted a divorce from his wife based largely on the fact that she had visited a nudist park, which was somewhere on Lake Motzen. The judge argued that for an honorable woman, any visit to such a facility was contrary to marriage.[30] This decision was reinforced by a 1931 opinion that stated that communal nakedness was indeed grounds for divorce, so long as one spouse opposed it beforehand.[31] Needless to say, nudists disagreed entirely, noting, again, that it was contrary to the nature of nudism for anything sexual to have occurred on the grounds of the nudist park, and that therefore the lady in question could not have done anything dishonorable or worthy of divorce from her husband.[32] Immorality, however appealing as an argument, would prove to be a very difficult issue to prove against nudism.

Until the very end of the 1920s, state or national campaigns against *Nacktkultur*, often based on the protection or promotion of public morality, were failures. Government officials only succeeded in getting Germans' clothes back on when it passed the much-ridiculed *Zwickerlaß*; it was not an attack on nudism as such, though that was clearly the intended target. *Nacktkultur* was widely recognized by state officials as a movement that was thoroughly morally inclined in its ambitions and in its practice.

In the same year that the Catholic Center Party called upon the Prussian Parliament to investigate the problem of *Nacktkultur*, a number of groups associated with the Lutheran Church began earnestly investigating the problem of social nakedness, and included in their scope an investigation of the nudist movement. The Lutheran campaign against nudism, like the investigation by the Prussian government, was quickly arrested by the discovery that nudism was an avowedly moral ideology and practice. Nonetheless, the prevalence of nakedness seemed to imperil German morality, and Lutheran attention soon shifted away from the actual nudists to their publications. Even after several years of effort against publications that featured nakedness only very modest success could be claimed.

Nacktkultur and the Weimar Churches

The Arbeitsgemeinschaft für Volksgesundung (AfV), a morality league attached to the Lutheran Church, opened its investigation into the extent of nakedness in German public life in the mid 1920s. There was the problem of naked calisthenics being performed in schools and homes, as well as the problem of naked campgrounds, air and sunbathing facilities, especially those at Rehbergen, Lake Motzen and at Spreehagen, all near Potsdam in the area of western Berlin.[33] The AfV also worried about the problem and growth of nudist magazines and other publications that used naked images to sell themselves on the streets, often in full view of anyone, youth included. There were the nudists themselves. Nakedness was everywhere, it seemed to the AfV, and in order to fight it the AfV needed to understand it.

The AfV made an important distinction, just as nudists and the state did, between nudism for health reasons and nakedness for erotic ends. The AfV sent out a questionnaire to its members in 1927 seeking information on seven basic questions regarding the prevalence of nakedness in society. Specifically they wished to know about naked images in periodicals and in photographs and postcards, how many naked publications were in bookstores, nakedness on stage and in the cinema, in sports such as calisthenics and swimming, and in the daily press. They also sought information about nudist leagues and clubs.[34] The AfV wanted to know how many of the examples of nakedness in the various media were obscene and how many were not. There was certainly an important distinction between, for example, a photograph of the Venus de Milo and that of a naked woman lounging suggestively on her bed. Naked cabarets, which were noted to be on the decline, were again quite different in intent than naked artwork, or even the Ufa film, *Ways to Strength and Beauty*. In an interesting caveat to the investigation, the AfV was careful to note that the difficulty in its endeavor rested in the fact that very often healthy aspects of nakedness were condemned along with the bad ones.

More than a year later, in 1928, the AfV published its findings about nakedness in Germany, and as noted in its report there were two quite different sets of results.[35] The AfV now had important information regarding the nature of nudism. The AfV outlined nudism's main points, its methods, its proliferation and possible effects on Germany, and most importantly its intentions as well as its threat to German morals. The AfV report noted the existence of a national nudist umbrella organization, the Arbeitsgemeinschaft der Bünde deutscher Lichtkämpfer (ABL), and estimated overall membership for all nudist organizations at around 200,000. What seemed like a great danger of both a religious and social nature, advocating something the nervous AfV termed the 'new morality,' which seemed ready to replace all traditional notions of morality and rectitude, did not in fact exist in the nudist movement.[36]

The organized nudist movement, the AfV noted, however much it rested on faulty conceptions and fundamentally mistaken ideas ('*abwegige*'), was 'quite harmless, especially when compared with publications.' Nudist circles were described as taking themselves 'very seriously'; and membership and participation at the various parks seemed to involve primarily those from the working class and the petite bourgeoisie, and only a few from upper classes.[37]

Importantly, the AfV report on organized nudism stressed that 'participation at the parks lets one easily detect that these people are filled with moral goodwill and no way appear to be the vanguard for a lax morality.' Members were 'convinced that their efforts would bring about a moral renewal of our *Volk*.' The AfV concluded, 'that we find here a true longing for sun and light, paired with the serious will to work on the health and healing of one's own body and soul, in part a reaction against the ugliness of life in the metropolis. This creed [*Bekenntnis*] of a new morality is primarily supported by a way of living through *Lebensreform*.'[38] Nudism did not present a threat to German morality so far as the AfV was able to determine.

The real danger to social mores and to youth came from the publications that utilized naked photos to sell copies. 'The naked movement assumes a new face entirely as soon as it becomes literary,' the AfV noted. However, in their condemnation of publications that had naked photos, some of which were nudist magazines, the AfV was careful not to condemn the books of the nudist movement. Works by Surén, Ungewitter and Seitz, and others like them, represented the so-called healthy nudist movement, and though they were just as rich with photos of naked men, girls and boys, and (especially) naked women, as were other nudist magazines such as *Figaro*, they were not to be considered dangerous to the *Volk* or to youth. Periodicals, nudist magazines included, however, represented the true threat to German morals. 'More and more,' complained the authors of the AfV's internal communiqué on nakedness in German society, 'one finds in street and train station kiosks magazines sold under the flag of idealism, but that basically in word and picture are nothing more than an excuse to show naked bodies, which must injure one's sense of responsibility.'[39]

The reason the threat posed to public morality by periodicals as greater than that posed by books was because the publishing nature of the magazines was fundamentally different. The AfV noted that the personal interests of the publishers often mixed very quickly into the format and stance of the magazine, all of which were further interfered with by the reality of needing to generate a profit. As one consequence, the magazines did not only limit themselves to the idealistic quest for beauty or perfect bodies, but rather they pandered to the sexual curiosity of the broad masses. The further away from pure nudist pursuits a magazine was, the likelier it was to print more photos of nudes, and those photos tended to be more sexually suggestive.[40]

As a rule of thumb, this principle is true not only of periodicals of the Weimar years, but also the post-Second World War era as well. Also worth mention, especially regarding magazines in the post-1945 era, is the relationship between declining sales and explicitly pornographic photographs. Typically, the closer to bankruptcy a magazine edged, the more pornographic its photos became, and the more singles-searching-for-singles advertisements appeared, becoming what the Germans call a 'contact-magazine.'

'Schund und Schmutz'

It is a characteristic feature of 1920s campaigns against *Nacktkultur* that they did not focus on the public or semi-public nakedness of nudists, though that was certainly an irritation to many a rural gendarme or village preacher. As we have seen, publications, not nudists, were the primary targets of government agents and church watchdogs. Naked or even suggestive images and dirty magazines or books were thought to contribute to the overall decline of moral standards. One Lutheran morality league, believing masturbation had reached epidemic proportions among youth, reckoned that 'whole school classes of boys committed it,' and no less than '120 *per cent* [sic] of girls suffered under self-pollution.' Clearly, the league concluded, this problem was the result of 'dirty advertisements, anal-art [*Afterkunst*] and the cinema.'[41] Great efforts were made throughout the period before the Nazis rose to power to expand the existing law against 'dirt and smut' (*Schund und Schmutz*) in literature and in public places in order to protect the youth from its obviously overwhelmingly destructive effects.[42]

Understandably, churches and church-based organizations can be expected to be at the head of any effort to promote higher moral standards and to restrict the most egregious displays of indecency. In the early 1920s, for example, a Protestant morality league publicly complained to the Reichjustizminister, Dr Blanck, about the declining morals of society, especially as they manifested in public displays of nakedness. In this letter, the naked dancing of avant-garde strippers like Celly de Rheidt, famous for a routine in which she stripped from a nun's habit to total nakedness, was especially condemned.[43] Indeed, the presence of nakedness on the Weimar stage was and is well known; however, it had little in common with the nakedness of nudism.[44]

The very earliest efforts to combat nudism occurred during the Kaiserreich (Wilhelmine era), and focused not on the fact that groups of people, children included, were congregating in communal nakedness in associations, but rather on the publications, often thick with photographs, nudist authors produced. Richard Ungewitter, for example, claimed in the 1920s that the Catholic politicians had attacked him before the First World War through Germany's district attorneys.[45] A member of a morality league based in Aachen attacked Ungewitter after the publication of each of his books for violating paragraph 184 of the penal code, which prohibited profanity, and for insulting the Catholic Church and the morality league.[46] Prior to the outbreak of hostilities in 1914, Ungewitter found himself involved in a number of court cases, most of which he either won or could claim as partial victories. His various defenses did, however, cost him a substantial sum of money.

The information about his various court cases comes primarily from Ungewitter himself, who typically began each book with accounts of his previous books' legal troubles. One of his first court cases was initiated by a Frau B. from Freiburg who accused Ungewitter of having sent one of his books, *Nackt: Eine kritische Studie* (Naked: A Critical Study) to a boy. Ungewitter admitted that he in fact had, but that the boy had ordered and paid for the book in full before the shipment.[47] His opponents also attempted to prevent the distribution of his books by prosecuting booksellers who sold or carried his books, a tactic that infuriated Ungewitter and led him to establish a mail-order only business. Although he won several lower court decisions, due in no small degree to the number of scientific and professional experts that wrote letters of support on his behalf. One such letter-writer was Dr Lanz-Liebenfels from Austria, a charlatan and aristocratic pretender who may have given Ungewitter many of his ideas in the first place.[48]

The courts generally agreed that his books advocated a nudist lifestyle, which was fine, and that he had not overstepped any bounds of decency.[49]

Importantly, the court decided that Ungewitter's photographs of naked people could only be immoral if there was also a sexually stimulating aspect to them. Since there was not, his photos were not held as immoral or indecent. Ungewitter is not clear about how many court cases he was ultimately involved in, though there appear to have been many. Eventually his luck ran out and gradually the Kaiser's judges began finding sections of his books indecent, and ordering those sections to be removed, until, as he bitterly complained, there was nothing left to his books. As an act of desperation he wrote Kaiser Wilhelm II a letter appealing for help.[50] The Kaiser does not seem to have answered his request. Ungewitter's legal troubles disappeared with the outbreak of hostilities in 1914, as did his hitherto vigorous publishing activity, which had resulted in a book about every two years. After the war he continued to publish books on nudism, though he does not appear to have been involved in any other lawsuits.

In the Weimar Republic, despite the constitutional guarantee of freedom of the press, certain standards and expectations of decency continued to apply, and once the chaos of the immediate postwar and revolutionary periods was overcome, efforts, public as well as private, were again made to restrict some of the more blatant violations of public decency in print and in behavior. As one example, the cabarets and naked dance revues that mushroomed in Germany's cities after the end of the First World War were condemned by many groups interested in restoring public decency and morality, including nudists.[51]

Generally, in the effort against indecent literature, known in German as the campaign against '*Schund und Schmutz*,' morality leagues associated with the Lutheran Church assumed the lead. In past campaigns against indecent literature, the main effort focused on the daily press – especially their pages of jokes, the features sections (*Feuilliton*) and the advertisements – cheap paperback novels (*Kolportageromane*), dramatic literature, New Year's and other greeting cards, as well as billboards, placards and other items.[52]

In the 1920s, now confronted with nothing less than the complete breakdown of the moral order as they saw it, the morality league *Weissen Kreuz* (White Cross), among others, initiated a campaign to strengthen the existing law against unsavory publications that dated most recently from 1905. At their meeting in Berlin in 1925, delegates condemned especially the literature found in train station kiosks as both dangerous and readily available to youth.[53] The city of Berlin would become a main target, as it was there, one group realized, that the erosion of shame, in particular among women, was the greatest, as was evident in prostitution, revues, film, billboards and magazines that featured nakedness.[54] Interestingly, this group did not agitate against *Nacktkultur*, whose explicit goal was the elimination of bodily shame in the promotion of nakedness.

An investigation was promptly launched to determine the extent of magazines that were dangerous to youth because of naked photos. In a survey of one train station's kiosk, for example, 1 per cent of magazines were determined to be of the nudist movement, another 5 per cent had erotic illustrations, approximately 5 per cent more were erotic, but had no illustrations, and just over 1 per cent were homosexual magazines.[55] The Hamburg police maintained a list of indecent magazines with over two hundred entries.[56] Berlin police promised to step up patrols of train station kiosks.[57]

By 1926, the new law against indecent or immoral publications was on the books and the struggle against such literature moved from private to government officials. In some cases, women's leagues submitted publications for review to authorities, including *Figaro*.[58] However, despite the new, tougher law, *Nacktkultur* publications and images of nakedness did not long disappear from either magazine stands or magazines.[59] A bureaucratic apparatus was established to aid in the determination of a publication being in violation of the *Schund und Schmutz*, and the committee's decisions to ban a work often had far less to do with the presence of naked photos in a publication and far more to do with the work's content or message.

Passages or photos deemed sexually stimulating or those that presented erotic situations were most often placed on the list of indecent works. Certain issues of some nudist magazines were placed before the committee, which sat in Berlin, often because of complaints made by authorities from Germany's Rhine provinces, a notably Catholic area. It is worth recalling the early decisions in favor of Richard Ungewitter's works that drew a distinction between photos that depicted nakedness in a natural or non-erotic manner and those that did not, as this same principle would guide the examining committee in the waning years of the Weimar Republic.

The early legal observation made during Ungewitter's trials that drew the distinction between images of erotic nakedness and the unerotic nature of nudism's nakedness would remain a staple of legal decisions regarding indecency in print, and often worked to the nudists' benefit.

Nudist publications were far less likely to be placed on the list of indecent works because they consistently passed the test of not being erotic. Nudist magazines such as *Eos*, *Asa*, *Soma*, *Lachendes Leben* and *Figaro* were all placed before the committee for judgment, and in the majority of cases they were not deemed indecent. Consistently, the natural, non-erotic nakedness of nudism, both in word and in picture, rested at the center of the committee's decisions not to ban the work in question.[60]

The examples of three magazines, *Lachendes Leben*, *Eos* and *Figaro*, which found themselves under the scrutiny of the committee, each with different outcomes, illustrate the distinction the committee observed. Ultimately, the decision to ban a work was based less on photographic representations of the naked body and more on other content. The complainant against the magazine *Lachendes Leben* noted in particular that the complaint itself 'did not involve the healthy nudist movement, only its outgrowths.' The magazine, the complaint maintained, among other things, showed so many naked women 'and propagandized for the nudist movement in a rather unsophisticated manner, and could only result in harm to the movement.' Based on this information, he concluded, it was obvious to all that the magazine represented a danger to the youth.[61]

In his defense, publisher Robert Laurer noted that although *Lachendes Leben* had a press run of nearly 25,000, it nonetheless operated at a loss; it was not, he claimed, 'a business.' He noted further, that images of nude women stood in the foreground of the magazine's content because it was difficult to obtain images of beautiful males. Finally, he observed that there was nothing worse in his publications than could be found in the daily press. The committee agreed, and the magazine was not banned.[62] In its decision the committee observed tersely that 'nothing in the magazine had any sexual suggestiveness. Much more the tendency of all the literary contributions was to health.'[63] Naked images alone did not make a publication indecent in the eyes of the law.

The complaint against *Eos* is less detailed, as are the reasons for the committee's decision to reject *Eos* as indecent. Rather succinctly the committee concluded that 'dangerous for the youth are far more the half-concealed figures than the fully revealed ones.'[64] *Lachendes Leben* and *Eos* both showed fully naked figures, which by the committee's definition were not erotic.

Figaro, the third nudist magazine placed before the censorship committee for review, had a press run of somewhere between 15,000 and 17,500. Again the committee recognized nothing untoward in the magazine's appearance, and although the magazine dealt with such sensitive issues as sexual hygiene, sexual pathology, sex education as well as nudism it did so in an appropriate, popular scientific manner. The committee found the magazine was not in violation of the law.[65] This decision, however, was reversed on appeal to the higher committee in Leipzig.

In five issues of *Figaro*, the same superior committee located in Leipzig found objectionable material, in that it was suggestive of sexual or erotic activity. Though not naked, the picture in issue 16 titled 'Queen Caroline of England is embraced by a lord,' showed Caroline's skirt lifted up and 'her naked legs were visible.' In issue 19, a picture showed a man watching through a window while a maiden literally picked fleas from herself ('*sich flöht*'). Most damning of all were some of the generalia and advertisements in the magazine; some of these discussed the consequences of *coitus interruptus*, or appeared to be a call for sexual activity.

In one advertisement, a couple announced that they were 'an elastic couple [*bewegliches Ehepaar*], naturally elastic,' which the censors admitted might be perfectly harmless, but that the common reader would not find it so. Finally, the singles advertisement 'which young, beautiful, thin maiden with an ideal body will grant a union to a blonde, beauty-thirsty young man for a future marriage?' was considered a blatant call for sexual intercourse outside the confines of marriage. The magazine also found itself in trouble for comparing the Pope to the termite queen, spending his whole life in the Vatican just as she did in her hive.[66] These and some other issues of *Figaro* were placed briefly on the list of proscribed works.

Nacktkultur and Nazism

Characteristic of the Weimar experience of countering nudism was the effort by state or religious authorities to restrict *Nacktkultur* primarily for moral reasons. Often such efforts failed because state and ecclesiastical authorities, except those in the Catholic Church, discovered that nudism was itself an exercise in morality, not immorality. Local police officials often simply ignored the nudists, as they tended to stay well behind their fences. The accession of the Nazis to power, by contrast, began an era of contradiction and confusion. In the Nazi state, nudism benefited from official recognition and state sponsorship, but at the same time, nudists endured intense police harassment, repeated Gestapo investigations, and were subject to endless bureaucratic wrangling as high Nazi officials dueled with each other over the value and desirability of *Nacktkultur* for the German race and nation.

The question of nudism's role, if any, in Nazi Germany generated considerable administrative and ideological conflict. The ban on nudism in the Third Reich was first promulgated in March 1933 and was only retracted late in the war, nearly a decade after *Nacktkultur* was fully integrated into the Nazi pantheon of approved leisure-time pursuits.[67] The schizophrenic approach to nudism is characteristic of the chaotic nature of Nazi administration as well as emblematic of the ideological rift of the Nazi Party itself. The effort by pragmatic Nazis like Hermann Göring and Wilhelm Frick to prohibit nudism was rooted in an interest in cleaning up the moral and political mess inherited from the Weimar Republic. At the same time, those Nazis like Rudolf Heß, Ricardo Darré and Walther Groß who sought to realize Nazism's racial goals to create a master race and healthy Aryan nation recognized *Nacktkultur* as crucial to their mission. In between these factions were the nudists themselves, who could be naked or not depending on the caprice of time and place.

Although they later understood it as a sexual and political threat, initially the Nazis opposed nudism on moral grounds. They claimed, like Weimar officials before them, that it was a moral threat to the German nation. The Nazi prohibition on nudism of March 3, 1933 was promulgated by Prussian Minister of the Interior, Hermann Göring. In 1934, Reichsminister of the Interior Frick issued an edict restricting nudist activity for the nation as a whole. Its wording is nearly identical to that of Göring's edict, and underscores nudism's moral threat to the nation.[68]

Although Göring recognized that nudism was a powerful tool to raise the *'Volkgesundheit,'* and that it was used above all by 'urban populations to make the healing power of sun, air and water subservient to their bodies,' he decided nonetheless that, 'the *Nacktkulturbewegung* must be rejected as a cultural aberration.'[69] Nudism was thus declared to be 'one of the greatest dangers for German culture and morality.'[70] In the Nazi mind, precisely because it was a moral menace, nudism also threatened German culture, and in Göring's opinion the links between immorality and declining culture were unmistakable. Nudism, he argued, 'destroys women's natural feeling of shame, and causes men to lose respect for women, thereby destroying the basis for any real culture.'[71]

The edict's provisions were thorough and aimed to eliminate any opportunity for nudist activity. It called for the police to place any nudist organization under the strictest observation possible. The police were instructed to exert pressure on the owners of lands nudists rented to invalidate rental contracts (a very effective measure, since almost all nudist clubs made use of rented land). In those cases where the rental contracts included explicit mention of nudist goals, they were to be considered null and void under paragraph 138. Communities that allowed nudist leagues to use municipal facilities were instructed to withdraw such support. Finally, public exhibitions of nudism, such as those given by Adolf Koch and his students, for example, were forbidden on the grounds that large numbers of people attended, which presented a threat to public order and safety.[72]

The decision to prohibit nudism was quickly reversed, however. At the same time that Göring was calling upon all police officials to combat the 'cultural aberration of nudism,' negotiations were already underway between von Hauff, leader of the Reichsverband für Freikörperkultur (RfK), the Kampfbund für deutsche Kultur and leaders of the Nazi Party to remove hindrances for practicing nudism in the new Germany.[73] These negotiations led eventually to the creation in April that year of the 'coordinated' (*gleichgeschaltet*) nudist organization, the Kampfring für völkische Körperkultur, which later became the Bund für Leibeszucht (BfL).[74] Led by Karl Bückmann, the Nazi nudist organization worked tirelessly to create space for naked Germans in the Third Reich.[75] As high-ranking Nazi officials investigated nudism's tenets, goals and ideology, they became increasingly attracted to it.

Within a month of its prohibition, nudism was officially readmitted to German life, and within the year nudism was again being practiced in Germany, with full state support. In 1934 nudism could be practiced in Anhalt, Hesse, Mecklenburg, Braunschweig and other areas.[76] In Thuringia restrictions on nudism were lifted in early January 1934, in response to the creation of the Kampfring.[77] In Kassel, Karwilli Damm, later the founder of the great nudist library in Baunatal, attempted to join a nudist organization, only to learn that despite having many members, there was no firm leadership in place; authorities here did not oppose it.[78] In Prussia, Baden, Bavaria and Württemburg only partial prohibitions on *Nacktbaden* (public nude swimming) existed.[79]

The creation of a national, Nazified nudist organization notwithstanding, local police forces and municipalities acted with vigor to close or to disband nudist encampments in their midst. Local and regional officials moved against nudist organizations under the authority of the Göring–Frick decrees. In areas near Hannover, for example, the prohibition from March 3, 1933 was satisfied in a number of different ways. In Kreis Burgdorf three nudist organizations avoided dissolution by agreeing to wear clothing, and were allowed to keep their rental agreements, unless they practiced *Nacktkultur*. The gendarmerie placed them under surveillance.

The nudist groups in Landkreis Lüneburg, home of the Liga für freie Lebensgestaltung (LffL), and Stadtkreis Harburg, home of the FLB-Harburg (the Freiluftbund or Free-air Group), escaped dissolution by promising to wear clothes and to conduct only sports activity. In the latter case, municipal permission to use the city's gymnasium and swimming pool, arrangements that had existed since 1925 and 1926 respectively, were withdrawn. In the city of Lüneburg itself, a nudist club of nineteen members without a park was placed under tight police watch. In many cases, areas known for *Nacktkultur* activity were simply placed under police surveillance. This was the case in Fallingsbostel-Soltau where Spöktal, a convalescent home dedicated to nudism, and in Glüsingen where Dr Fränzel's Lichtschulheim, a school for coed naked education, were located, as well as in Landkreis Harburg, home to the Sonnenland Egestorff.[80]

For most of the rest of 1933 and all of 1934, counties around Hannover dutifully reported to their superiors whether any nudist activity existed. The towns of Celle, Dannenberg, Gifhorn, Oldenstadt, Uelzen and Burgdorf reported that *Nacktkultur* no longer existed in their communities.[81] By no means does this suggest that nudists stopped being nudists, however. Isolated examples of families or groups of individuals practicing nudism appeared throughout the duration of the edict of March 3. The occasional discovery by local police of naked Germans frolicking in the woods and fields near Hannover confirmed official suspicions that nudists were secretly violating the law.[82]

Some, like Dr Fränzel of the Lichtschulheim in Glüsingen and H. Bescheke, the lessee of the land in Egestorff where nudism had existed for years, doggedly fought the prohibition in an effort to win back their businesses. Their efforts created a minor storm of paperwork, lasted years and produced only limited results. Bescheke argued, for example, that the decree forbade only public nudism. His guests, he pointed out, were not in public and that they could not be seen by the public, as they were well hidden behind thick vegetation. Moreover both he and his guests were all official members of the Nazi nudist organization the Kampfring. These arguments did not persuade local authorities and the prohibition against nudism continued at Egestorff. Bescheke and his guests, however, continued to practice mixed-sex nudism, to the increasing irritation of local authorities. The final resolution to the matter cannot be concluded from the file, though it is likely that Bescheke continued his appeals and the authorities continued their crackdown.

In Hamburg, police harassment is particularly revealing of local authorities' attitude towards nudism and nudists. 'Coordinated' nudist organizations, many of which had existed for decades and had belonged to various umbrella organizations and cartels, some socialist oriented, some not, endured ongoing police harassment under the pretext of both Frick's and Göring's edicts. When members of the former FLB, now 'coordinated' into the Kampfring, contested the edicts' provisions and their persecution by police authorities, they were told that the FLB, 'has not been forbidden because of its membership in the [Weimar-era] Arbeitersportkartell, that is of ancillary nature. It has been forbidden because the police authorities in Hamburg do not want *Nacktkultur* leagues.'[83] Hamburg's nudist groups, all operating as members of the Bund für Leibeszucht (BfL), were eventually allowed to practice mixed-sex nudism in the city's facilities in 1937, after enlisting and gaining the support of Senators Richter and von Allworden.[84]

Göring's edict against nudism recalled the moral concerns of *Nacktkultur*'s Weimar opponents, and it did not strictly forbid all nudism, only that involving both sexes. Thus in 1935, Frick expanded the edict of March 3, 1933 to bar all public nude swimming, which the original had not done. His reason for doing so had to do with Nazism's fear and loathing of homosexuality. 'Furthermore, I would like to stress,' he wrote, 'that those circles that actively call for the communal naked swimming of persons of the same sex are on occasion composed of persons of sick disposition.' Instances of persons of the same sex caught swimming naked together would need to be decided on a case-by-case basis for possible violation of paragraph 175, which criminalized homosexuality.[85] Though few nudist groups were ever persecuted under this provision, it does indicate how the regime dealt with the problems presented by public nakedness. Homosexuality was understood as a grave danger to the regime.[86]

Nacktkultur in Nazi Politics

Finally, and most seriously, efforts to restrict *Nacktkultur* in the Nazi state were driven by Nazism's pathological pursuit of communists and communist cells. Here again, the familiar rift in the Nazi Party over the nature and future of nudism in the Third Reich can be observed. Fears of nudism being a Marxist idea or a Marxist breeding ground propelled a number of investigations into it.

In Leipzig the major police crackdown on nudist organizations occurred on September 6, 1933. Citing Reichminister Frick's decree from February 28, 1933 for the 'Protection of State and People,' the police dissolved and confiscated the means of most of Leipzig's nudist clubs, including the Bund für Sonnenfreunde (BfS), the Vereinigung für neuzeitliche und gesunde Lebensgestaltung (VgL), Licht und Sonne (Liso) as well as its non-nudist parent organization the Möve Lodge, Bund der Licht und Sportfreunde (BLS), which had belonged to the Leipzig branch of the Liga für freie Lebensgestaltung (LffL), Freikörperkulturbund Leipzig (Fkk-Leipzig). On September 8, the Adoa workers' bank was asked by police to freeze the accounts of eight free-time organizations, under suspicion of being Marxists, at least five of which were nudist groups, and one of which was a communist association.[87]

Being banned by the police could but did not always spell the end of a nudist club's existence. The clubs and their members were always investigated by police. In some cases, the political economist, Georg Fischer, was assigned the task of sorting out who was a Marxist and who was not. His decision that a club was 'politically as well as morally unobjectionable' meant that the club could continue to exist, but it did not mean that their nudism could be practiced.[88]

In some instances, small, politically unobjectionable clubs were dissolved; their members often joining one of the larger Nazified organizations. Such was the case with the BLS, which had fifty members. The BLS was formed by a group of nudists who broke away from the LffL in February 1933. Both groups were subsequently dissolved in September 1933, and whereas the LffL and its property were liquidated, the BLS was cleared of suspicion in December 1933 by Fischer. By then, however, its members had all joined the Kampfring (later the BfL), and it was never refounded.[89]

Key Nazi officials such as Frick and police agencies like the Gestapo were convinced that nudism was little more than an opportunity for Marxists to meet, and they repeatedly subjected nudists to background checks and investigations. Other high-ranking Nazis, such as Hitler's deputy Heß, Agricultural Minister Darré and Racial Policy chief Groß, however, were equally convinced that nudism was in no way a Marxist phenomenon. It was not, in their language, a 'November phenomenon,' a reference to the social and political chaos of November 1918 that ultimately saw the fall of the monarchy and the birth of the Weimar Republic.[90]

In 1934, after sifting through the short history of nudism, Party Deputy Rudolf Heß acknowledged that Marxism was often present in nudist leagues, but that the effort to characterize nudism as being permeated with Marxists was a result of church efforts to force the state or Party to reject nudism. In his opinion, 'the party and its State have no reason to be pulled into such a position.' In his decision, Heß declared that 'the basic formulation of the *Freikörperkulturbewegung* [nudism] is healthy and must, from the standpoint of a nature-based and nature-oriented renewal movement, be welcomed.'[91]

Dr Walter Groß, head of the Office of Racial Policy, supported nudism for many of the same reasons as Heß.[92] Moreover, Groß expanded Heß's position in an important way, claiming it was beyond the ability of the Nazi state to end nudism. In an argument that needs to be read twice to be believed, Dr Groß, a man who would become intimately responsible for the murder of millions, argued for allowing nudism into Nazi society because eliminating it 'would mean a powerful intervention of the state in the lifestyles of the [nudist] members.'[93] Such an intervention by the state in the lives of its citizens, Dr Groß continued, 'could only be justified when it was in the interests of the public and of the *Volk*. This necessity,' he confessed, 'cannot be considered as a given.'[94]

German nudism eventually found a home in the Nazi state as a sports club. The decision reached by Reichssportführer von Tschammer und Osten, under whose leadership all German sports were 'coordinated,' echoed those made by Heß and Groß.[95] Nudism, until the efforts by Adolf Koch in the 1920s, had been known almost exclusively from the works of such men as Richard Ungewitter and Hans Surén, the latter of whom was now in the SS. Moreover, Heß's report noted that towards the end of the 1920s, a number of nudist groups joined the RfK, which took a political turn towards pacifism and liberalism, causing a general decline in member groups' participation. He recognized nudism's goals as being 'a reasoned way to live, physical strengthening of members through exposure to the air [*Freiluftleben*] long distance walking and sports. [Its] participation in the racial improvement and ascendancy [*Aufartung*] of the *Volk* and its demands for proper culture are to be thoroughly welcomed.'[96] He further suggested that because of its apparent close association with Marxism, the term *Freikörperkultur* be dropped from use, which it was.[97]

Despite 'coordination' and integration into the Nazi state, nudists continued to experience considerable suspicion and harassment from state officials, in particular from the Gestapo and SS police forces, who remained convinced nudists were Marxists until well into the Second World War. In 1937, for example, Gestapo officials in Dresden began to revisit the question of Leipzig's nudist leagues and Marxism. A number of individuals and groups who had been declared 'politically and morally unobjectionable' by Fischer, and who had joined the BfL, the official nudist club, had their files reopened for investigation by the Gestapo.[98] In both of these cases, the matter appears to have ended with a report from the Leipzig Gestapo office detailing events through 1934.[99]

The institutional fear of communism and security forces' suspicion of nudism is further illustrated by the example of a BfL movie that toured Germany at the end of the decade. In 1939 a nudist film deemed 'educational' (*volksbildend*) by Goebbels' ministry, titled *Natürliche Leibeserziehung* (Natural Body Education) toured Germany accompanied by Karl Bückmann, the leader of the Bund für Leibeszucht (BfL).[100] It was shown throughout Greater Germany including Vienna, Dortmund, Berlin, Erfurt, Wesermünde, Essen, Hamburg, Chemnitz and Stuttgart.[101] In a hotel in Lüneburg on June 2, 1939, the film was shown before a group of roughly seventy-five people, including approximately thirty women, but almost no youths. The goal of the evening, announced the host and long-time nudist, Dr Fränzel, 'an elderly man who leaves the impression of a "nature man" [fullbeard],' was to help the BfL gain a foothold in Lüneburg.[102]

Before the presentation, Bückmann gave a little speech outlining the history of nudism and its function among the ancient Germanic peoples as well as the BfL's goals, which included eliminating prudery and returning Germans to their age-old custom of communal naked bathing. A second goal listed by Bückmann was the creation of an understanding among modern Germans of nakedness and nudity free of sexual connotation and meaning. Again this hearkened back to the innocent, natural nakedness of the ancient Germans, among whom nudism was a way of living, for the purpose of breeding a superior race. He ended with a warning to the audience that the film was not for those who were there 'to indulge in curiosity.' The Lüneburger authorities tersely described the film's contents: Shot on a beach, 'the film showed pictures of members engaged in sport and play. Offensive images were not present.' Authorities in Lüneburg certainly found little offensive about the film, the presentation or nudism, and only reprimanded Fränzel and Bückmann for misusing the title *Reichsleiter* in the invitation.[103] In Lüneburg, nudism apparently carried no political dangers, moral threats or subversive messages.

In Munich, however, where the film was shown about a month earlier on May 11, authorities were much more suspicious and much less willing to believe that *Nacktkultur* was neither Marxist nor immoral, and that it was acceptable in National Socialist society. This time local BfL representative Martin Kürsinger, an inspector for the Reichsbahn, hosted the evening. Before the Nazi assumption of power Kürsinger had been the leader of a nudist group that belonged to the Arbeitsgemeinschaft für Freikörperkultur und Lebensreform (AgFL). Kürsinger introduced Bückmann, described by officials as giving the impression of an ascetic, who then delivered a familiar speech on the naturalness and moral purity of the ancient Germans in matters of the naked body and bathing. Again, SS officers were present to observe the meeting.

In his speech, the SS officer noted, Bückmann relied heavily on the works of Ricardo Walther Darré, the Reichsbauernminister, and Dr Groß, to support his arguments in favor of nudism and its ability to create a healthy, racially pure *Volk*. Bückmann, the report indicates, then showed the film, which is described as depicting a folding boat on the Baltic Sea near Mecklenburg sailing into a nudist summer camp, where the focus then shifted to show the life and activities of various north German nudist leagues. The film showed club members of both sexes naked and together. The police report concludes that nudism could not lead to a new moral conception among the German *Volk*.[104] Far more interesting, however, than their opinion of nudism's chances for success are the police comments on the audience and members of the Munich BfL.

About 400 mostly elderly people attended the film's showing. The police observer noted with a touch of irony that the 'youth who were to be the bearers of the new conception of the body were completely absent.' The only youths who were present at the film were those who played a 'melancholy recorder' in an effort to provide the film with its musical accompaniment. These youths appeared to the police observers to have been members of the 'former Marxist *Nacktkultur* and *Lebensreform* leagues that have come over [to Nazism].' The members of the audience, the report states, 'greeted each other warmly, though seldom with the "German Greeting",' and it appeared to the observer that 'the majority all seemed to know one another from some camp somewhere.' Importantly, the report says that 'known Marxists were not observed.' In an investigation of the backgrounds of the members of the Munich branch of the BfL, which consisted of sixty-three men and fifty-one women, only ten could be identified as having supported left-oriented parties before the Nazi 'seizure of power.'[105]

The authorities in Munich were prepared to find Marxists either in the audience or in the Munich BfL, and could scarce believe otherwise. Of the 114 nudists in the Munich BfL, just ten had been supporters of left-wing parties before 1933. This was clearly not a hotbed of Marxist activity, and the police observer is forced to admit that 'an immediate connection to Marxist or even federated [*bündisch*] efforts cannot be established.' However, his disbelief registers in his comment that 'the outward appearances [*äussere Rahmen*] of the gathering suggest Marxist or federated tendencies.' No matter how closely he looked, however, could any 'Marxist tendencies' actually be uncovered either in the BfL nudist group, in the film or in the film's audience. This police report found high levels of readership in the Nazi hierarchy, and raised interest in *Nacktkultur* among top Nazis. By the end of July 1939, the Reichsführer-SS, Heinrich Himmler, had requested a copy of the film for his own viewing.[106]

Chief of Security Reinhard Heydrich, like his officers below him, believed nudist organizations to have been heavily infiltrated with Marxism in the Weimar Republic. Much of the resistance in the SS and SD (Security Police,

Sicherheitsdienst) for allowing nudism to flourish stems from his conviction that it would lead to the construction of new political cells, and provide a meeting place for Marxists to organize. In 1938 he promised a lengthy and decisive memorandum on the matter. Unfortunately, it is not known if Heydrich ever produced the memo.[107] It seems unlikely that a final decision was ever reached, and *Nacktkultur* enthusiasts continued to experience sporadic Gestapo and SS investigations and inquiries throughout the last years of the regime. Not even the national nudist organization could avoid scrutiny. In 1943, almost ten years after being 'coordinated,' the Sicherheitsdienst of the SS requested a full membership list of the BfL-Leipzig, 'for inspection and review.'[108]

The Politics of *Nacktkultur*

In the 1930s, nudism was caught in the unenviable position of being lost in a Nazi bureaucratic wilderness. It was both legal and disallowed at the same time. Nudists were persecuted by party officials and investigated by security and police forces while simultaneously nudism was embraced by the party and practiced by Germans. Clearly, no small amount of confusion existed among Nazis as to the political nature of the nudist movement. This confusion has lingered on in the historiography of the movement.

In historiography it is common to assume three nudisms existed in the Weimar era, and historians write of the '*völkische Nacktkultur,*' the 'proletariat *Nacktkultur*' and the '*bürgerliche Nacktkultur*' as separate and not necessarily related entities.[109] An exception to this is Arnd Krüger's excellent essay, which provides a very nuanced view of the various directions *Nacktkultur* took in the early twentieth century.[110] Many of the secondary sources have been deeply influenced by Georg Pfitzer's 1964 study, which provided much biographical information about the early important nudist figures.

Some, like Wolfgang Krabbe's landmark 1974 study do not address the post-First World War era and discuss only the *völkisch* nudism of the Kaiserreich.[111] Others take the opposite approach and give brief mention of the racism and *völkisch* nature of nudism before concentrating on the workers' nudism of the 1920s; they thus leave one with the impression that socialist nudism was the sole nudism of the Weimar Republic and that the Nazis terminated nudism altogether.[112] The later communists of East Germany never recognized nudism nor any communists who had been nudists prior to the Nazi regime.[113] Still other histories are narrowly focused on one aspect of nudism or nudity, such as sexuality or dance, and their overall relationship to modernity. These do not address directly the political aspects of nudism, declaring '*Nacktkultur* was too mysterious to project any clear political identity.'[114] Michael Grisko rightly argues against the assumption that nudism was fundamentally anti-modern.[115]

Finally, in the post-Second World War era nudists themselves, perhaps understandably seeking to gain distance from recent events, avoid mention of any political association of nudism, especially any association with the Far Right.[116] In these works, the past is not ignored as much as it is minimalized, with a hope perhaps that certain aspects of it can be forgotten. To suggest, however, that vast political or class divisions sharply divided nudism during the Weimar Republic would be both an exaggeration and a mischaracterization. Nudist ideology sought to unite all Germans based on a common naked experience and was, at best, politically amorphous.

Nacktkultur appealed to Germans from across the political spectrum, but was itself apolitical. Indeed, one of its goals was to undo the damage caused by party politics, and then create a national nudist community freed from politics altogether. The source of the Nazi state's ideological and administrative confusion rests on the one hand on the Weimar nudist experience and on nudist ideology on the other.

The impression that nudism was a Marxist expression was due in part to the figure of Adolf Koch, a nudist noted for his work among the working classes, and possibly a socialist. At the very least Koch was a socialist sympathizer. Koch and his naked students were unique among German nudists for their level of public self-promotion, a fact that undoubtedly contributed to the general impression that nudism was a socialist phenomenon.

Koch and his students would hold public performances of naked calisthenics and rhythm exercises throughout Germany. These performances attracted a good deal of attention both from the press and from authorities. For example, a performance in Ludwigshafen in 1928 drew tight police control as well as a crowd of 800 to watch.[117] It was for a similar performance while a public schoolteacher in Berlin-Moabit that Koch found himself embroiled in a very public controversy that eventually cost him his position at the school.[118]

Those Nazis who supported nudism concluded that the real reason *Nacktkultur* was so readily associated by the general populace with Marxism was due especially to the degree of persecution of Koch's group by government authorities under then Prussian Interior Minister Severing.[119] The Nazis observed that the public, 'experienced little from other groups.'[120] There were many kinds of nudism, but Koch's group garnered more than its fair share of the press.

Koch, in offering his own views of nudism's politics, provided a second explanation for why so many readily associated *Nacktkultur* with the Left; one that nevertheless hinged on a popular perception of the movement. *Nacktkultur* was apolitical, he explained, however, its awareness of hygiene needs and work conditions caused it 'to coincide with the demands of the free trades' unions, the socialist youth clubs and the parties of the Left in cultural-political terms.'[121] Though some of its goals mirrored those of political parties, allowing it to appear closely related to a political position, nudism in fact never was. Nudist ideology remained free of political ideology.

The ideology of *Nacktkultur* acted as a powerful magnet, promising to promote physical health and to better the nation through the naked experience. It could draw together the traditionally most antagonistic political positions and foster a spirit of cooperation and of unity among them in ideology and in practice. Although nudism undeniably attracted Germans who hated and feared socialism, it also attracted socialists. Guided by the nudist vision and influenced by nudist practice, nudists from both political extremes found considerable middle ground in the nudist experience. In two key ideological regards – the goal of nudism and the means to achieve that goal – *Nacktkultur* drew adherents from the far right and far left, building a kind of naked consensus at the nudist park.

In its earliest manifestation nudism opposed socialism, but this opposition did not run deep enough to cause a split in *Nacktkultur*. For example, the early *Lebensreform* magazine *Deutsch Hellas*, which promoted nudism, anticipated the day when 'the fertile soil of socialism would be made sterile.'[122] Richard Ungewitter, deeply frightened by the specter of communism in Germany, continued the animosity towards Marxism in *Nacktkultur*. He repeatedly warned that the only way to prevent a Jewish-led Soviet horde from occupying Germany – a path that in his mind began with the Catholic Center Party, democracy and social democracy – was through the 'solution to the racial question,' made possible through nudism.[123] However, by the 1920s nudism was being practiced by the very group Ungewitter feared so much, Marxists, yet his response to this development was both unexpected and uncharacteristic: he welcomed it.

Although virtually all nudist organizations made at least an official effort to remain apolitical or to establish their organizations free of political affiliation, leading nudists were often of very different political ideologies.[124] However, in the quest to build a naked state, political differences among nudists could be easily and unequivocally laid aside. Ungewitter, an early member of the Nazi Party and long-time *völkisch* nationalist, declared in one of his publications his outright support for the leftist nudist Adolf Koch, who, as we have seen, had run afoul of Berlin's school authorities in 1923 for his work among the schoolchildren of Moabit.[125] 'I can and must point out that the efforts of Koch can only be described as noble. And I take him into protection against the aspersions cast by his enemies, despite the fact that he is my political opponent. However, in matters of moral and health education, he is my comrade-in-arms.'[126] In matters of politics, Koch might look for the solution to the class struggle through 'war against those classes that oppress us,' and Ungewitter might seek the reversal of Germany's decline through the solution to the racial question, but in matters of the naked body the two could meet.[127] Ungewitter at least was publicly willing to compromise.

None of the close association with anti-socialism or anti-bolshevism prevented nudism from finding strong support among communists and socialists. Adolf Koch, often acknowledged as the leading figure of 'proletarian *Freikörperkultur*,' adopted and popularized nudism as a way to heal workers and especially their children in the 1920s. To further his goals and nudism in general he founded or co-founded the Sparte für proletarische Lebensreform und Freikörperkultur, which was loosely associated with the Verband der Volksgesundheit (VVg), a Wilhelmine era umbrella organization that covered a number of reform movements, including *Nacktkultur*.[128]

Despite its efforts, the VVg remained largely unknown in the broader socialist movement milieu. Its effectiveness in reaching German workers has been called into serious doubt by its historians, Franz Walter, Viola Denecke and Cornelia Regin, who concluded that 'with its lectures, presentations and transparencies, the "Verband der Volksgesundheit" did not reach the working classes.'[129]

One principle on which nudists from the Left and the Right could find common ground was the primacy of breeding and eugenics in creating the new, nudist Germany. *Nacktkultur* was an ideology designed to purify the German race, by strengthening the viable and slowly weeding out the weak and those deemed undesirable. Koch, as a spokesperson of the political left, could sound remarkably similar to those nudists on the far right on the need for breeding and nudism's role as an agent of purification of the German race. Koch recognized the potential for racial improvement in nudism, remarking that 'the *Nacktkultur* movement is thoroughly set to racial biology,' a statement that many on the right would have seconded, if not produced.

Koch's friend and ally in bringing nudism to the working classes was Dr Hans Graaz, and it is through him that the need for breeding and eugenics finds some of its clearest expression. Graaz saw moral and physical degeneration all around him, and he blamed it on poor reproduction. Much of people's basest behavior and moral shortcomings including 'the disposition to intellectual degeneration, unsociability, quarrelsomeness, vagrancy, restlessness and other unsocial tendencies' were often inherited from one's parents. Predisposition to physical ailments, too, was the fault of parents. Graaz continued: 'the disposition to not effectively resist infectious diseases, flu-like infections, that lead to bone suppuration, crippling, deafness, kidney and heart diseases ... to tuberculosis, diseases of the blood ... to weak physical construction ... to an over-sensitive nervous system (hysteria, neurasthenia) and to an early old age, are inherited from parents.' One-third of men, he believed, suffered from some type of venereal disease.[130]

Living in a modern society only exacerbated the problem. Because they often worked, women, Graaz believed, were unable to nurse, and children were forced to nourish from cow's milk, causing them ill health.[131] Women, lamented another observer, had long since stopped nursing their young, something that led to a slow death of the nation as it contributed to higher infant mortality.[132] Graaz proposed as solutions to the rampant problem of ill health – often genetically inherited – better nutrition including vegetarianism, nudism and movement or exercise.[133] The reason for people's and society's health problems, and the continuation of those problems into future generations, was humanity's careless sense of reproduction. In the wild, he explained, the weak or sick died off and could not reproduce. Human society had altered this natural law, enabling anyone to reproduce, often at great expense to society.

With alarm, Graaz demonstrated how devastating and costly poor reproductive criteria could be for society, using the example of one Ida Jurke, born in 1740. By 1893, Ida Jurke and her children had produced 834 offspring; of these, 106 were illegitimate, 142 were beggars, 64 were alms recipients, 181 became prostitutes, 76 were thieves, and 7 were murderers. The total cost of the Jurke legacy was in excess of five million marks. The meaning of Jurke's legacy was equally clear: when the wrong types reproduced, and they did so in large numbers, society suffered. Like most nudists, Graaz did not propose sterilization, murder or other negative eugenics measures to deal with the problem of the weak or sick. As part of his broader nudist view, he wanted to return humans to a state of nature, where, presumably, natural laws would again assert themselves and only the strong would survive to reproduce.

The goal of reordering society by creating healthier, stronger Germans appealed to many; socialists were no less influenced by the works of Darwin and Social Darwinists than were others, and by the 1930s had begun to endorse the idea that one's life was directly related to one's economic value. Historian Alfred Kelly has shown that the 'bulk of popular Darwinism's influence was on the left half of the political, cultural and social spectrum.'[134] *Völkisch* nudist Richard Ungewitter, for example, like his counterparts on the left, was profoundly influenced by the works of Darwin popularizer Wilhelm Bölsche, whom he quoted at length.[135] When nudists formed leagues they carried their ideology into practice, and did not necessarily exclude because of a prospective member's political beliefs. The image of *Nacktkultur* as a manifestation of the left, or of being thoroughly dominated by Marxists, is a fiction manufactured by those who did politicize it.

The *Volksgemeinschaft*

One final, albeit important, area in which considerable similarity between the two political extremes can be found is in the longing for a unified *Volk* and nation, sometimes expressed as the desire for a *Volksgemeinschaft*.[136] This desire for a racially homogeneous, politically and socially harmonious nation was also characteristic of *Nacktkultur*.

During the Weimar era, the dream of uniting the fractured *Volk* had broad appeal. A carefully constructed piece of propaganda, the idea of 'the *Volksgemeinschaft* was embraced throughout the political spectrum, by Anarchists, Catholics, Jews, Protestants, Social Democrats, Liberal Democrats, Conservatives, and National Socialists,' notes Jeffrey Verhey.[137] For many it might mean a return to the heady days of August 1914 when the Kaiser's call for national unity (*Burgfrieden*) in the face of the enemy was enthusiastically received, though it did not endure the conflict that gave birth to it.[138] The hope for unity and harmony within a deeply divided and war-scarred *Volk* found voice in popular fiction from right and left authors during the Weimar Republic as well.[139] The term *Volksgemeinschaft* conjured different images to different groups, but for almost everyone it meant some kind of national or social unity. For National Socialists it carried, among other notions, a distinct racial agenda. For nudists it meant accepted, widespread social nudity, as well as social harmony.

The nudist Magnus Weidemann spoke both as a German and as a nudist when he lamented from his stormy enclave on the island of Sylt in the North Sea, 'we still do not have the *Volksgemeinschaft* for which we long.'[140] Among nudists, whose ideology was deeply rooted in the idea of creating a wholeness and unity among *Volk* and nation, the call for a *Volksgemeinschaft* could be found as well. Richard Ungewitter, for example, dreamed of a *Volksgemeinschaft* based on racial purity and unbridled Germanness.

Nudist endeavor and the ideology of *Nacktkultur*, both of which strove for the creation of a nudist utopia, could cause normally vicious political differences to subside, at least among nudists, in order for the larger and more important goal to succeed. This, too, is indicative of nudism's ability to draw disparate groups together in common cause, bringing with it harmony and wholeness, and is also a characteristic feature of the *Volksgemeinschaft*. At least one nudist called for Germans to combat party politics, presumably to avoid the divisiveness they brought with them, and to live freely, purely and naturally in the sun, air and light.[141] Nakedness was truthfulness before one's fellows. In the quest for social unity and harmony, nudist groups could and did claim that they had, in effect, already established the *Volksgemeinschaft* in the naked experience.[142]

Based on his own experiences, one author writing for the left-oriented nudist publication *Urania* was able to report that nudism furthered a sense of community or communal living (*Gemeinschaftsleben*) because *Nacktkultur* made people familiar with one another in an honest and direct manner, a necessary requirement for a community to succeed.[143] Noting that at the nudist park both sexes as well as all ages, professions, backgrounds, classes and those with varying levels of education got along quite well together, the Nazi Wolfgang Reichstein explained this was 'because everything that contributes to class hatred and antagonism is missing here and,' he continued, 'because in our nakedness we face each other person to person, recognize in the other person only a friend and comrade-in-arms for a common idea.'[144] Communists and Nazis could sound remarkably similar when discussing nudism and its benefits.

One of the most fundamental features of nudist ideology throughout the first part of the twentieth century was its desire to lead Germans and Germany to an idealized future where the problems of contemporary society had been overcome and eliminated, a place where Germans could again live naked in racial purity and national community. In the society *Nacktkultur* envisioned, all barriers between Germans would be dismantled in the common naked experience, including those built on sexual and class differences. The simplicity of nudist practice promoted its unifying impulses, for 'in contrast to other movements, nudism offers a way of life that is obtainable by everyone, as it requires no preconditions other than good will and a pure mind.'[145] 'Separations and fragmentation into smaller and smaller groups does not exist with us,' explained a Berlin nudist.[146] Magnus Weidemann called for nudists to remain free of politics.[147] Nudism combated division in its ideology and through its practice, and in it one could find the basis for a new age of German social unity and harmony.

One way in which nudist ideology claimed it could overcome the social divisions that plagued German society was by allowing anyone to join a nudist club or league. Nudists made the claim that their clubs and organizations did not exclude on the basis of religious or political belief. At the nudist parks, proponents alleged, all backgrounds, classes and Christians met happily. Although when considering a new member, an applicant's moral or racial background might be investigated, especially by the organization led by Richard Ungewitter, nudists claimed to admit anyone into their clubs. 'By the acceptance of new members, no religious or class differentiation will be made, rather only the personal value of the person is relevant,' claimed Wilhelm Kästner.[148] For others, too, the growth and success of the movement was far too important to allow it to founder on differences of class. A club should accept, 'people of all classes, from the high-ranking prominent to the lowliest craftsman, regardless of political affiliation, even people from various age groups are necessary.'[149]

In the ideology of nudism, social transformation was held to be the eventual result of transforming Germans, and nudists wrote of creating 'new people' or a 'new generation' through their endeavors. Only through naked activity 'will a powerful generation and a healthy *Volk* grow,' reminded one author.[150] The new generation of Germans, raised in nakedness at the bosom of nature, would possess characteristics that set it apart markedly from other generations of Germans. This generation would moreover 'pave the way for *Nacktkultur*,' and finalize nudism and nudist living as the new patterns of German life.[151] 'The goal of nudism,' claimed Hans Surén, 'must be oriented to the construction of a whole new German, of a German warrior, of a German woman with a majestic body from whose expression and movement beams a self-confident spirit, one that was accustomed to victory.'[152] The nudist generation would embody and exhibit nudism's most important principles, and bring them to the *Volk*.

Conclusion

In the final analysis, there were few major attempts to restrict nudism for most of its history. Neither Germany's confessions nor the various government and police officials, whether under the monarchy or the Weimar Republic, made any serious efforts to prohibit nudism. Instead, a spirit of indifference or acceptance, however begrudging or benign, appears to have prevailed. Remarkably, those individuals and organizations that sought to make society more decent by restricting images of naked people and access to those images, especially of youth, did not consider the organized nudist movement to be a threat to either public morals or to youth. *Nacktkultur* was apparently beyond the scope of the problem of declining public morals, or at least did not appear to contribute to it. That view would change, though only briefly, with the rise of the Nazis to power in 1933. Nazis understood nudism as a threat, though scarcely a moral one. *Nacktkultur* was integrated into National Socialist society once its racial value was identified.

Nacktkultur was seldom recognized as harmful to the nation or to the *Volk*; indeed, quite the opposite was the case. Many in the uppermost echelons of the Nazi administration recognized nudism as an important and powerful measure to ensure public health. It is among the Nazi elite that nudism, especially as a popular expression and alternative form of health, exerted its greatest influence and gained its greatest acceptance.

Reintroducing the naked body to German society and habituating Germans once again to its presence and observation was an important goal of the nudist movement. Indeed, accustoming oneself to the sight of a naked body, both one's own and that of someone else, was one of the most profound and important effects of the nudist experience. It was vital to the success of nudism and its utopian dreams of regenerating Germans into an organic, unified *Volk* that lived naked and chaste at the bosom of nature, and the German nation into the modern incarnation of the ancient, tribal whole, unmarred and unmolested by the pernicious, disintegrating effects of artificial religious, economic, social and sexual divisions.

Nudism's professed ability to overcome division of all kinds under the banner of regenerating the German *Volk* and nation was evident within the movement itself. Nudists came from a variety of backgrounds and held convictions that ranged across the political spectrum; yet unlike those in the political arena nudists did not allow these differences to dominate or to derail their collective effort of transforming Germany into a nudist utopia. Nudists were united in their criticism of German society, in their vision of the future configuration of society and the belief that the means for building that society would originate from the naked body.

Nudism's promise to make Germans physically and morally healthy was part of what made it an appealing ideology to broad sections of the population, and similarly its vision of a united *Volk* attracted believers from across the political spectrum, including the far right and far left. Thus could Adolf Koch easily reconcile his socialism and his nudism, ideologies that both sought to create a more equitable society, and call for a new 'configuration of life in the spirit of socialism.'[153] The Nazis, who first banned then re-allowed a 'coordinated' nudism, issued some of the strongest calls for nudism to become a part of daily life in order to create a better kind of German. Clearly, they were attracted to its racism, which fit nicely into their own, and its promise of health and renewal. '*Freikörperkultur* . . . is also an expression for a Nordic way of life that is connected to nature as well as a morally pure physical education and physical hardening, in which the movement of the unclad body in light, air and water is only the means to an end,' explained the Nazi nudist magazine.[154] The appeal of nudism was broad and penetrated deeply into many aspects of German society.

–3–

Nudism and Medicine

In the period from the beginning of the twentieth century to the end of the Nazi regime in 1945, the relationship between nudism and the state was marked by little interaction. What interaction there was between the state and nudism was often characterized by a spirit of indifference or antagonism, often motivated primarily by political concerns, such as the Nazi hunt for Marxists. Unconcerned with politics, the idea of nudism was rooted in a number of popular beliefs and prejudices against science, especially medical science, and scientific conceptions of the body. In stark contrast to the growing importance of science in the nineteenth century, in nudism, the body remained organic, natural, animate and whole.

Nudism functioned primarily as a reform movement. Nudist reform efforts focused both on long-term degenerative influences such as lifestyle and estrangement from nature, as well as on more immediate threats to Germans and Germany, such as disease and even the methods and theories by which doctors attempted to treat disease. Conceived as a movement that sought to regenerate Germans, their culture and their society to be more racially viable, nudist ideology focused foremost on health issues – a focus that changed little over the following decades.

Nudism was not a static ideology, and as it grew and evolved it dropped its initial hostility to science and incorporated whatever scientific discoveries and principles reinforced its own ideology, increasing its already strong appeal. Interest in nudism spread throughout German society in the twentieth century, and by the time of nudism's inclusion in the National Socialist regime some of its most central tenets, especially the healing power of the sun, fresh air and light, had become central to medical and state-sponsored disease prevention efforts. Nudism's strongest appeal stemmed precisely from its non-scientific understanding of the body and promise of health.

Science versus Organicism

At the turn of the century, health, healing and medicine were poised at the entrance to the modern era of treatment, but proved incapable of crossing the threshold – a situation that gave rise not only to frustration and uncertainty but also to alternative practices. Nudism offered an alternative view of disease and prevention that stressed the individual over the medical professional, natural cures over medicines, and environmental factors over biological ones. Nudists extended their attack on medical science to its theories, methods of treatment and even to doctors, who found themselves in an awkward position.

Advances in medical science had provided doctors with the understanding of what caused disease but with neither the knowledge nor the ability to cure diseases. Medical practice was becoming increasingly marked by scientization. The nineteenth-century union of biology and medicine had been a fruitful one, producing important theoretical advances, especially the theory of germ-based infection. However, it was also in this same period that non-scientific cures and treatments, such as nudism, originated and flourished.[1]

The importance and presence of the doctor was expanding in the years just before the twentieth century, a situation cultivated by doctors themselves. Due in some degree to the better training and education they were receiving, a consequence of the increased funds the new German nation was devoting to research and university education, the doctor's position as expert on medical issues was becoming widely accepted.[2] The presence of a doctor at the side of the sick was becoming more common as well, itself a result of national health insurance.

The passage of Bismarck's health insurance package in 1883 caused the number of doctors to swell, as it increased the likelihood of payment for treating the lower classes, who in any event became the focus of widespread efforts to make Germans more hygiene oriented.[3] Moreover, after years of struggle doctors sought to secure for themselves a monopoly on the entire body of the ill and unhealthy by eliminating from an already overcrowded field traditional and non-scientific healers and health practices through the passage of the so-called anti-quackery law in 1908.[4] Not everyone accepted the arrival of the scientifically trained professional doctor with enthusiasm, however, and many, nudists included, chafed under the anti-quackery law.

The early twentieth-century persistence of alternative treatments in the face of growing scientific and professional presence in health and healing speaks of a sense of frustration among some contemporaries not only with doctors' inability to cure disease but also with doctors themselves. Throughout the last third of the nineteenth century, doctors had attempted both to raise their status in society by professionalizing medicine and healing and also to establish a monopoly for themselves in medical treatment. Though ultimately successful, the efforts to professionalize medicine from the top down, to create areas of specialty for doctors and to monopolize the sick, also produced protest and reaction against doctors, of which nudism was one voice. Nudists and others strained under the anti-quackery law and complained that doctors themselves were the quacks who hurt and killed thousands each year with their medicines and theories.[5] In early nudist ideology, doctors were dangerous individuals with a misguided approach, whose theories and practices endangered people's lives and created suffering.

Nudists and doctors held fundamentally different views about the nature of the body, and this was the source of many of the complaints nudists made about doctors. The twin processes of professionalization and scientization within the medical profession created doctors who were better equipped to diagnose patients, but who had lost sight of the fact that patients were people.[6] Furthermore, these same processes, nudists argued, created a cadre of healers whose entire approach was mistaken. Specialization was the most egregious example of doctors' misguided approach to health and healing, and the nudist rebuke underscored the basic theoretical differences between the two camps. Doctors, nudists charged, treated symptoms not illnesses, organs rather than whole bodies.[7] As far as nudists were concerned, any attempt by doctors to cure victims of illness or to promote health among Germans could only result in failure because they lacked the proper holistic understanding and approach to treatment.

Holism and Naturism

The nudist contribution to the discourse on health and prevention was unique. The early nudist writers opposed medical science's approach to health, its claims to authority over the body and its very theoretical foundations. To begin with, the very different ways in which nudism and medical science conceived the body dictated their approaches to healing. For nudists, deeply influenced by the long tradition of homeopathy (*Naturheil*), which itself was a potent combination of holism and vitalism, the body was an unbreakable, unified whole that lived as a part of a larger natural whole.[8] Homeopathic treatments, claimed nudists, had for decades cured thousands.[9] Future efforts to treat the body needed to stem from a similar holistic approach.

Holism stressed the interdependence of the body's parts to one another and of the body to its environment. No one organ or body part, for instance, could malfunction without grievous consequences for the whole organism. Similarly, bodies suffered when they lacked some element from nature. One proposed cause of pulmonary tuberculosis that illustrates this point comes from nudist Richard Ungewitter. He suggested that since skin was covered by clothing, it could not assist the lungs in breathing, which was one of its natural functions. As a result, lungs were forced to work too hard, eventually becoming exhausted and tubercular.[10] In holistic thought, measures to cure illness, such as medicine, that treated only the areas producing symptoms could not succeed.[11]

In the homeopathic tradition, ideal cures returned the body to a more natural setting. Homeopathic cures featured heavy doses of water, sun, air and light, but could also prescribe vegetarianism and hypnosis and were occasionally conducted naked.[12] A fundamental difference between homeopathy and *Nacktkultur* was the nudist requirement that the body be completely devoid of clothing in order for the natural elements to achieve their full effect.

The influence of holism and homeopathy in nudism was one of the guiding forces in its own attack on the contemporary medical profession, which nudists derisively called *Schulmedezin* (school-medicine), a term they inherited from their homeopathic forefathers. The term *Schulmedezin* first appeared in 1876 in homeopathic journals, and was used in context of the homeopathic argument against immunizations and medicines, arguments nudists incorporated wholly into their own ideology. Homeopathic treatments, unlike medicine which was theory based, university taught and scientifically oriented, were founded on personal experience, not scientific or theoretical knowledge, and were rooted in naturism. For nudists, one's medical credentials were one's own body and own experiences, not one's theoretical knowledge or framed diploma.[13]

Naturism, the other major influence on nudism, was also a legacy from the Enlightenment and has been traced to Rousseau. Essentially, it taught that one's relationship to nature was vital to one's existence and that one should live with

Figure 3.1 The power of nature was awesome in nudist ideology. Here a woman ascends a mountain peak. Image from *Ideale Nacktheit*, 1915. Original photo by R.A. Giesecke. Courtesy of ANRL.

nature, not contrary to it.[14] Nature was believed to possess more power than humans could comprehend; it was 'in its omnipotence always stronger than the human mind.'[15] It was from the so-called 'nature-doctors' of the nineteenth century that nudism learned the healing value of sun, air, light. By the 1880s many recognized a relationship between contact with water, whether during bathing or swimming, and healing and health.[16]

Although important to homeopathy, nudism was less enamoured of water, and its usefulness was downplayed in nudist ideology. Nudist Hans Surén believed water 'draws too much warmth, magnetism and electricity from the body.'[17] 'I struggle exclusively against the "water-only believers," who expect water alone – be it hot or cold – will cure everything,' wrote the nudist J.M. Seitz in his contribution to the debate about the elements.[18] Heinrich Pudor agreed, saying that water was better as a drink than as a cure. A so-called *Wasserheilbad*, Pudor continued, was perhaps only useful insofar as it required one to be naked.[19] For him it was

Figure 3.2 Like sunshine and air, water was important in building a healthy body. Nudists often traveled to Germany's waterways to practice nudism. Image from *Ideale Nacktheit*, 1915. Original photo by R.A. Giesecke. Courtesy of ANRL.

clearly not the water that counted, but the nudism it demanded. In nudism, the most important elements, because of their ability to interact with the skin, and thus prevent infection, were sun, air and light.

Nudist ideology denied the ability of medical science and its practitioners to cure or even to prevent infection, as nudists believed medical science lacked the proper theoretical understanding of the body, disease and health. University trained doctors held a mechanistic view of biology, and were not disposed to consider nature therapies as practical.[20] For some nudists, doctors' refusal to admit the benefits of sun, air and light in combating disease was perceived as both a consequence of formal university training and general stubbornness. 'Good nutrition and *Nacktkultur* are shown to be the path to healing. *Schulmedezin*, which feels itself called upon in this respect to be the sole authority not only does not comprehend this so easily understandable sentence, but it even acts directly contrary to it.'[21] Nudists were well aware that no matter how simply they formulated their doctrine, medical science lacked the desire to grasp it.

While theoretical differences regarding their understanding of the body and the proper path to health were important forces behind the nudist rejection of medical professionals, not all of the nudist reaction against them was grounded on theoretical differences. There was a practical element to the nudist protest against doctors. Nudism was free; doctors and their prescriptions, one nudist rightly pointed out, were costly.[22] Worse than their medicines were doctors' uses of surgery, considered by nudists to be nothing less than a cruelty.[23] Unlike virtually all of their patients, doctors were university educated and spoke in medical jargon, an odd and baffling code, to describe even stranger illnesses, symptoms and procedures. One's health and body were quite literally in the hands of another.

In early nudist ideology there was little room for a university trained doctor. Even during its evolution from fringe phenomenon in the early 1900s to popular movement in the 1920s, when nudism discarded its initial vitriol against doctors, doctors' methods and authority were never accepted. The *Nacktkultur* of the 1920s considered doctors primarily as a group who could benefit from the practices of nudism, not as authorities on health matters. Eventually, once *Nacktkultur* and its practices triumphed in Germany, medical institutions and doctors would no longer be needed. The hospital would come to be known as the 'house of health,' and in this era people would always be cured according to homeopathic means. Finally, there would be a retraction of any compulsory immunizations.[24]

Nudism was constructed in such a manner that the individual German was always in control of his or her own personal body and health. It was inexpensive and easy to do, features that made it available to large sections of the population.[25] The practice of nudism established a pattern of daily rituals and practices, which, if properly followed, guaranteed a disease-free life. A nudist could completely control his or her own health by spending more or less time in the air or sunshine, for example. The nudist, not the doctor, made the decision to go outside, for how long and when.

In nudism, healthiness was an immediate result of exposure to the purifying elements of sunshine, fresh air and light, and was not dependent on the diagnosis of a doctor or on somehow preventing unseen germs from penetrating the body. There was no reason to consult a physician in nudism. Nudism existed outside the medical establishment, something that in the minds of many gave it greater legitimacy.[26] Nudism was a frank belief, with no alien jargon, no unfamiliar scientific language and, initially at least, no disease causing bacteria.

Modern nudism made its appearance in the pre-antibiotic era, and claimed itself to be both a cure and a prophylactic. Nudism taught that it was not possible for a healthy body to succumb to infection, and that the key to a healthy body was plenty of exposure to sunshine, fresh air and light, which cleansed and rejuvenated the body, keeping all of its interconnected parts functioning as a whole. Without periodic exposure to air and sun any healthy person would fall victim to illness.[27] Nudism was a utopian ideology and its believers and ideologues always remained confident that disease and illness would wither away once Germans devoted themselves to nudism. *Nacktkultur* was imbued with the power to heal, to prevent and to eliminate disease from the personal and racial body.

The most vituperative nudist attack on contemporary medicine concentrated on medicine's central theory. The crowning achievement of nineteenth-century medical research had been the development of the theory of germ-based infection. Growing knowledge of the body, its functions and anatomy, combined with the discovery of bacteria and other micro-organisms, led to important theories about contagion and disease that climaxed with the formulation of the theory that germs were the source of disease. Conceived by such men as Pasteur and Virchow, germ theory was first applied to anthrax (1876) and tuberculosis (1882).[28] Later it was confirmed and expanded in the great Hamburg cholera outbreak of 1892.[29] With the advent of germ theory, the cause of infectious disease was finally being truly understood, and medical science was on firmer theoretical footing. Unfortunately, however, this advance brought doctors no closer to being able to cure victims of disease, something that would remain largely outside their ability until the arrival of antibiotics after the Second World War.

Initially, nudists believed their movement capable of preventing infection and illness because of their conviction that disease was caused by estrangement from the natural environment, not by germs. Early nudists rejected the scientific explanation of disease, namely that bacteria and other micro-organisms were the root of illness. Using the example of tuberculosis to argue against germ theory, one nudist noted that although science had found tuberculosis bacilli, they must be rejected as a cause of the disease. His argument rested on circular logic, explaining that since bacteria needed to eat they would naturally be attracted to (and hence be found in) tubercular lungs. They were a consequence not a cause of the disease, he concluded.[30] Blaming bacteria for illness, this same nudist argued in a later work, was nothing more than a latter-day equivalent of the medieval practice of assigning blame to demons.[31]

The implications of germ theory for one's own agency in controlling health and protecting the body must be considered. Invisible without the aid of microscopes, bacteria and other germs could not be easily avoided; one could never be certain where they were. Also, one had to trust the doctor that germs even existed. It was far more comforting to believe in a familiar world where the sun nourished, the air refreshed and one's body was one's body rather than in a world of invisible armies of pathogens, defense against which was difficult. In proclaiming the existence of bacteria, creatures that only scientists or other specialists could see, yet were unable to kill or otherwise neutralize, doctors faced a kind of 'credibility gap' that nature-oriented movements such as nudism filled and exploited.

Nudists bolstered their arguments against germ theory with observations from contemporary doctors' offices and hospitals. If germs truly were the agents behind infection, then it seemed only natural that those who were most exposed to them should fall ill more often. To one early nudist observer, this, however, was not the case. Doctors and nurses, nudists pointed out, who dealt with victims on a regular basis, were simply not dying in numbers proportionate to their exposure.[32] Furthermore, doctors did not seem to be spreading illness among their patients during office hours, as it seemed they should be according to germ theory. Evidence such as this reinforced early nudist conviction in the error of germ theory. The position that infection was the result of environmental causes, or even genetic predisposition which was then exacerbated by living in a poor environment, dictated the nudist approach to prevention, which was to create and maintain healthy bodies through exposure to any of the natural elements of sunshine, fresh air and light. Nudist prevention efforts remained the same, and even gained validity by eventual acknowledgment of the existence of germs.[33]

In early nudist thought, the same environmental factors whose omission led to illness were also those that could cure or prevent it. Devoted as it was to germ theory, medical science, nudists were convinced, could never actually prevent infection or even cure illness. Immunizations, the main weapon against disease in a doctor's arsenal, were doomed to failure, since, as nudists argued, diseases were caused primarily by clothes, immorality and a lack of exposure to sunshine and fresh air.[34] One example nudists used repeatedly to support their assertion that wearing clothes caused illness was that of non-civilized hunter-gatherer tribes. They wore no clothes and showed no indication of tuberculosis, for example.[35] Moreover, the practice of immunizing was believed especially dangerous by nudists, as it not only did not prevent infection, but also actually introduced poisons into the body, corrupting and weakening the blood.[36] The nudist stance against immunizations was fueled in part by the belief that cowpox, commonly used to immunize against smallpox, and syphilis shared a common origin.[37] For nudists, immunization amounted to blood poisoning or infection with a most insidious disease.

Nudists were even more critical of medical science's reliance on chemicals and medicines to cure illness than they were of doctors' approach to healing. Guided as they were in the belief that environmental or moral factors caused infection, rather than bacteria or other micro-organisms, nudists held that chemicals and other medicines administered to sick patients ultimately caused more damage than they repaired. The pills prescribed to patients, as in the case of anemia to counter iron loss, were not only expensive, but also did not solve the problem.[38] Medicines, nudists argued, damaged the body's cells. Worse, the medicines and chemicals prescribed by doctors for treatment of disease ultimately created new diseases by altering a body's chemistry.[39] Doctors, it seemed, did not promote general health among Germans, but rather created conditions for infection. To become a healthy person, nudists countered, one needed not pills and chemicals, but 'the spring of strength and health [is] air, light, wind and weather, water, simple nutrition, moderation and alternating peace and motion.'[40]

Early nudist writers accused medical science and doctors of, in effect, inventing diphtheria, tuberculosis, influenza, polio and other diseases through the use of medicines on patients.[41] Moreover, any effort by medical science to find a cure for a particular illness was doomed to failure and would only result in more poisonous concoctions for patients to drink or swallow, ultimately worsening their condition or causing a new one altogether.[42] Only gradually, over the next two decades, did nudism accept the role of bacteria in causing disease, even as doctors came to accept the power of the sun, fresh air and light as prophylactics.

Unlike medical science, which identified numerous diseases, all caused by different germs, nudism identified only one cause for disease, the accumulation of 'self poisons' or the 'accumulation of metabolic residue' within the body.[43] One nudist even proclaimed that 'the poisoning of the body' was the only disease.[44] The 'accumulation of metabolic residue' or self-poisoning was related to environmental or moral factors, or a combination of the two. Infection was believed to be a result of living contrary to the natural environment, in cities or clothes, for example. The absence of just one element could lead to illness. Lack of sunlight was thought to be one reason behind the high incidence of working-class illness.[45] A German who practiced nudism could expect to be healthy. A nation living as nudists could expect to see the disappearance of disease completely.

Nudists fully believed that their movement, once adopted by and completely integrated into society, would extirpate disease. The Danzig nudist Adolf Weide centered his entire book, *Verjüngung absolut*, around this principle. Weide stated quite simply that there should be no disease. Practicing *Freikörperkultur*, he argued, would accomplish just that by creating a healthy body and a joyous individual, neither of which could act as vessels for disease.[46] Although by the time

Weide's book was published nudism had come to accept the theory of germ-based infection, exposure to natural elements remained the key to establishing and maintaining health, either by curing illness or preventing it altogether.

The nudist conversion to germ theory was abrupt. Sometime in the early 1920s, nudist authors simply stopped denying its veracity. As we have seen, the 1920s was an era of growth for the nudist movement. Its ideals and practices were becoming more widespread and accepted, and early leaders like Richard Ungewitter, the Stuttgart-based nudist gardener-cum-baker, were becoming less visible. As participation in nudism spread up and down the social scale and across the political spectrum, membership diversified. It was a natural consequence of that growth that certain aspects of *Nacktkultur*'s ideology would also change. Acceptance of germ theory did not change the nudist conception of health or its approaches to disease prevention in any significant manner. In a sense, acceptance of germ theory enabled nudism to move beyond its staunch early opposition to doctors and criticism of medical science to a position that sought to reform and influence them both. If, as nudists maintained, the tools doctors used to repair the sick body were incorrect, then these could be exchanged for the proper ones, readily supplied by *Nacktkultur*.

Nudism did make use of science and scientific discoveries, and was thus neither an anti-intellectual movement nor opposed to science, however much it occasionally appeared to be. Beginning in the 1920s, nudism increasingly integrated scientific discoveries into its own ideology and practice. Even the most obdurate, anti-mechanistic, anti-scientific nudists began to include discussions of scientific advances, especially those from the field of spectral analysis.[47] The result was a more potent, mainstream nudism whose message of health and prevention had the added strength of scientific support. Nudism utilized scientific discoveries throughout the 1920s, especially those with regard to the nature of light, not only to broaden its message and appeal to Germans, but also to place further pressure on professional medicine to overcome its own prejudice against *Nacktkultur* and to adopt some of its principles as legitimate in preventing and curing disease. And there was some success: by the 1930s, medical science, too, was proclaiming the benefits of sunlight.[48]

Just as *Nacktkultur* eventually accepted some scientific theories, such as germ-based infection, its antipathy towards doctors – the practitioners of medical theory – underwent a transformation from its original outright rejection to a position that advocated reform through cooperation. In the 1920s, when nudist activity was at its peak, enthusiastic nudists began to envision the day when doctors and the state would embrace nudism for the good of the *Volk*. Nudists hoped that once doctors began to 'observe nudism from a health standpoint and were free from their superfluous morality, they would urgently greet nudism, and not only for a small portion of the population, but for the whole of it.'[49] Calls were made for the state and medical establishment to recognize nudism and nakedness as legitimate therapies in raising the level of the nation's health.[50] The vituperative nudist Richard Ungewitter even bestowed his blessings on two doctors, Dr Max Becker and Dr A. Rollier, whose own experiences with sunshine, he believed, led them to conclusions similar to his own oft-repeated convictions.[51] One can only guess at the doctors' response to this honor.

Although official state adoption of nudist principles actually occurred under the National Socialists, the hope that doctors would wholeheartedly embrace nudism was never realized, even when it appeared that they understood the health value of *Licht, Luft* and *Sonne*. Writing near the end of the 1920s, one optimistic nudist who foresaw the eventual wholesale promotion of nudism by the state, believed that nudism was already gaining ground at the highest levels in his own day. 'More and more,' he wrote, 'the gates of the *universitas litterarum* are opening to the new movement.'[52] Such expressions of hope for cooperation between doctors and nudists espoused in the decade of the 1920s were unthinkable in the early ideology of *Nacktkultur*. By the 1920s in addition to healing the personal body from illness and the racial body from degeneration, nudism hoped to reform the medical body from its false practices – an endeavor that met with some degree of success.

Doctors made some acknowledgment in the later 1920s of the health benefits to be had from sport, light, air and sun, such as acquiring a 'good pulsing blood,' an important defense against contracting tuberculosis.[53] One particularly strong call for state promotion of nudism employed both its healing and prophylactic advantages. 'Sunbathing facilities should be erected not only for the goal of healing, but also mainly for the **prevention** of diseases. **The state should supply such facilities**' [bold in original].[54] Despite such obvious logic and strong calls, nudists remained dissatisfied at the pace with which the state acted to build facilities to accommodate and to utilize *Nacktkultur*.[55] In the next decade, however, calls for sun, air and light therapy to combat certain diseases began to come from official quarters, and nudism was embraced, in part, for its role in promoting health, especially in its ability to prevent infection.[56]

The importance of disease prevention in the pre-antibiotic era cannot be underestimated. The need to assist doctors in prevention efforts was a real one, as their power to fight existing infection was limited, obvious and widely perceived. As one turn-of-the-century non-nudist observer noted in the *Blätter für Volksgesundheitpflege*, the journal of the Verein für Volkshygiene, 'the doctor stands all too often powerless against his malignant enemy, despite his passionate struggle against disease, despite his selfless exertions and self-sacrifices.'[57] In the absence of effective, reliable cures, the most doctors and medical science could hope to accomplish was the prevention of disease.

The discourse of prevention often centered around lifestyle, with particular emphasis placed on hygiene. The discourse of prevention and hygiene was moreover one in which nearly any individual or organization could participate.[58] During both the Kaiserreich and the Weimar Republic – the so-called Golden Age of Hygiene[59] – greater efforts were made to reach the public on topics concerning health and hygiene through exhibitions and massive public education efforts. The most famous and most important of these was the 1911 Hygiene Exhibition in Dresden and later in 1926 the federally sponsored 'Week of Health,' which also included representatives from the famous Hygiene Museum located in Dresden.[60]

The purpose of exhibitions such as the 'Week of Health' was to introduce to the largest number of Germans possible the principles and practices of good health and hygiene. Important topics such as proper nutrition, the need to curtail alcohol and tobacco consumption, especially smoking, the necessity of physical fitness and of proper clothing, the need for air, light and movement were presented.

Importantly, the exhibitions conveyed the message that through their individual effort and in particular through their devotion to a natural way of living that Germans could improve their health, strengthen themselves and increase their personal happiness.[61] Racial hygiene and the importance of health for the race as a whole were also important topics covered at such exhibitions.[62] The desire and the effort to improve the general health of the nation through the promotion and awareness of the ideas of basic hygiene in the home and of the body were important public health measures and remained the cornerstone of official efforts under the Nazis.

Official emphasis on prevention over cure lasted well into the Nazi era. Nazi health officials, however, unlike their Weimar colleagues, were much more open to the ideas and methods of alternative medicine, including those advocated by nudism. Prevention was elevated to the level of one's duty, and various calls were made for doctors to become Führer der Volksgesundheit.[63] Dr Wagner reminded doctors that they were Volksführer, and that their service was to the German Volk.[64] In the Third Reich, the figure of the doctor remained important but his methods needed to be revised, and for this the nature-oriented movements from the turn of the century supplied the blueprints.

Under the Nazi regime, alternative healing practices gained a more equal footing with scientific ones. The theme of 'Preventing is Better than Curing' formed one of the topics of the 1938 meeting between Dr Gerhard Wagner's Hauptamt für Volksgesundheit and representatives from the Reichsarbeitsgemeinschaft für naturgemäße Lebens- und Heilweise and the German Lebensreformbewegung.[65] Exploring alternative paths of healing became a patriotic responsibility as well. Dr Gerhard Wagner instructed doctors to be less dogmatic in their approach to and understanding of medicine.

> In his thinking and practice, the German doctor must become closer to nature. He should no longer swear solely and only by the dogma of his university acquired

Schulmedizin-based knowledge. Rather, he should also master the methods of *Naturheil*, homeopathy, and *Volksmedezin*. We National Socialists subscribe neither to economic nor intellectual dogma, we only know one dogma: The well-being of the German *Volk*.[66]

The elements of light, sunshine and air, long promoted by nudists as important ways to prevent disease and to maintain a healthy population, even to heal the injured, were given more serious consideration by Nazi officials. In the 1930s, efforts to prevent tuberculosis infection, in particular, increasingly relied on convincing Germans to practice regularly sun, air and light therapy, either fully naked or in as little clothing as possible.[67] In this respect, children were considered especially important, as it could become a lifelong habit for them. In the 'Ten Commandments to Living a Healthy Life' Dr Hördemann, the Reichsarzt of the Hitler Youth, charged his boys in the 'Second Commandment' with remembering that light and air were the key to keeping their bodies clean and healthy.[68]

In his broader discussion of those aspects of civilized living that eased daily existence and softened the struggle for survival, Dr Hördemann commented that many of these aspects must be characterized as 'enemies of life.'[69] 'I am thinking here,' he wrote, 'not only of living quarters [*Wohnform*], but I also draw into my observation aspects of personal conduct of life, like nutrition, clothing and misuse of pleasurable intoxicants [*Genußgiften*], and so on.'[70] Efforts to persuade Germans to sun and air themselves naked or in as little clothing as possible were not restricted to the youth, however.

The retired army officer and active nudist SS officer Hans Surén became under National Socialism the special plenipotentiary of the Reichsbauernführer, Walther Darré. In his capacity as Darré's special plenipotentiary, Surén worked to instruct Germans on how to become and to stay healthy, in an effort to achieve a particularly Germanic body. He penned articles on general body care, all associative with concerns of body culture that taught, for example, proper breathing, exercising, nutrition and how to fight off tuberculosis infection. Here, too, the prescription was for copious amounts of sun, air and light on the nude body. The effect of 'sunbeams on tuberculosis [was] especially astounding,' he wrote.[71] Further, bathing the body in sun, air and light would result in a thoroughly Germanic way of living and a healthy body, one that hearkened back to the lessons of venerated *Turnvater* Jahn himself. 'Full utilization of sun, air and light for the naked body, solid living, proper nutrition . . . provide for a lifestyle outlined in *Deutsche Gymnastik*.[72]

During the Second World War, air, sun and light were seen by Nazi officials as important and useful ways to keep the German population healthy and productive. By the second year of the Second World War, ambitious plans for the construction of air and sunbathing facilities were being presented to some state governments, in order to maintain and improve the health of workers and mothers and to heal those already wounded in combat. The SS captain and leader of Württemburg's

Prießnitzbund, a homeopathic, nature-oriented organization, K. Maier, submitted to the Interior Ministry of Württemburg a proposal calling for the erection of a large, easily accessible facility near Stuttgart.

Recognizing that the needs of the war had increased the demands on workers' bodies and psyches, Maier realized that time in the healing elements was now of paramount importance. The facility he proposed would be broken into a number of sections to accommodate whole families, single adults, combat injuries and those who wished to be totally naked, and was intended to offer everyone 'the possibility to visit daily after work, on the weekend, or during recovery or vacation periods,' in order to relax and to rejuvenate themselves physically as well as psychologically from the day's toil.[73]

Maier's proposal also reveals the level which the curative and regenerative promise of the homeopathic and nudist movements reached in the Nazi system. In accordance with the wishes of the Reich Health Minister, who envisioned every German town and village having its own *Luft-* and *Sonnenbad* (air- and sunbath) facility after the war, Maier wanted the proposed facility near Stuttgart to become the prototype and model (*Musteranlage*) for all of Greater Germany. The mass construction of air – and sunbathing facilities would not be restricted to urban or semi-urban areas, but would also be made available for the rural population, for whom, 'such facilities are a dire necessity, because for them the questions of personal and public health are quite poor.'[74]

The scope of the curative power of the elements is evident in the proposal, as is the hope placed in them for creating a better *Volk*. Maier believed that in their section whole families would play sports and perform calisthenics, gradually becoming healthier and learning how to incorporate the principles of the airbath more and more into their daily lives. In the section reserved for soldiers, the men wounded in the war could expect to heal nicely, especially with regard to their psychological trauma, ultimately speeding along their full return to society. In their section, soldiers could expect 'to overcome the inhibitions and feelings of inferiority that they often possess early on. Freed of their artificial limbs, they can completely relax, and quite by itself their feeling of self-confidence returns, and they can soon return to and enjoy the Family Section.'[75] While it was important to heal soldiers' psyches and to help them return to their families and society as quickly as possible, the *Volk*'s future was also important, and could be secured in this facility.

As one might expect from the National Socialist regime, the purpose of medicine, healing the *Volk* and the individual, whether through scientific or through alternative, homeopathic, nature-based remedies, was to improve the racial quality of Germans. The Nazi press reminded its readers that it was their racial responsibility to remain healthy, especially those men in the SA and SS, the racial vanguard of the new era.[76] A 1938 manuscript from the Verein Deutsche Volksheilkunde

(German League of Homeopathic Medicine), itself titled *Preventing is Better than Curing*, baldly declared, 'the maintenance of health of the individual and the gene pool [*Erbmasse*] is more important than caring for and curing the sick.'[77] The desire to improve not only the health of the individual German, but also that of the German race as a whole through exposure to the natural elements is evident in Maier's air- and sunbathing facility, as well.

At the proposed facility, the section reserved for naked air- and sunbathing was deemed especially important for Germany's women. Here 'growing daughters, expectant mothers and mothers with small children up to age four, could air and sun themselves, and expose their bodies to light.' On one level, the naked airbath and sunbath were expected to increase and to improve women's glandular functions. They were also expected to help these women develop a greater sense of 'naturalness, especially the harmony of the natural experiences, the will to beauty, gracefulness, charm, elasticity, and awaken greater spiritual and physical capabilities.'[78] Creating strong, capable women, who were also beautiful and charming, was important for the future of the race, since it was assumed that weak or ugly women would produce similarly weak or sickly children. The physical beauty and strength of the next generation needed to be created in the present one.

Racial health and efforts to improve the race were never far below the surface in Nazism or for that matter in *Nacktkultur*. The Nazis only made official what many had preached, believed and practiced for decades. The idea of a racially pure, socially harmonious and united Germany was one that found broad resonance across the political and social spectrum; it shaped nudist ideology and propelled nudist activity no less than the same idea formed Nazism.

Conclusion

Nudism's roots as a reform movement are most visible in discussions of its nineteenth-century origins. Nudism was very much a product of alternative medicines that persisted in the face of growing pressure from doctors and the state. Nudism and science conceived the body in very different ways. Nudists saw the body as a whole unit, science saw it as not necessarily interrelated parts. This theoretical difference informed treatment and was at the forefront of *Nacktkultur*'s rejection of scientific knowledge and medicine. Over the course of the twentieth century, nudism and state medical authorities gradually moved closer together in their opinions of treatment, until, by the 1940s, some key nudist ideas were being taken seriously by the state.

Nudist medical reform ideas gained a fair amount of acceptance by the Nazi regime. Looking to the future, leading Nazi doctors began inculcating among the youth the important notions of body health through proper nutrition, movement, light and air exposure. These are key tenets of the broader Life-Reform and nudist movements. The health of the body, the health of the race was everyone's business.

Indeed, the driving force behind nudist activity was to improve the German race by first making all of its individual members healthy and beautiful so that they could then repopulate Germany. The task of creating healthy Germans in the naked experience was really only the first step in a larger nudist vision of creating a racial utopia. A better Germany began with a better body, one forged in nakedness and in nature.

–4–

The Healthy Body

The promise of good health and a life free of both disease and doctors was not only a selling point of nudism, it was also a central tenet of the ideology. As we have seen creating healthy Germans was considered vital to the overall success of the race, and was the first part of the nudist equation to regenerate the *Volk*. The nudist preoccupation with Germans' physical health was driven by equal parts racism and nationalism. Fears of Germany's racial or national degeneration figured prominently in early nudist thought and served as the motivation behind much of its activity. To recast Germany as a racial utopia that was both defined by and a product of mass *Nacktkultur*, forces of degeneration that ranged from disease and racial mixing to Christianity and body shame needed to be fought and eliminated. The groundwork of the better German race nudists hoped to build was health.

Creating healthy Germans was the all-important first step in regenerating Germans and making Germany into a nudist racial utopia. The promotion of physical health was important to *Nacktkultur* as nudist plans to deliver Germany to its new era of national and racial harmony were largely based on breeding. Nudism strove to make Germans into a healthy, beautiful people because nudist ideology held that a natural consequence of this would be healthy, racially pure children. Healthy, beautiful Germans, the idea ran, would select appropriately healthy and beautiful mates and would then reproduce. The children from these pairings would continue the pattern set by their parents until all members of the *Volk* were healthy, beautiful and racially fit. Those people who were not racial Germans would lose the birth contest and eventually die off on their own, theoretically leaving the Germans a *Volk* and a nation without problems. Physical health and beauty were thus serious matters for the nudists, and something they believed their movement actively cultivated through the interaction of sun, air, light and the nudist's own body.

Nacktkultur offered every German who practiced it the possibility of establishing and regulating her or his own health; no doctors or other medical professionals were necessary to diagnose, advise or order, and no medicines were needed to heal. Once healthy, nudist ideology assured, a nudist could not fall victim to illness – a healthy body could not become a sick body. Becoming a healthy German was, according to nudist ideology, as simple as stepping out of one's clothes and stepping into the elements of the natural world, bathing one's naked body in light, air and sun. Staying healthy was no less difficult than becoming healthy, with the exception that it required constant nudist activity. The immediate goal of opening oneself up to nature was to make the body impervious to infection by reviving and fortifying the skin.

The Importance of Skin

The skin is an organ with which people experience much of the world. Its role as medium through which air and other elements passed was already known and promoted by a number of nineteenth-century doctors.[1] Nudists, however, considered skin to be the *only* way humans experienced the world. Dr Max Grunewald reported in an article, which essentially became a medical endorsement of *Nacktkultur* for the nudist magazine *Das Freibad*, that *Körperpflege* (hygienic care of the body) 'wants above all else to mediate the relationship between one of our largest organs, namely the skin, and the outside world.'[2] Grunewald was specifically thinking of preventing tuberculosis and rickets infection. The skin was the key to all physical health and subsequently to all racial regeneration. Nudism posited itself as the primary means to cultivate and to care for a healthy skin, guaranteeing the body full benefit from its encounters with the outside world.

From the standpoint of nudism the most vital organ the human body possessed was the skin because of its primary role in protecting against infection. It was also the most neglected by modern humans, especially by *Zivilisationsmenschen*. Care and color of the skin betrayed a person's or a *Volk*'s awareness and knowledge of the skin, indicating either their racial vigor as *Kulturmenschen* or their degeneracy as *Zivilisationsmenschen*.[3] The skin's functions were central to a body's survival, and its health and vitality were paramount in preventing infection and in building a beautiful body.

The skin was the way that nudists were able to utilize the health benefits of the natural world. Air, light and sun first affected the skin, which then filtered their effects throughout the rest of the body. One manner in which nudists themselves viewed skin was as a medium between the inner body and the outer world.[4] Inner organs, for example, could not be healthy unless the skin that surrounded them was healthy. Nudism constructed healthy Germans through the construction of healthy skin.

In the assessment of many nudists, the skin was the most important factor in a person's health.[5] Skin color was an indicator of one's overall health, and tanned individuals were believed better able to resist disease.[6] Pale or white skin was an obvious marker of degeneration. Paleness, for example, affected the immune system and probably meant that its owner suffered from anemia.[7] Proper care of the skin was the most important element in becoming and staying healthy. All attempts to improve one's health necessarily involved improving the skin, simultaneously strengthening it and making it more capable of responding to the nudist therapies. One enthusiastic nudist spared no restraint in his evaluation of the skin. 'The skin is the seat of health,' he wrote, 'It is on the skin that we must begin, pursue and achieve our efforts to cure. The skin is the seat of life itself. Life proceeds from the lungs and the heart, *but it sits on the skin*' [emphasis in original].'[8]

Physically speaking, the skin functioned in a number of different ways, all of which were identified by nudists as vital to a person's well-being. Nudists considered the skin to be an interior as well as an exterior gland, and described it as having the ability to protect against disease from within and, after accepting germ theory, from without. As an inner gland, the skin was able to influence a person's health by preparing secretions and directing them into or out of the body, maintaining health. One essayist believed that the skin regulated the construction and decomposition of materials basic to a body's structure (*Körpersubstanz*), especially calcium. Finally, as an inner gland, skin was capable of killing bacteria.[9] Skin was thus a doubly important organ in the struggle against disease; it could prevent infection from the outside as well as on the inside. This last property of skin provides a good insight into the way nudists incorporated and molded scientific fact to jibe with their own ideology.

Unlike the relatively late nudist acceptance of the scientific discovery that ultraviolet light possessed bactericidal properties and that sunning oneself was a useful prophylactic because it killed any agent of infection on the skin's surface, nudist ideology asserted from its earliest days that healthy skin would benefit the internal organs.[10] The effect of light on the skin was also to 'raise the general condition [of health], accelerate the inner metabolism, increase the number of red blood cells, raise the energy consumption of the central nervous system and also bring about an increase in the ability of the brain.'[11] The absence of air or sun on the skin made one 'unable to resist infections, sickly, highly susceptible for tuberculosis, rachitis, scrofula and skin infections, headaches and dizziness,' noted one author.[12] The interaction of the elements, in this case sunlight, with the skin caused a number of reactions that made nudism capable of preventing and curing disease.

The very early nudist writers determined the usefulness of light on the skin based on the assertions of the homeopathic movement, whose influence was so heavy in *Nacktkultur*, and on their own conviction. Light was, early nudists believed, healthy for the internal organs simply because it was a natural element, and because it drew the blood from the inner organs closer to the skin.[13] The presence of blood in the skin was crucial for good health. 'Should a person again become healthy, so must the nerves first be stimulated, blood must again flow in the skin,' explained one.[14] The skin acted as a filter for light, bringing it into the body, where it benefited the internal organs by keeping them healthy.[15] As *Nacktkultur* gradually accepted and incorporated scientific principles, less and less mention was made of the skin's role in filtering light to the inner organs. This belief, though, was never retracted; it remained a relic from nudism's early and somewhat more mystical days. Skin was much more than just a filter for sunlight, however, and served far more important functions.

In nudism, skin was considered a breathing organ,[16] and by far the most important function of the skin was breathing.[17] Nudists claimed that skin-breathing had been discovered by the Italian scientist Sanctorious three centuries prior, but was only now becoming fully understood and appreciated, especially in its capacity to combat and prevent disease.[18] Skin-breathing promoted the exchange of gasses between the body and the air, causing the skin in effect to act as a kind of second lung. Although most nudists agreed that skin-breathing primarily supplemented the lungs, some essayists went further. A Dr Küster wrote that skin worked with both the lungs and the kidneys to metabolize and eliminate substances from the body. In his view, nudism was essential to this process because one's health was related to the metabolism, and the more skin exposed to the air meant a higher metabolism, which generated greater health.[19] One nudist writing in a rather poetic moment likened human skin to a leaf, specifically comparing their mutual function of breathing.[20]

Skin-breathing was admittedly not as efficient as that of the lungs, but it was vital for the maintenance of good blood and healthy nerves. Not allowing the skin to breathe, warned some nudists, caused the blood vessels to die, resulting in less blood to the skin, which in turn caused the elasticity of the skin to decrease, ultimately leading to an early death.[21] Tuberculosis was seen as a consequence of inefficient skin-breathing, since blocked by clothes, the skin could not exhale the body's poisons.[22] Nerves, it was revealed, required oxygen, and were particularly dependent on the oxygen acquired through the skin.[23] Breathing with the lungs occurred in a central location, skin-breathing by contrast occurred in the peripheries, a place where the lungs could not effectively penetrate.[24] Skin-breathing pulled more blood into the skin, which further aided and increased one's metabolism.

In later nudist works, after the influence of science was apparent in the movement, the ability of skin to filter light to the internal organs and to supplement breathing were combined. Nonetheless, the overall result remained the same. Sunlight striking the skin would cause the capillaries to fill with blood and to expand, lowering internal blood pressure and increasing circulation. According to one author, the increased circulation would prevent colds, by keeping the body warm, and also arteriosclerosis, rickets, chlorosis (greensickness), anemia and tuberculosis.[25] An increased metabolism would cure such skin disorders as gout, rheumatism and scrofula.[26] Increased circulation and metabolism were the crux of how skin-breathing promoted health and prevented infection.

Nudists believed that the skin interacted with the sun, air and light to prevent disease on and in the body. The increased blood flow and a higher metabolic rate,

Figure 4.1 The sun held enormous power and appeal for nudists. Poses such as this were common in nudist publications. Image from *Ideale Nacktheit*, 1915. Original photo by M. Breslauer. Courtesy of ANRL.

it was thought, decreased the possibility of infection and promoted a better functioning, healthier body. 'Skin is a protective covering for the inner organs, a means to regulate circulation, metabolism and body heat, for the body's secretions and its detoxification, and finally it is a way to influence the state of our souls, our mood.'[27] However, the skin could only perform these functions when it came into direct contact with the air, the sunshine or other light. The more skin one exposed, the healthier one would be.

The Sunbath

The interaction of skin with the elements of sun, air and light occurred in twin nudist practices of the *Sonnenbad* (sunbath) and the *Luftbad* (airbath), considered of the highest importance regarding one's health.[28] Together they could cure tuberculosis, for example.[29] The sunbath and the airbath could and often did occur simultaneously, and in fact were closely related. Although designed to accomplish similar goals, namely the utilization of sun and air on the naked skin for improved health of the nudist, the *Sonnenbad* and the *Luftbad* were different in some key regards. Nudist authors themselves often addressed them as separate practices. Each carried different precautions, for example, or could bestow different benefits on the nudist. In both instances, nudists lamented, too many Germans remained ignorant of the sunbath and the airbath, their benefits and the proper methods by which to utilize them.

Both had similar origins in popular medicine.[30] The distant roots of the sunbath, however, were traced by nudists back to the Assyrians, Babylonians, Egyptians and even the ancient Germanic tribes.[31] The Ancients, nudists believed, knew the healing value of the sun in the battle against rheumatism.[32] Locating the origins of the sunbath in ancient times was a function of nudist nationalism and the nudist attack on the Catholic Church, which it held responsible for the corruption of Germanic virtue and purity. In many ways, whether in sunbathing and knowledge of the healing power of the sun, or as the model for the future, the ancient world supplied much of the vision of nudist ideology.

The origin of the modern sunbath was located in the nineteenth century and was often attributed to Swiss German Arnold Rikli.[33] One nudist's account has him 'rediscovering' the ancient Germanic knowledge of the sun.[34] Sun therapy treatments had been around for decades prior to the arrival of nudism, claimed one nudist, but the participants committed the mistake of wearing swimsuits and segregating themselves according to sex.[35] Whatever the origins of the sunbath, and it seems likely that Rikli did in fact open the first ever sunbathing establishment in Veldes in 1855, nudists were in agreement that the power of the sun to influence health was strong.[36]

There were also cases of individual nudists making the discovery of the effects of the sun on their own. Adolf Weide, for example, was in the habit of lounging in a hammock in the woods, when he noticed that the sunshine first dried then cured his moist feet, a problem from which he had suffered since childhood. He then reasoned that applying sunshine to his own admittedly wretched body would cure it as well. At the age of forty, he claimed he was a 'regrettable man,' his body was used up, he had a weak heart, was constantly dizzy from his heart medication, plus he drank and smoked too much. His accidental discovery of the sun was his eventual cure, even if at first it hurt more than helped. He dedicated himself to helping others, particularly the youth, to learn the value of the naked sunbath, by spreading his knowledge of nudism through doctors, the press but most importantly through schools. He declared, 'we must orient ourselves more to the natural sunbaths and modern body culture, then we will certainly distance ourselves from diseases, for which we mostly have ourselves to blame.'[37]

In explaining both the effects and importance of the sun, nudists drew comparisons with plants and took their examples from the world of nature. In human biology, just as in nature, the role of the sun was crucial to sustaining life. Nudist Emil Peters believed the sun essential to life itself, and to humans' ability to function, 'we are born from the sun. Our nervous system received its laws from the sun.'[38] The sun's effect on human blood and the circulatory system was especially valuable.[39] Sunlight increased electric impulses in the cells and encouraged cellular protein.[40] The twofold health effects of the sun were light and warmth; the former being the more important of the two. As light hit the skin, it pulled blood from the inner organs into the skin making them healthier.[41] It also increased one's energy.[42] Human hemoglobin was likened to chlorophyll, in that it too was a result of sunlight and essential to life. Moreover, like plants, the more sun humans received the larger and healthier they would grow, which as one doctor noted was one characteristic of the peoples from the tropics, where sun was plentiful.[43]

Sunlight obviously possessed certain properties that enabled it to work such wonders on nudists' bodies, and nudists attempted to understand and define just what those properties were. Most were in agreement that the sun supplied the 'thermal, physical, chemical and the electrical stimulation' to humans, but no one seemed to know exactly how.[44] Sunrays, argued one nudist, existed on several different levels, all of which could be received in the sunbath.[45] Ether rays could effect the 'liveliest stimulation and activity' of the skin.[46] There were, claimed Strassmann, cosmic rays, which increased cellular energy; warm or chemical rays; electric and magnetic rays, the full effects of which were still not entirely known; and finally there were light rays. Light rays, continued Strassmann, themselves consisted of many different colors, each one having its own distinct effect on the organism.[47]

Other nudists identified only three components of sunlight as being important to the skin: chemical, electrical and magnetic. Of the three, the chemical was considered the most vital as it contributed, among other responses, color to the skin. Here too, the electrical and magnetic components were not clearly understood.[48] Still another explanation suggested that a sunbeam essentially consisted of metals, thus skirting the electrical-chemical-magnetic debate altogether.

Proposed by the autodidact[49] and fiery patriarch of the nudist movement, Richard Ungewitter, the 'metallic sunbeam theory' held that sunrays were healthy because of the metals they contained. Ungewitter made specific mention of magnesium, iron, sulfur, radium and mercury, of which the most important in his opinion was mercury. His praise for mercury was high and he excitedly described how it was transmitted through a ray of light, 'the refined properties of quicksilver become dissolved and intermixed with the light wave as a delicate fluid, and which are then absorbed by the skin. The high sun brings nothing other than a refined metal cure!'[50] The possibility that mercury was present in sunlight and that it could be so easily brought to and absorbed by the skin was indeed a tantalizing prospect for Ungewitter.

Ungewitter, like many nudists, was a rabid anti-Semite and an ardent advocate of eugenics and breeding as the best means by which to renew the German race. He was also deeply frightened by such diseases as syphilis, which had the potential to infect and destroy the German germ-plasm, result in sterility or birth defects and ultimately thwart his fantasies of Germany's rebirth through breeding. His rapturous description of mercury's presence in sunlight must be considered in this context, as it becomes a justification for nudism. If an individual suffered from syphilis, then a visit to the sunbath, but only a nude visit, would allow the mercury present in the sunlight to penetrate the skin and sores of the afflicted genitalia and effect a cure.

Ungewitter was not the only nudist terrified by the prospect of syphilis, nor was he the only one to seek its cure in the sunlight. The nudist Emil Peters noted the importance of the sunbath in treating this dread disease, as well as gonorrhea. He believed that the sun would force the syphilis to be excreted through the pores. 'Specifically with regard to syphilis,' he wrote, 'the sunbath has a phenomenal excretory effect.'[51] In nudist ideology the genitals occupied an important position, 'for it is in our sexual potency that we find that seat of our entire life-strength [*Lebenskraft*].[52] While the benefits for the body as a whole might be discussed by nudist theorists, the genitals were often singled out for special attention. Many nudists, though not always discussing syphilis, were avid about the importance of and need for the genitals to receive sunlight. A Danzig nudist reminded that 'sun and air must be free and unhindered in getting to all parts of the body, and especially the sex organs. These most valuable organs should receive sun and more sun.'[53]

Attempting to cure syphilis with concentrated mercury was an available but dangerous cure in the early twentieth century. The presence of refined, dissolved mercury in sunlight would have been a safe, cheap, easily available cure. The sunbath in Ungewitter's theory becomes a healthy practice not only because it raises the metabolism, improves circulation and relieves the inner organs, but also because it could cure a vicious disease, protect the German germ-plasm and eliminate a major contributor to racial degeneration. In other authors' versions, the sunbath would cause a person to sweat out the mercury administered in a medically prescribed treatment.[54] Nudism could rectify medical science's dangerous attempt to cure syphilis and supply a healthy one of its own. Sunlight was quite literally the miracle antidote for the scourge of the pre-antibiotic era and eugenicist's nightmare, venereal disease.

For all the health benefits to be had from the sunbath, there were dangers as well, and one needed to exercise caution when participating. Taking a sunbath was not a simple matter of taking one's clothes off and going outside; there was a right and a wrong approach to the sunbath. Nudist magazines supplied much advice to both the beginner and the advanced nudist on such topics as when to sunbathe and how to maximize their use of the sun once there. There was no one correct way to soak up the sun in a sunbath, and a preexisting medical condition might alter one's approach entirely, for example.[55] If weak or ill one needed to procure a doctor's permission before proceeding with a sunbath.[56]

Beginners were cautioned to expose themselves only to very early or late sun, especially during the first eight days of a nudist regimen.[57] Obviously, the threat of sunburn was something nudists constantly faced, and while no one was certain how long it took to burn, some people needing as little as fifteen minutes, many stressed caution when sunbathing nude.[58] Magazines cautioned against spending too much time in the sun but there were other practical issues to consider as well.[59] A sunbath should never exceed an hour in length as that could result in a burn, nervousness, a headache or general agitation, nor should it be conducted on a full stomach. A final admonition warned women and girls not to visit the sunbath during menstruation.[60]

A sunbath could occur in any season. The magazine *Lachendes Leben* (Laughing Life) reminded its readership that even in winter the nudist could and should venture outside for the sun.[61] Most nudists agreed that beginners needed to initiate themselves gradually.[62] Some suggested that beginning nudists should only take their first steps during warm conditions; their first sunbath should occur in the

Figure 4.2 The nudist's body was steeled by the elements to extremes of temperature. Three nudists play in the snow. Image from *Lachendes Leben* Jahrgang VII, Heft 2. Courtesy of ANRL.

springtime.[63] Other nudists recommended a much longer period of acclimatization. In this view, a nudist should begin in January by moving about the house naked, slowly getting used to the sun. By March the windows could be opened, to begin accustoming the body to the air and unfiltered light. Eventually, as temperatures warmed, the nudist could venture outside and bask in the direct rays of the sun and the fresh air.[64] Still other nudists encouraged the beginner to alternate between sun and shade, especially during the summer months.[65] During summer, the midday sun was to be avoided by all.[66] Advice for the sunbath, however, extended to the seasoned nudist as well. Hans Surén believed that before taking a sunbath, the nudist should cover the skin in a thick layer of oil.[67]

Preparation was essential for a successful sunbath, otherwise instead of furthering one's health as it should, the sunbath would sicken and hurt the nudist, perhaps through a burn. It was because Germans lived under the domination of the tailor in the first place, argued nudists, that the skin was a weakened and sickly organ, having lost its ability to perform its most natural function, namely breathing. The magazine *Figaro* provided the most thorough advice for the sunbath, recommending moving about the house naked for several hours some

Figure 4.3 Nudists working in a quarry. From Richard Ungewitter, *Nacktheit und Kultur: Neue Forderungen*. Courtesy of ANRL.

days before having a sunbath, but also exercising naked in an open window, washing the body in cold water followed by a thorough rubdown of the skin, to prepare it for breathing.[68] These preparations complete, one was ready to go outside naked to the sunbath, to soak up the sun's rays and become healthy.

The sunbath was not just an act of lying around or sitting in the sunshine, sweating out self-poisons (or mercury or even syphilis, for that matter), it required movement of some kind. Sleeping naked in the sun was to be avoided under all circumstances.[69] The sunbath required movement or exercise for full effect.[70] Constant movement, play or sports activity were the only way for the good effects of the sun and air to reach all parts of the body. There was a consensus among authors that after every sunbath, the nudist should bathe or swim in cold water.[71] When bathing, the nudist needed to be careful to insert each body part slowly into the water, the head last.[72] The measure of whether or not a sunbath was done properly was 'the highest feeling of physical well-being and an elevated, joyful mood' for the participant.[73]

The Airbath

Equally important to one's well-being, though in different ways than the sunbath, was the *Luftbad*, or airbath. The *Luftbad* was quite similar to the sunbath, in that 'one freed the whole body from its shell of clothes, and bathed in the air.'[74] Parents were encouraged to give their infants and children a daily airbath, as infants would benefit from five to ten minutes of naked air-breathing per day, older children a bit longer.[75] Taking an airbath was not as potentially dangerous as a sunbath, though one still needed to exercise a certain degree of caution, and after the temperature reached more than 86°F (30°C), an airbath automatically became a sunbath.[76]

Unlike the sunbath, which possessed the ability to cure disease, the airbath was primarily prophylactic in nature.[77] Although it could influence a number of diseases and conditions, it was especially notable for being able to establish a healthy nervous system. Like the sunbath, the airbath was important for the creation of a healthy skin, blood and metabolic rate, but also for its ability to alter one's entire lifestyle. The airbath was the all-important foundation for subsequent nudist activity and health; it was in fact the 'master of *körperkultur* [sic].'[78]

The airbath's origins are similar to those of the sunbath, coming out of nineteenth-century popular medicine and homeopathy. Historian Karl Rothschuh has credited Adolf Just with building the first air-huts for airbathers, after personal experience with airbathing helped him recover from a sickly childhood. Later Just founded a sanitarium called Jungborn in the Harz mountains near Bad Harzburg and Ilsenburg. Just was influenced by the ideas of Louis Kuhne, a fellow nature therapist, and Rousseau. Just believed in the power of the Earth, water, air and light to cure victims of illness. In his view, not only were women's clothing, alcohol, tea, coffee, salt, sugar and spice considered unhealthy influences, but also trains, technology and science. Just published his ideas in 1892 in a book titled, significantly, *Kehrt zur Natur zurück* (Come Back to Nature), which then influenced others to attempt similar cures by airbathing.[79]

Although nudists called upon the state and local governments to establish airbath facilities both to raise general health and to secure the future of the *Volk*, one could take an airbath anywhere.[80] Ideally, an airbath should be near one's home, be easily accessible, and have air, light, sun and some water.[81] Theoretically, a nudist could take an airbath anywhere prying eyes could not penetrate. In cities one could do it in one's apartment, with the windows open, or, better, on the roof of one's building using a sheet as a shield.[82] However, this same nudist cautioned, taking an airbath in one's own home could be dangerous because of the neighbors, therefore he recommended that one live on upper floors or at the city's edge. If attempting an airbath in the garden, which he highly encouraged, sheets should be used to block the view.[83]

Aside from location, a nudist needed to be concerned about the temperature and quality of the air. Two aspects that determined the overall efficacy of the airbath were air temperature and strength and direction of the wind.[84] Like a sunbath, an airbath could be taken in all seasons and in all weather, if the nudist exercised proper caution. One should not become too cold, for example.[85] Other nudists believed that it was not possible to become too cold at an airbath, as the body produced its own warmth and was generally able to acclimatize itself to cold temperatures. In this view, 'the increasingly strong, increasingly powerful, livelier skin, well-supplied with blood, acquires greater resistance.'[86] The airbath was a contributor to the skin's resilience. One author cautioned that below 68°F (20°C) one risked catching cold and should move about. However, in warm temperatures, this same author noted that one could, for example, work comfortably at one's desk while taking an airbath.[87] The tubercular could safely withstand temperatures as low as 50°F (12°C). Those with heart problems, by comparison, could easily benefit from an airbath with temperatures as chilly as 41°F (5°C), but not those above 59°F (15°C).[88]

There was a range of advice concerning the airbath. Length of time spent in the airbath was determined by one's level of nudist experience. Generally, nudist authors agreed that beginners to the airbath should limit themselves to ten to fifteen minutes a day, and gradually build up from there.[89] Nudists suffering from kidney or bladder ailments should restrict their time in the airbath even more.[90] Even infants would benefit from the airbath, and it was recommended they receive five to ten minutes a day, on their stomachs if possible.[91] Some believed that beginners should only take an airbath on windless days, until their resistance was stronger.[92]

Time of day could be a factor in the airbath's overall efficacy, though many nudists did not specify a time of day. Heinrich Pudor endorsed an early morning

Figure 4.4 The comfort and ease of living as a nudist is shown by these three women having a snack. From Hans Vahle, *Zielskisse der Freikörperkultur: Ein Leitfaden für Leibeszucht und gesundes Leben*. Courtesy of ANRL.

airbath. 'One should get up with the sun, or even earlier, and waltz through the dew moistened grass or flax or wheat. If circumstances allow it,' he continued, 'one should also take a long naked walk [*Spaziergang*], barefoot if possible.'[93] J.M. Seitz maintained that the airbath was most beneficial when conducted in the morning at one's home with open windows.[94] Generally speaking, an airbath was better if conducted out-of-doors, though in a pinch it was acceptable to do it in one's home, with the windows open if possible.[95]

Although better for the skin and health of the nudist, taking an airbath out-of-doors could present certain problems, such as rain or cold, that called for extra measures. Hans Surén warned that in rain, one should wear foot protection at the airbath, and limit one's exposure.[96] In wet conditions, sandals were favored over shoes and socks, which under no circumstance should be worn at an airbath.[97] While the average nudist might consider rain healthy and a reason for joy, a nervous nudist needed to be careful in it. Nudists with fragile nerves needed to protect themselves in rain, as it could cause brain and spinal cord agitation, as well as damage to the nervous system.[98] However, an airbath could prove particularly advantageous to those suffering from nervous conditions, though they needed to be carefully monitored while at the airbath.[99] Essential to a healthy body, nerves were among the first casualties of wearing clothes, which weakened them.[100] The combination of air and nakedness present in the airbath regenerated shattered nerves.

Cold temperatures were another matter of concern for the nudist airbather; however, these too could be mitigated, especially through movement. One essayist found little cause for alarm in chilly conditions writing that, 'an airbath should not be avoided in cloudy, windy and cold weather. It is then especially refreshing and strengthening. One need not fear catching a cold, provided that he or she moves about in a lively fashion and runs afterwards.'[101] One nudist foresaw the disappearance of colds from the realm of human illnesses because of the airbath.[102] Movement for this author was the key to a successful airbath. He noted further that arriving at the airbath, 'one should immediately undress, run, jump, play and perform calisthenics [*Turnen*].' Heinrich Pudor, one of the self-proclaimed founding fathers of nudism, stated that an airbath could be done in all weather, even storms.[103] One of the reasons that an airbath could be done in all seasons was because of its ability to inure the nudist to all weather.[104]

Nudists hardly suffered at the whim of the weather. To be sure, weather conditions were often influential regarding a person's health, as was the season. Despite

Figure 4.5 Having fun with friends in the snow. Nudism returned a sense of joy to Germans. Image from *Lachendes Leben* Jahrgang VII, Heft 2. Courtesy of ANRL.

the fact that exposure to the air in all types of weather was considered healthy, some diseases had meteorological origins, or could be exacerbated by them. 'Those suffering from heart disease, rheumatism, nervousness, neurasthenia,' for example, 'can tell you all about the oppressive and suffocating influence of bad weather,' cautioned one nudist. A sinking barometer signaled the onslaught of digestive problems, for instance. The control of weather over a person's health, however, could be modified or weakened by nudist airbath activity, in a process nudists called *Abhärtung* or inurement.[105] Inurement was a way to stave-off the atrophying of the skin, which could result from its neglect or improper use; read: wearing clothes.[106]

In the process of inurement, which essentially consisted of being a nudist, braving all types of weather and conditions to air the body, one diminished the negative effects of the weather but not the beneficial ones. Emil Peters explained, 'in the same ways in which we get our pale skin used to air and wind, we also make our physical and our spiritual state of health independent of all kinds of weather influences, as well as increase the measure of our ability to perform and our health.'[107] Some nudists went to great lengths to inure themselves to the weather. Nudist K. Finckh reportedly took an all-day airbath every day in an effort to harden the body.[108] One could not expect to become a healthy person without following the 'iron law of the constant airbath.'[109] The air was interpreted by one nudist, based on his reading of Scripture, as nutritive.[110] Inuring the nudist to weather was part of the broader goal of strengthening a German against degeneration.

The airbath was a powerful tool in the nudist effort to create and maintain physical health among their contemporaries. Primarily, the airbath kept the healthy from becoming sick, but it could also effect cures to an astonishing variety of illnesses.[111] The airbath detoxified and de-acidified the blood, making it the so-called 'alkali blood,' which prevented infection.[112] It could, by allowing the lungs an opportunity to rest, heal sick lungs through skin-breathing.[113] At least one nudist believed he escaped the influenza pandemic following the First World War because of the airbath.[114] It simultaneously helped obesity, by increasing the metabolism, and malnourishment (*krankhafte Magerkeit*), because it excited the fat glands. Gout, rheumatism, scrofula, rickets, anemia, chlorosis (greensickness), catarrh, heart diseases, blood congestion, kidney ailments, skin conditions, nervous disorders and hemorrhoids, as well as a number of other diseases, could all be treated and cured in the airbath.[115]

The reach of the *Luftbad*'s power was not restricted to physical ailments, and it could act as a powerful palliative for immoral behavior and bad habits. Nudists noted that the natural lifestyle of the nudist would draw the drinkers from the beerhalls, in itself a healthy feat.[116] Touting the usefulness of the *Luftbad* in reforming behavior, Professor Kreuzberg cited a letter in his possession that claimed the airbath helped the author of the letter exactly because it kept him out of the pubs.[117] Thus were the calls for massive construction of airbaths in Germany's cities rooted in arguments that they would benefit the common health of all Germans.[118] Nudism, armed with its twin practices of *Sonnenbad* and *Luftbad*, exerted a moralizing influence on Germans as well as a healthy one. It could calm the excited, disarm the masturbator, calm the sexually excited and squelch sexual fantasy.[119]

Nudism provided for the greatest amount of skin exposure possible to the regenerative and restorative natural elements of sun, air and light. Every inch of a nudist's skin was actively engaged with the natural world, busily employed at discharging the body's poisons, preventing the accumulation of 'metabolic residue' and 'self-poisoning,' increasing blood flow throughout the layers of the skin and raising metabolism. A nudist was a vigorous and active German, who possessed increased mental ability and physical resistance to disease because of the interchange between the skin, air and light. A nudist's body, bathed in light and air, was able to withstand infection and was itself deadly to germs. A nudist's skin was itself a symbol of health and vitality. Tanned skin radiated health, fought germs and signaled one's racial value to contemporaries. A nudist was the apotheosis of health, incapable of becoming sick.

Conclusion

There is a strong temptation to liken German nudists to German Romantics from the nineteenth century. Both groups thought of cities as essentially bad places where bad things happened to either individuals or to the race, or both. *Nacktkultur* was deeply influenced by Romantic thought, but nudists were drawn to the medical curative power of nature, not its ability to rejuvenate them spiritually. For nudists, the city was where the race went to degenerate and to die, but nature was where Germans would go first to rejuvenate themselves and, through their efforts, the race.

Nudists did not embrace nature for the sake of embracing nature, however. They were profoundly mistrustful of it. No nature-loving Romantic would ever devise the quite detailed rules and regulations for comporting oneself in nature, as the nudists actually did. To be sure, nature and the natural setting were by themselves important for nudism and naked physical recovery, but theirs was a nature that was strictly regulated. Temperatures, conditions, seasons, times of the day, shade, direct sun, all these variables had specific response for beginning or advanced nudists, for men and for women. Nature was not carefree, and neither were the nudists. Work on the body was a serious business for the race was at stake.

The nudist program to regenerate Germany was predicated on the twin convictions that Germans were unhealthy and that only by repairing and rejuvenating the personal body could the national or racial body benefit. Regenerating the personal body began with healing it through exposure to the curative and restorative elements of sun and air, which nudists believed capable of preventing and curing disease. Sunbathing would tan skin to a healthy color, airbathing would heal the lungs, and both were capable of killing deadly germs. Germans would become physically healthier in the nudist experience.

Healing Germans and curing them of disease, however, were only the first steps in the nudist vision of transforming Germany into a nudist racial utopia. In the process of building a better personal body, the national body would be healed, regenerated and beautified. The idea of successfully constructing a natural and harmonious society, the modern incarnation of the imagined and idealized tribal past, rested on first constructing Germans who were themselves natural and harmonious, whose bodies were robust, healthy and, most importantly, beautiful.

–5–

The Beautiful Body

The driving force behind *Nacktkultur* was concern for the welfare and the future of the race. As important as health and healing was the nudist quest to build beautiful bodies. In *Nacktkultur*, the preoccupation with Germans' health was part of an effort to reverse the widespread physical degeneration that nudists maintained came from living in burgeoning metropolises or from toiling in filthy factories. Good health was also considered the first step towards creating beauty, which as one author explained was 'the symbolic expression of inner and outer health.'[1]

However common and widespread, illness and disease were only two kinds of physical decay; other indicators were paleness, ugliness and weakness, characteristics many Germans possessed. In order for there to be a true regeneration of the *Volk* and nation, bodies, nudists realized, would need to be beautiful as well as healthy. 'Through *Nacktkultur* beautiful people must first be bred and healthy bodies must be realized,' declared one author. 'For us,' he continued, 'intensive nudism must be practiced to eliminate the seeds of disease and epidemics from our bodies before beauty can be expected. Beauty is not the prerequisite for *Nacktkultur*, but rather the path to health and beauty leads through nudism.'[2] In nudism, the body, aided by the natural elements, was the instrument of its own transformation, physically and symbolically, and that of Germany.

Body culture in general and nudism in particular challenged old notions about the body and society. Nudist activity transformed the body into a pure, healthy vessel worthy of an equally pure and moral soul, and a home for both a strong, fully formed personality and sharp intellect, a precondition for transforming the race and nation.[3] One needed to be naked as much as possible for the full benefits of the naked experience to be realized. Again as Fritz Thies, a former leader of one of nudism's failed umbrella organizations, realized, 'the cultivation of nakedness is the condition for the attainment of these goals [of transforming body, life and society].'[4] Not only would whole lifestyles be changed by nudism, including sleeping, working, even eating and drinking, but also more importantly *Nacktkultur* would create a new body and a new society.[5] The healed, beautified German would lead to a flowering of German culture, reminiscent of the accomplishments and glory of ancient Greece.

102 • *Naked Germany*

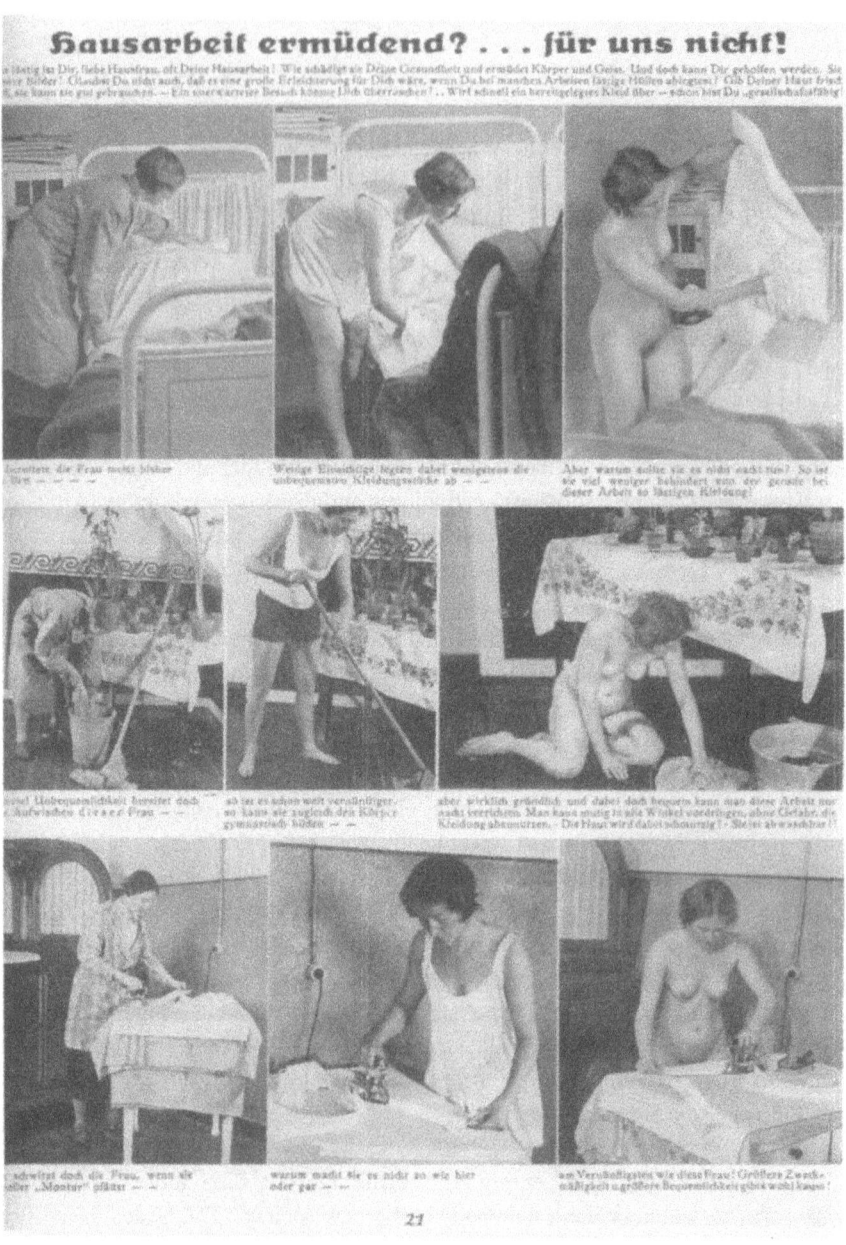

Figure 5.1 All manner of work could be performed while naked, to the advantage of body and spirit. Here in a series of panels is a demonstration of housework done in increasingly comfortable and 'practical' circumstances. Daily chores are best done while naked. The title reads: 'Does housework exhaust? Not us.' Image from *Lachendes Leben* Jahrgang VIII, Heft 3. Courtesy of ANRL.

The Ancient Model

The importance of the classical civilizations of Rome and especially Greece in the development of modern Germany cannot be underestimated. Created in the Prussian school reforms under von Humboldt in the early nineteenth century, the famous German secondary schools (*Gymnasien*) had as their very foundation the study of ancient languages, in particular Latin and Greek.[6] The domination of the curriculum by the Ancients began to be replaced only in the post-Second World War era, despite an early awareness of its impracticality for the twentieth century.[7] Among intellectuals, in the realm of so-called 'high art,' too, the accomplishments of the Greeks in sculpture were considered paramount, thanks largely to J.J. Winckelmann, who in the mid eighteenth century formulated and codified the aesthetic greatness of the Greeks and their bodies in his tome, *Geschichte der Kunst des Altherthums*.[8] No less a personage than Richard Wagner, the most quintessentially German of all composers, was himself deeply influenced by the legacy of Hellas.[9] That German philosophical endeavor over the course of the last three centuries centered on the effort to build an 'aesthetic state,' one scholar has argued, is itself traceable to ancient Greece through Winckelmann's lingering truisms.[10]

For German nudists, as for so many of their contemporaries, the example of the ancient Greeks and their society was of vast importance, supplying them with the standards of physical beauty, examples of desirable body types, and even providing the model of the cultural and artistic heights a society that embraced nakedness could achieve. Greek culture was able to ascend to its lofty heights, nudists determined, because of its relationship to the body, especially the nude body.[11] The foundation of Greek and Roman society was nakedness; they literally 'built upon a healthy nakedness.'[12]

Nudists held that the Greeks realized the naked body was god-like, and their appreciation of it fueled their cultural accomplishments.[13] Through *Nacktkultur*, assured one author, the Greeks had been able to overcome their fractious city-state politics; an assertion that must have resonated with readers frustrated and wearied by the Weimar political experience.[14] Nakedness, argued another nudist, was what enabled the Greeks, and later the Romans, to become great. So integral was nakedness to the Greek that once 'in clothing he could neither breathe nor think.'[15]

Like the Romantics a century before them, nudists worshipped the Greeks for their beauty.[16] Exploring the mystery of the origins of Greek physical beauty, one author decided it stemmed from a combination of 'climate, diet and intellectual and physical dynamism.'[17] Whereas Germans could not replicate the climatic conditions of the ancient Greeks, they could imitate their diet and physical and intellectual dynamism, and their nakedness. German nudists believed it was precisely the casual and accepted social nudity of ancient Greek society that made the Greeks such a beautiful people. Living as a nude society also enabled the Greeks to formulate a concept of beauty based on their own bodies, which they applied to and captured in their art, especially their sculpture.

Later, as Greek society buckled and collapsed under the onslaught of Christianity and crumbled from within with the arrival of luxury and aristocratic decadence, its view of the body as well as its concept of corporal beauty were also lost. This initiated a general decline in European art and culture that continued up to the nudists' own day.[18] Moreover, when ancient Greek society collapsed, the pure, nude body largely disappeared with it. Fortunately, the principles of body beauty formulated by the Greeks were rediscovered by J.J. Winckelmann in the eighteenth century, which, when published, initiated a transformation in middle European art that slowly reintroduced the nude to society – a process that was culminating in the modern nudist movement.[19]

Nudism, in the form practiced by the ancient Greeks, provided modern Germans with a powerful model with which to redirect the fate of the German *Volk* and nation. 'We greet in *Nacktkultur* a rediscovered educational force, lost since the downfall of the ancients, that will physically, intellectually and morally strengthen our *Volk*,' noted one nudist.[20] For precise instruction in teaching modern Germans how to construct the proper body form and to aspire to higher beauty standards, nudists relied on art, especially classical Greek examples, because as one nudist explained art was the 'teacher of peoples.'[21] Nudists believed that the statues and other artistic works from classical Greece were portraits of ancient life, captured and forever set in marble, which would serve both as reminders and as guides for future generations attempting to raise themselves. Greek art achieved the highest levels of perfection because it, like all great art, was a reflection of life.[22] Sculpture was proof of the Greeks' beauty and nakedness.

So fundamental to the culture and success of the Greeks was the nakedness of the body and so highly developed was the Greek sense of art as an expression of that nakedness that even the famed Olympic Games were thought by nudists to be a result of the combination of the two. The Olympics were important for state and *Volk* in the Greek system, decided Hans Surén, and brought joy to the audience and to the athletes. 'In ancient Greece, one knew, for better or worse, how very much the flowering of a *Volk* was tied to true *Körperkultur*.'[23] The Greeks achieved greatness because 'for centuries nakedness and gymnastics were the source of the power and health of the Greek *Volk*.'[24]

Surén was not, however, the only nudist who believed the Olympic athletes were naked. Pleased by the recent growth of people engaging in sports while naked, nudist Walther Brauns likened these athletes to the ancient Greeks. He richly illustrated his book with highly stylized photographs of nude Germans imitating classical or Olympic-style poses, throwing javelins, tossing hammers, shooting bows and arrows or wrestling.[25] These photographs, like the activities they depicted, were useful in furthering the idea of nudism through their imagery. Walter Heitsch described the ideal Sunday visit to a nudist park. He imagined friendly beautiful Germans being led in calisthenics (*Gymnastik*) by a degreed instructor, then throwing spears, heaving shot puts and tossing discuses.[26] Olympic imagery and imitation is prominent in nudist iconography and activity.

The Purpose of the Naked Body: Founding the Greco-Germanic *Volksgemeinschaft*

The advanced state of Germany's degeneration at the dawn of the twentieth century, nudists suspected, was due in large part to the loss of the ability to view the naked body, especially in the manner of the Greeks.[27] Modern Germans were further hindered in their attempt to regenerate themselves by the fact that almost no one knew how a healthy, normal body should appear. Germans knew only distorted, damaged and sickly bodies.[28] Whereas the Greek felt 'complete' in his or her nakedness, modern Germans felt 'empty.'[29] The Greeks both understood and were comfortable with the naked form in living and in art. 'Among the peoples of ancient Greece, nakedness was always at hand. Nakedness was dealt with while at play, in sports and in their body care. The beautiful body was admired and idealized not only in artwork but also in nature, as a paragon.'[30] In nudist ideology, the naked body not only characterized Greek society and culture, it also in a certain sense created it. Just as *Nacktkultur* had made the Greeks lofty, so too would it save Germany.

Recovering this lost sense of the body, its beauty and its nakedness would propel German culture to new levels, just as it had for the Greeks.[31] 'The ancient model justifies the expectation that a new renaissance will spring from present *körperkultur* [sic],' assured Hans Vahle.[32] Applied to Germany, *Nacktkultur* would strengthen, heal and revive culture, foster appreciation of the nude and inspire the arts.[33] 'Even in the interest of art one must demand that people be returned to the condition of the ancient Greeks, so that they may have the [opportunity to] view the naked human body and become capable of viewing its pure nakedness with pure eyes.'[34] In the naked 'airbath, art and hygiene meet, in order to elevate the human species.'[35] 'The air- and lightbath are the aesthetic cure forms,' decided one nudist.[36]

The German nudist vision of the ancient Greeks was important for a number of reasons. By positing their nudism as part of the inheritance from the classical civilizations, nudists could claim a measure of legitimacy against the charges of indecency that opponents might level at them. Nudists could portray themselves as part of a long tradition in European culture dating from its earliest, most exalted moments. Nudists could present themselves as the purest variety of latter-day humanists, attempting to help Germany recover first from Wilhelmine decadence and later from the national collapse in the First World War. Other humanists' efforts were doomed to failure because they left out the essential ingredient of the Ancients' recipe for greatness, namely nudism.[37]

The ancient Greek example also provided nudists with a convenient means for criticizing their own society's moral or physical follies, as well as supplying the means for correcting those follies through the cultivation of beauty through nakedness. Many nudists were also vehement nationalists, and believed that through their efforts the German *Volk* and nation would recover from the depths to which they had sunk in the 1920s, and here too classical Greece supplied distraught nudists with a model: Sparta.

Modern body culture (*Körperkultur*) meant more than simply being naked – it entailed a good deal of work and appreciation of the body. *Nacktkörperkultur* in particular carried with it notions of discipline and an awareness of the racial value of the body. Unlike their decadent metropolitan counterparts, who, over-stimulated by their urban environments and unnatural lifestyles, could only thrive on the sight of artificially sexualized women in naked dance revues or other erotic nightclub-like situations, nudists were a strong, strenuously self-disciplined group who did not engage in wanton sexual behavior. 'Modern body culture is not a rebirth of the bacchanalia and the orgies of lust [*Wollust*], but rather a rebirth of Sparta and true human life.'[38] In nudism, the body, once freed of its clothes, did not become a vehicle for outrageous behavior, but instead became a constant, living reminder to its owner of the need for restraint, sobriety and pure living.

The nudism of the Ancients brought glory to the body, and made its owner want to cherish his or her physical being and not to tarnish it in any physical or spiritual way. Being naked and practicing nudism not only advanced a sense of health and beauty to the nudist, but also one of cleanliness, especially self-cleanliness. Once overcome by an awareness of his or her own corporal beauty, a nudist would not want to jeopardize it by courting disease or infection, possibly leading to disfigurement or death. The sense of cleanliness exerted control over the nudist's sexual behavior, so that, for example, a male nudist would not dirty himself by visiting a prostitute.[39]

Nudism was responsible for a purer morality, one that did not tolerate lasciviousness, and here too the moral discipline was Greek in origin. 'Spartans, like ancient Germans, had no patience for prostitution. Affirmation of life and joy of the body lead to moral purity and a noble humanity.'[40] Modern German nudists acted vigorously to rekindle the positive ancient disposition towards the body among their contemporaries. Nudists were the heirs of the Spartan tradition of body glorification and strong people, argued one.[41] The long dormant spirit of Sparta was to be brought back to life by nudists in *Nacktkultur*:

> Sparta – magical name from a long lost era – it reawakens in us! It lives in us not only as the place of physical discipline, severity, fitness and excellence [*Straffheit und*

Figure 5.2 'An idealized communion with nature.' From *Ideale Nacktheit Naturaufnahmen menschlicher Körperschönheit*, Zweiter Band 1915. Courtesy of ANRL.

Tüchtigkeit]: but also as the school of self-discipline, modesty and straightforwardness. Nudists [*Lichtkämpfer*] hold yourselves to this ideal! Spartan tradition and simplicity – that spirit is your spirit![42]

In order to grow and to mature properly, modern German youth, like the Spartan youth centuries before, would need to throw off its clothes and swim in a sea of light.[43] In gender relations, which nudists also hoped to transform, Sparta again provided the model. Citing Bebel, one nudist noted that Spartan women were wholly accustomed to the sight of a naked man.[44] Nudism's effort to claim the inheritance from ancient Sparta also fit nicely into the later National Socialist regime's worldview of struggle, racial purity and vigor, and militarism. For example, when the Nazi nudist Hans Surén called forth the spirit of the ancient Greeks for nudists to follow, it was the Greece of Lycurgus and Sparta not of Solon and Athens that he meant.

German nudism borrowed a good deal from the ancient Greeks, who nudists thought had practiced the first conscious nudism in history. The cultural accomplishments of all Greeks and the legendary military invincibility of Sparta were attractive images for a movement that decried as degenerate the artistic and cultural trends of its own era and for a nation that suffered defeat in war and humiliation in the peace that followed.

The awesome figure of the beautiful Greek body loomed large in *Nacktkultur*'s own quest for beauty. 'Our beauty ideal is embodied in Greek imagery,' explained one nudist, 'and everyone should improve his or her own body, should strive for it for his or her own person!'[45] However, regardless of how heavily German nudists relied on ancient images for their inspiration, it would be mistaken to consider the goal of their movement as a return to that past. Rather, nudism was more properly viewed, suggested one nudist, as the inheritance from the ancient world.[46] In *Nacktkultur*, the Greek legacy of nakedness would merge with other traditions to shape the nudist German future.

Figure 5.3 The lure of the imagined tribal past was powerful, and nudists sought to recreate in themselves their Greco-Germanic ancestors. From Richard Ungewitter, *Die Nacktheit in entwicklungsgeschichtlicher, gesundheitlicher, moralischer und künstlicher Beleuchtung*. Photo by R. Ungewittter. Courtesy of ANRL.

Apart from the ancient Greeks there was one other ancient people for whom nakedness and the appreciation of the natural, unadorned and beautiful body was a way of life, and who served as an example for modern German nudists to follow: the ancient Germans. Conjuring the ancient Germans served much the same purpose as conjuring the ancient Greeks – it was a way for nudists to criticize their fellow modern Germans. Among the ancient Germans, nudists argued, the naked body was 'natural, holy, beautiful, and a joy.'[47] It was a symbol of health, power and purity – in short, a symbol of their Germanness.

The ancient Germans had a number of uses for nakedness, such as protection from spooks and evil spirits.[48] In ancient Mecklenburg, claimed one nudist, it was customary to sit naked beside the fire before retiring to sleep in an effort to ward off nightmares. The ancient Germans' natural, healthy sense of nakedness was completely alien to the sensual charm of the nakedness of stripping.'[49] Like the Greeks, once the ancient Germans began to lose their relationship to the naked body and ability to appreciate it in its natural, non-erotic pureness, they too became degenerate.

Like the ancient Greeks, Germans' relationship to nature, nakedness and purity was eroded by 'racially alien influences, international efforts and ecclesiastical forces,' which had been at work for generations destroying Germany.[50] Nudists were able to ascertain in the present day physical degeneration and ugliness in German society oozed from the top down, and gradually afflicted the whole nation. Observing the 'leadership echelon of our *Volk* over the course of the last few decades,' wrote Hans Surén in the 1930s, one could see that 'the physical strength and beauty that should characterize our race is missing totally.'[51] Obviously a criticism of the Weimar leadership, Surén's comment could just as easily have been aimed at Wilhelmine society, thought in the popular mind to be riddled with scandal. It also gave Surén the chance to praise Germany's new leadership, the National Socialists.[52]

Though nudists detected some essential differences between the *Nacktkultur* of the ancient Greeks and the ancient Germans, the two peoples bore a number of similarities and were often equated with one another in nudist writings. One major difference was the meaning of the nudism each practiced. For the ancient Greeks, nudism was primarily a means to achieve beauty, to produce art and to create culture. For ancient Germans, *Nacktkultur* and physical conditioning were thought to have been used to strengthen themselves against weather, for the hunt and for war.

Nudism helped the ancient Germans develop high moral standards, unlike contemporary Germans whose 'depraved morality . . . happily characterizes nakedness as immorality, for it really does always whip up the erotic passions of impure persons.'[53] Other minor differences existed between the two ancient tribes. For example, whereas the Greeks played at the Olympics as a way to maintain their naturalness, the ancient Germanic equivalent focused on 'competitions of strength, the beauty of strength, racial stature and chivalry.'[54] In both cases, however, nudism was a catalyst for all other social and cultural developments.

Restoring to modern Germans their original tribal qualities of naturalness, nakedness and the ability to appreciate that nakedness as the foundation for all subsequent cultural activity meant diminishing or eliminating the influence of those forces that continued to eat away at the racial body. It also meant awakening in every German a sense of his or her original tribal qualities, and reacquainting Germans with their true selves, so to speak. This would be a relatively easy task since, 'in every person, despite our civilization which has led us astray, there slumbers a tiny piece of primordial Germanness that only needs to be awakened.'[55] Here nudism would play the pivotal transcendental role.

To awaken the slumbering ancient German within them, modern Germans, nudists enjoined, needed to revive the ancient customs, such as bathing their children year-round in Germany's rivers and practicing nudism. 'One would be surprised how quickly everything would configure itself and healthy life would unfold and spread before everyone,'[56] assured Heinrich Pudor. Nudism was capable of reawakening the primordial German hidden within his or her modern counterpart, since practicing it called forth 'old sagas of naked heroes and tales from long forgotten times.'[57]

Nature and nakedness were profoundly important for the ancient Germans, and deeply intertwined. The ancient Germanic religion, the organic product of its climate, celebrated not an invisible and fickle deity or group of deities but the sun.[58] The sea, especially the Baltic and North Seas, exerted a lasting influence on Germans, which led one nudist to conclude that northern Europe was the 'cradle of all Aryan tribes,' and that returning naked to the waters or beaches of either sea to swim or to play would bring joy to the German.[59]

Surén noticed a transformation among those with whom he practiced nudism, one that was joyful and soulful at the same time. 'All of my comrades who have tried nudism and have exerted themselves [*trainierten*] while naked were overcome by a deep longing for a return to the life in the time of the ancient Germans.'[60] Moreover, the ancient Germans belonged to nature, but nature did not belong to the Germans. In other words, private property did not exist among the ancient Germanic tribes – 'everything belonged to the whole' and its advent helped bring to ruin all the great ancient societies, including those of the Germans, Greeks and Romans.[61]

In *Nacktkultur*, the future Germany would be constructed from elements that combined the ancient tribal past and the legacy of Hellas. The idea was to 'reorient German life along the eternally fertile soil of the ancient Hellens in a Goetheian, Schillerian and Wielandian sense, permeated to the soul with the German cast of mind and spirit.'[62] The groundwork for the fusion of Greco-

Germanic nudism had already been laid in the eighteenth century, as nudists liked to acknowledge. The master of German classicism, J.W. Goethe, had praised nudism in the *Letters from Switzerland*.[63] Each ancient civilization would contribute its special qualities to this new Germany. 'This nation [*Reich*] of the future will be called German-Hellas [*Deutsch Hellas*]. German is the embodiment of all manly virtues, as Tacitus gloriously preserved them for posterity, and Hellas embodies the virtues of freedom, beauty and goodness.'[64]

Practicing *Nacktkultur* allowed the separate forces of strength and beauty to combine and to merge into a new force that would result in the creation of a new German and a new Germany, where all were naked, close to nature and whole. Germans would be physically and economically free, discord and internal strife would fall aside and private property along with its companions 'need, suffering and poverty' would disappear under a new system of land rights that did not force people into crowded cities where high rents further exploited them.[65] The land reform ideas of American Henry George and German Adolf Damaschke carried a powerful appeal among nudists. Private property along with body shame and clothing were alien to the German character and the German body. Their removal would set the nation once again on a more proper path, and one originally begun by the ancient Germans.

The union of ancient German and ancient Greek virtues and cultures would proceed smoothly, nudists assured, since the Germanic racial type was largely responsible for the advent of all culture. 'The fact is well known,' wrote Richard Ungewitter, 'that the dominant blonde-haired (and blue-eyed) race is the German race, the bringers and spreaders of the culture of the entire planet. Not only,' he continued, 'did this race fertilize the European cultures, but also through its migrations in the pre-historic era did it create the cultures of the Greeks and Romans.'[66] German culture, Ungewitter continued, had also achieved the Italian Renaissance, all visual arts in France, as well as all medieval French literature, the discovery of bronze, the creation of ceramics, and finally all classical art.[67]

Nudists were no strangers to racial nationalism. Hans Surén further developed the idea that Greek culture was in fact Germanic culture. Upon careful inspection, Surén was able to conclude that the ancient Greeks were in reality ancient Germans, which at least helped explain why the former's cultural achievements were possible. The Greeks 'were Nordic forefathers, racial brothers of our present *Volk*.'[68] 'Both come from Aryan origins, both have equal talents and inclinations in character. Their forms only changed because of climate and external circumstances.'[69] In any event, whether following the Hellenic, the Spartan or the Germanic legacy, or all three, Germany's rebirth would involve reviving its own past and the German people looking to its Nordic, Aryan roots for guidance. Even the climate of ancient Greece and southern Germany, informed one author, were similar.[70]

German nudists deliberately invoked the legacy of the ancient Greek and Germanic tribes to explain the goals and ambitions of their ideology and movement. 'Hopefully,' explained one author, 'we will arrive quickly to the point where just as in ancient Greece we will find nothing objectionable in complete nakedness.'[71] *Nacktkultur* was not only a way to 'make humans stronger, healthier,' but also a way to make them physically beautiful.[72] Like the ancient Greeks, once Germans embraced nudism on a large scale then they too would rise to cultural dominance and national strength. Nakedness was a way to mitigate the harmful effects of clothes, and was also a prerequisite for beginning the process of making the body healthy and beautiful.

The Beautiful Body and Modern Germans

Although beginning the process of self-beautification was simple, involving little more than removing one's clothes and embracing nature, air, light, sun and nakedness, determining beauty could be difficult. Crucial to nudist ideology, nudists established only a loose guide for determining what a beautiful body was or what beauty meant. Building a beautiful body began first and foremost with nakedness. Idealism and ideology aside, nudists struggled with creating and understanding beauty.

For nudists, beauty in some instances was quite simple. For many nudists the naked body in and of itself was a thing of beauty. Artists, nudists noted, typically depicted the nude human form in their works, further justification that raw nakedness was beautiful.[73] 'The human body,' rhapsodized an anonymous nudist author was 'the most beautiful accomplishment that organic nature has achieved.'[74] For Heinrich Pudor simply being naked made one beautiful, 'the cult of the naked is simultaneously the cult of the beautiful, for nakedness is beauty. The naked human form is the highest of all that organic nature has given.'[75] For him, cultivating nakedness meant cultivating beauty. Wilhelm Kästner found the pinnacle of beauty in the naked body when it was engaged in exercise (*Turnen*) or at play.[76]

Often in nudist discourse the concept of beauty was connected to nature, itself understood to be an unadulterated or pure condition. Nudist rhapsodies on nature could assume an outright religious tone. Hans Surén, for example, described how being naked in the forest made the forest itself into a cathedral.[77] Wilhelm Kästner held that everything natural was beautiful, and the naked body, disencumbered by any sign of civilization, was the natural body. The half-naked was an abomination, ugly, immoral and a threat to public decency, linked as it was to eroticism.[78]

For some, the beautiful body was a combination of simplicity, naturalness and the discovery of one's true form. Those who could not take pleasure in simplicity or in nature often could not bring themselves to be naked either. Nudists believed the inability to enjoy nature or to be naked was a powerful sign of degeneracy. City dwellers in particular were thought incapable of returning to nature because they were so far removed from naturalness and simplicity. 'To be natural is too simple for them, and because it is too simple they cannot be naked. They cannot bear simplicity,' concluded Karl Bückmann.[79]

For Surén, removing one's clothes was a simultaneous stripping of the trappings of civilization, making the individual again part of nature, at peace and happy. Describing the experience of nakedness to the reader, he wrote that once naked it was 'with innermost pleasure that we feel the cool freshness of our skin. In this naked, fresh skin we sense the true-to-life person.'[80] Nakedness was humans' natural form, and as nudists were fond of reminding their readers, people were born without clothes ('Nature created humans naked, therefore nakedness is natural' was the oft-expressed sentiment), and they should remain so.[81] However, simply being naked did not necessarily always qualify one as beautiful; there was a good deal of work that accompanied the creation of beauty. Moreover, there was a serious debate among nudists as to whether everyone could be made beautiful.

The question of physical ugliness and what could be done with it, if anything, was not one that received a clear answer in *Nacktkultur*, and nudists wrestled with the problem. Some cleverly argued that those who practiced or supported nudism were automatically beautiful and those who opposed it were not. Opponents, this nudist argued, were not only ugly but were also physically deformed and perverse. 'Those who warn against nudism are hypocrites and prudes, jealous, perverse, depraved individuals, whose bodies are incomplete and deficient,' explained Richard Ungewitter.[82] This simplistic equation of nudist supporters possessing beauty and opponents being ugly was not one that found universal support. Others believed that one was beautiful or one was not, and in the case of the latter no amount of covering could ever conceal what was beneath.[83] Some nudists argued from a strictly aesthetic position, and claimed that the ugly could not participate in *Nacktkultur*.[84] This position, however, ignored and negated one of nudism's most basic tenets and powers, that is, its ability to transform bodies.

J.M. Seitz recognized that physical ugliness among nudists and potential nudists was a serious problem. He appreciated the views of those whose concerns were primarily aesthetic, and placed them at the opposite extreme of nudism's racial concerns, which called for everyone to participate in order to improve the race.[85] Seitz also proposed a compromise to mollify aesthetically oriented nudists that would allow for the so-called physically ugly to visit a nudist park and to better themselves while not offending those nudists possessed of a strong sense of aesthetics.

One solution to the problem of how not-yet-beautiful Germans could visit an airbath or sunbath and become beautiful while also not offending anyone was for a slight garment to be worn. The ugly, explained one author, could wear to their '*Luftbad*, a light [weight], airgarment [*Luftgewand*], easily penetrated by light and air, that would hold a natural, pleasing shape.' As long as the garment was worn out of aesthetic concerns and not because the wearer harbored any feelings of body shame, then this was considered an acceptable solution. Seitz understood that his society was in a 'transitional state,' and that many were adversely affected by having worn clothes most of their lives. Only by allowing these people the opportunity to improve their bodies through nudist activities such as 'sports, calisthenics, walking, and rhythm exercises' could they ever expect to acquire physical beauty.[86]

The question of unappealing or ugly bodies was above all else a lopsided one, and it throws some light on nudist attitudes towards women. Little to no mention of ugly men is ever explicitly made. At most, only a hint of their existence is intimated, such as in the formulation of the problem in terms of what to do with those people 'especially women,' who are no longer beautiful.[87] The nudist preoccupation with physical ugliness concerned itself primarily with women's physical ugliness, with attention especially focused on the condition of women's breasts.

Unlike with men's bodies, which could not be (or were not) analyzed or evaluated in terms of just one component, the shape and form of women's breasts were considered the key to understanding the beauty of the entire feminine form. 'The beauty of the whole female figure,' one nudist argued, 'is strongly dependent on the formation and shaping of the breasts.' Moreover, he continued, 'all women and girls quite naturally long for well-formed breasts.' Unattractive breasts were those that were underdeveloped or saggy, and girls and women who possessed them should not appear without tops on Germany's beaches.[88]

The concern over whether or not women possessed beautiful breasts transcended mere aesthetic concerns, however. Beautiful breasts were important for the health and preservation of the race since they were thought by nudists to be more capable of producing milk, which would better nourish Germany's infants, eventually leading to a more robust race. Cow's milk could not be expected to nourish Germany's babies nearly as well as mother's milk, for cow's milk 'did not contain all of the essential ingredients of mother's milk.' Practicing *Nacktkultur*, or at the very least toplessness, could help girls develop and women maintain beautiful breasts; however, it could not repair them.[89]

The need for beautiful breasts forced Hans Surén to advocate drastic measures that were seemingly incompatible with nudism's emphasis on naturalness. For those women and girls for whom it was too late, whose breasts already sagged or were otherwise not beautiful, Surén recommended hormone therapy, which he believed had for several years busied itself with studying how to improve breasts and their milk production. He claimed further to know of one gland-based compound that caused underdeveloped breasts to develop completely and that tightened the loose skin on saggy breasts.[90] Racial improvement was a serious matter, and women, future mothers all, needed to be on top form by whatever means to ensure any successes in the next generation.

Figure 5.4 A healthy, well-built body was the ideal. Nudists worked diligently to create it through calisthenics. Image from *Lachendes Leben* Jahrgang VII, Heft 10. Courtesy of ANRL.

Building a beautiful body was not necessarily an easy task, but a sometimes complex process that involved constant attention to one's body. In the effort to construct the ideal body, along with breasts, various body parts, such as the feet and the skin, were identified as especially important and needful of extra attention. Feet needed to be washed and cleaned often, though not necessarily daily. Socks and shoes should never be worn, and foot exercises needed to be performed often, admonished one concerned nudist. Occasionally one's feet should be soaked in moss, clay, sand, peat or other rich soils, though never for more than half an hour.[91] Easily the most important part of the body, given its role in transporting toxins out of the body and air and light into the body, as well as being the one that required the most attention and care, was the skin. Remarking on the attention now being given to skin and skin-care, one nudist author proclaimed that the 'discovery of the skin is one of the most important for our era.'[92]

A nudist needed to have healthy, strong skin for a number of reasons, not the least of which was its importance in the *Licht-* and *Luftbad*. Human health, argued Hans Graaz, was a result of the meteorological conditions and humans' own secretions. Healthy skin ensured a healthy interaction between the elements and the body's inner organs, in particular the glands, which in turn would produce better secretions, detoxifying the body.[93] Acquiring healthy skin was a fairly simple matter, involving little more than water and oil. Nudists advocated daily washing, though without soap. Soap stripped the skin of its precious fatty deposits.[94] For readers' benefit, Richard Ungewitter passed along his personal example. He bathed every morning in the kitchen, using only water and his hands. He strongly cautioned against using soap, sponges or washcloths.[95]

Nudists varied in their recommendations for daily hygiene, but many offered their own examples to follow. Hans Vahle recommended using soap as well as an abrasive sponge in one's bath, which should be conducted in front of an open window or outside, for maximum benefit. He suggested that afterwards the body should be thoroughly rubbed, first from hand to shoulder, then foot to thigh, until dry.[96] Hans Surén maintained that daily bathing was best done in a brook, stream, spring, under a waterfall or with rain water.[97] Adolf Weide recommended that upon waking, one strip one's clothes off, have a quick rubdown using one's hands, followed by a 'nose airbath,' which involved vigorously blowing air through the nostrils in order to empty them, a bowel movement, a shave and combing of the hair.[98] Daily hygiene was essential to building a healthy, beautiful body.

Alongside cleanliness, a skin's color was considered an important factor in an individual's as well as a race's overall health. Skin that had been long encased in clothing was pale and sickly in appearance. Not only was such skin unaesthetic, complained Wilhelm Kästner, but it made the person look like a corpse. Pale skin was the color of death, whereas the color of life was the red-brown of the sun.[99] Moreover, the meaning of tanned skin had deep cultural and historical implications. The revered Greeks believed that tanned skin 'was the first requirement of a man, pale skin was seen as completely unmanly,' noted Hans Surén. Surén even went so far as to suggest that the Greek victories over the Persians were due to the inspiration the Greeks drew when they saw that Persian prisoners were pale-skinned and therefore 'effeminate.'[100] Skin was vital to an individual's health, and even to national survival. Skin-care was a subject nudists took seriously.

Virtually everyone recommended the use of oil on the body. Ungewitter claimed to oil himself once every three to four weeks, soaking his body in olive oil, almond oil and even poppy seed oil.[101] His personal endorsement fell on Diaderma brand olive oil.[102] Hans Vahle advocated a daily oiling, best done after one's bath.[103] Surén, whose books often featured photos of him posed naked and very obviously slick from body oil, discouraged use of any animal-based or synthetic oil, suggesting instead any plant-based oil.[104] By the 1930s, manufacturers had become aware of nudists' needs, and a small market niche for skin oils developed. Advertisements for a skin oil called Jadeöl, appeared in nearly every issue of the Nazi nudist organ, *Deutsche Leibeszucht*, for example. Other brands made periodic appearances.

Using olive oil or some other type of oil on one's body was an important tool in the sunbath, where it helped keep the bather calm and reduced overall sweating.[105] Body oil replaced soap in the nudist's daily hygiene routine, as it could remove dirt that soap could not. Perhaps even more importantly than its practical uses was its historical and cultural meaning. Again connecting themselves to the ancient Greeks, nudists excitedly reminded readers that the ancient Greeks were known to have practiced daily body oiling. Whatever its practical uses in the *Luft-* or *Sonnenbad*, the practice of daily oiling reinforced nudism's claims to be the heir of Hellas. One nudist proclaimed that a culture's status could be determined by its consumption of skin oil.[106] The skin also needed a certain amount of massaging to be fully healthy and receptive of the elements. To this end a daily self-massage was recommended. One began by cutting fingernails, relaxing all muscles and then began rubbing at the head, pushing blood in the direction of the heart, while simultaneously conducting breathing exercises.[107]

Central to the nudist endeavor of building a better, more beautiful personal body was its nakedness. Nudists were well aware that in the human primeval and classical eras, people had been naked, innocent and pure. The advent of clothing together with the degeneracy of civilization and the cancerous growth of religion, especially Christianity, had worked throughout Western history in a potent alliance that devastated whole cultures by malforming bodies and perverting attitudes about the body. Now in the twentieth century, nudists believed, Germany, long a bulwark of racial purity against the forces of degeneration, was also beginning to succumb to their relentless onslaught. *Nacktkultur* was desperately needed to stem the tide and to regenerate Germans.

Conclusion

Communal nakedness in a natural setting created the basis for a new morality, one better suited to Germans and designed to foster a cultural Golden Age. *Nacktkultur* was partly a liberation from negative attitudes about the body developed in the nineteenth century and earlier, and partly the basis for a breeding program that would reestablish Germans' racial purity. Building the beautiful body began with stripping off clothing in order to return the body to its original, natural appearance so that, guided by classical principles, bodies could be crafted into works of living art, the literal embodiments of the Aryan racial ideal.

Further advances towards nudist society could only be made when everyone was comfortably naked and comfortable around the nakedness of others. 'When the *Volk* is used to seeing a naked body with an unencumbered view, then we can go a bit further,' explained one author.[108] When one removed one's clothes, not only were layers of fabric being taken off, but so too were artificial social distinctions. The concepts of truth, morality and beauty all intersected at the nexus where humans and nature met.[109] Forging a new German and building a better body entailed peeling away not only clothes from the body, but also stripping away from the body any association with shame, sexual activity and erotic suggestion. In nudism, Germans would cure, beautify, steel and eventually redefine their bodies in order to regenerate the racial nation, the modern incarnation of the Greco-Germanic tribal past.

–6–

The Nudist Woman

Sometime before her marriage, the woman who would become Frau Doktor Schmidt-Blankert was embarrassed to learn that her beloved was a nudist. Her embarrassment quickly gave way to shock when she pressed him for information about his nudist activities and more generally about nudism. Eventually, she must have pressured him to quit his involvement with *Nacktkultur*, as she later confessed that his public nakedness became a source of friction in their relationship. Sometime later, her beloved tricked her into visiting a nudist park with him, which she admits she finally assented to do with only the greatest reluctance. Her fears were considerable; she was being asked to appear naked before an unknown number of total strangers, all of whom would also be naked and looking at her naked body. 'I believed,' she wrote, giving voice to her initial worries, 'that people were going to observe my body, examine and scrutinize it.' The future Frau Dr Schmidt-Blankert was expressing a basic concern, namely that her naked body was going to be placed on semi-public display for anyone, people wholly unacquainted with her as well as her beloved, to see, to observe, to ogle, to inspect or simply to view.[1]

The future Frau Dr Schmidt-Blankert was not, however, visually inspected by a horde of nudists. Nor was she ogled, leered at or even stared at. In fact, as she later acknowledged, to her private chagrin she was hardly even seen. She reported, 'it was as if no one saw my body at all. It almost angered me.' During her first visit to the nudist park, she met other nudists, including a military officer with whom, she noted, introductions were made as formally as if at a ball; life at the nudist park, it seemed, proceeded as normally as if in Society. It was not long before she forgot altogether that she was among a group of naked people and quite naked herself. 'I was no longer aware that I, along with everyone else, was naked. It was all so natural, so obvious, so matter of course, as if it had always been thus.'[2]

She enjoyed herself so much at her first airbath that she quickly became a convert to nudism. It was difficult to convince women to attend nudist parks, and the problem of increasing women's participation was one nearly every nudist commented on. In *Nacktkultur*, the women's question was part practical and part ideological.

Though the practice of nudism applied itself to the transformation of every German and every German's body, women were of especial importance to the ideology of *Nacktkultur*. In the process of reproducing the race, women, as the sex that bore children, naturally assumed a greater importance, and nudist ideologues

120 • *Naked Germany*

Figure 6.1 There were a variety of activities to busy the nudist at the nudist club, including song and companionship. Image from *Lachendes Leben* Jahrgang VII, Heft 8. Courtesy of ANRL.

recognized this. Intended ultimately, of course, to benefit the race, *Nacktkultur* and the experience of nakedness promised a number of benefits to women in general and to women's bodies in particular that would more obviously and more fundamentally transform them than was the case with men and men's bodies.

More importantly, nudism would bring to women a certain measure of emancipation. In the nudist experience, women would not only be changed physically, something that was itself pregnant with a number of important consequences for women, but in the process would also realize a shift in their social positions, if not their basic role as mother to the *Volk* and nation. In nudism women would experience emancipation, though in a manner peculiar to the German women's movement.[3] In nudist ideology, women continued to be thought of primarily in biological terms, but the sex reform inherent in nudism promised an elevation of women's status within heterosexual relationships, from passive to active agent in every level of the union.

Nudism's View of Contemporary German Women

The modern economy had been particularly harmful to women, nudists argued. Generally, nudists acknowledged that industry and industrial work brought harm and decay to the worker's body and mind. However, there were specific effects it had on women's bodies that drew nudists' ire. The sickened state of the *Volk* by 1929 could be traced back to women working in the factories. The magazine *Das Freibad* declared that cases of sickness among gainfully employed women were five to eight times higher than among non-working women. The author of the magazine continued, drawing attention to the real problem that arose when women worked, 'among these [illnesses], one finds numerous illnesses of the all-important reproductive organs.' The magazine further warned that, 'where women suffer, so too suffer children!' Its conclusion assigned to all 'understanding humanity,' the 'task of working against the fate of so many women.'[4]

Further consequences of industrialization and rising luxury included the suspicion that women would begin to lose their ability to nurse, and their fertility in general would decline. Slowly, the effects of prosperity, industry and luxury would make themselves felt in the coming generations, as 'weakness, pre-disposition to tuberculosis and epilepsy, feeble-mindedness and idiocy, as well as perversity and criminality' were passed on to children.[5] Even worse, explained one author, was the fact that the modern economy based on industry created prostitutes out of otherwise healthy, wholesome German women. Capitalism, for example, sucked women from the countryside to the city, only to pay them with lower wages, eventually forcing them to seek supplemental income, usually as prostitutes.[6]

The message was clear from the nudist perspective: industrial work was destructive to individuals and to the race. Modern work endangered the *Volk* by employing women, whose bodies were consequently made incapable of producing healthy offspring, when it did not transform them into prostitutes. 'Thus the industrial-hygienic women's question is not only a special one of welfare work, but instead a question of fate for the entire *Volk*,' concluded *Das Freibad*.[7] Nudism was presented as the opposite to industrialized society, especially the society that emerged from the nineteenth century.[8]

For nudists, national regeneration through the glorification of the naked body and purification of the race through breeding and eugenics were well-established tenets. In their eyes, it remained only a matter of implementing these principles in Germans' lives for their effects to begin to be realized; this was an aspect of nudism that relied heavily on the role of women as men's equal partners and as the race's future mothers. The nudist commitment to eugenics and breeding, however, was well tempered with the emancipating and liberating effects of sex reform, which, broadly speaking, anticipated a kind of emancipation of women by first liberating them sexually.

Nudism combined eugenics and sex reform as a means to produce a better race and society by rooting sex and sexuality in knowledge, rather than in ignorance, hearsay and superstition, as it had been in the past, and by producing gender equality within relationships, promoting the love-match and the companionate marriage as a prelude to social equality and as the means to create the nudist racial utopia. Nudism would produce a new Germany, but it would do so within the confines of traditional structures, in particular the family unit, reformed and altered according to nudist principles.

Nudism would emancipate women but also keep their feminine qualities intact; 'this struggle, this rising up, should never hinder or oppress women's natural disposition,' commented one.[9] In *Nacktkultur*, biology was still destiny, and emancipated women nevertheless remained mothers of the *Volk* and nation.[10] Although nudist ideologues continued in the Enlightenment tradition of conceiving of women and women's roles in biological terms, namely as mothers of the race and nation, their concept of femininity did not.

Unlike the thinkers of the Enlightenment, nudists did not conceive of sex as being rooted in biology. The nudist separation of sex and eroticism from the naked body also had the effect of generating an inherent equality between the sexes, as one body was now no longer only sexually passive or sexually active both men and women could initiate or reject a proposition to engage in sexual intercourse.[11] Furthermore, the path to women's sexual pleasure during intercourse, also an aspect of sex reform and the modern sex ethic, and something not happily acknowledged by good bourgeois of the nineteenth century, was now open.[12]

The Nudist 'Call to Women'

In what must be considered the most thorough and the most explicit attempt to address the differences between men and women as well as to understand the position of women in German society at large, nudist Wilhelm Kästner published a collection of essays titled *Ruf an die Frauen!* (*Call to Women!*), before the First World War, most likely in 1912. Kästner realized that as a movement, nudism had attracted few women; this was a problem, he also realized, that was not adequately addressed in nudist literature. *Call to Women!* was his solution to both problems. It would on the one hand help persuade women to try nudism, and would on the other hand address the problems particular to women and nudism. Kästner, however, was unique among nudists for his actions only in the fact that he collected his ruminations on women in a volume; most nudists addressed the topic sporadically, each arriving at more or less similar conclusions: the race would improve from a new kind of woman and nudism would create her.

Generally, nudist authors possessed a negative view of contemporary women. The conviction was deeply rooted in chauvinism and sexism, but was also both critical of the society that produced such women and kept in character with that society's views of women.[13] If women of the lower classes suffered from cruel factory conditions and inadequate housing, their bodies perhaps irreparably damaged from their industrial experiences, women of the middle classes were 'tiny, charming creatures with naïve, playful, prattling chatterbox-mouths.' Women's minds and pursuits – as well as their bodies – required urgent attention and reform through nudism. There was a general call in nudism to elevate the status of women in German society in general, and even to heed those calls from the women's movement that would place women on a higher plane.[14] Improving women, their bodies and their status in society was directly related to bettering the race and nation, more directly even than improving men's bodies.

Nudist authors understood a number of differences between men and women in both their physical construction and in their social roles and functions, all of which, they stressed, would be diminished, if not outright eliminated, through nudist activity. Women's beauty, for example, only first fully emerged between the ages of thirty-six and forty.[15] Physically, women were smaller than men, but also more graceful, and competition could cause nervous breakdowns in women.[16] Women's hips were stronger and higher than men's.[17] It was women's nature to be catty and shy, to use instinct rather than reason, to gossip, to be loose and wanton, to misuse their charm to excite, to be inconsistent and coquettish. This was in marked contrast to men who were loyal, stable, trustworthy, reliable, dependable and used reason. Men, however, were not perfect and were easily given over to licentiousness, gambling, drunkenness and likely to misuse their strength.[18]

According to nudists, women differed from men not only in their physical construction and in their inclination to act on emotion rather than to reason, but also in their overall intellectual capacities. Nudist authors devoted considerable energy in the effort to understand women and to motivate them to become nudists.

Generally, their conclusions about women's intellectual composition and capacity smack of nothing less than outright sexism. An acknowledged chauvinist, Richard Ungewitter, a man whose views mirror exactly those of the anti-feminist movement of the pre-World War era, commented that cultural achievements were beyond women's abilities, as were all state-building endeavors.[19] A political woman, for him as well as for others both within nudism and German society at large, was an aberration of the most despicable kind. 'I, however, conceive of the effort to draw women into political life, a consequence of sexual degeneration, as the highpoint of the sickening over-stimulation of perverted minds.'[20] Ungewitter was by no means the only nudist to evaluate a woman's intellectual ability as low, and the belief that women held no place in politics was endemic to *Nacktkultur*.

Improving women's health, dismantling their body prejudice and teaching them to be socially naked and comfortable around others who were naked were all vital to the success of *Nacktkultur*. Although damaging to everyone and to every body, civilization and urban living, nudists recognized, had been especially unkind and harmful to women, their personalities and to their bodies. For Kästner, the woman question *was* the clothing question.[21] Clothes had caused women's bodies, in particular, to degenerate; corsets 'crippled the liver, disturbed the circulation, digestion.'[22] 'Through clothes and corsets is a beautiful body artificially, externally feigned, while without these it is inside ugly and sickly,' reminded one author.[23] Recent history, conceded Fritz Stube in the mid 1920s, had been much harsher on women than on men. War, revolution and inflation had all taken a heavy toll on what he unabashedly called the weaker sex.[24] Participation in nudism would undo the damage wrought upon women's bodies by the custom of wearing clothing as well as by daily life in a modern, industrial society.

Women's bodies, much more so than men's, were harmed through clothing, especially the corset, a practice reinforced by widely accepted, though no less harmful, concepts of feminine beauty. Corset wearing damaged women's most sensitive and most precious organs. 'Above all else,' explained Hans Fuchs, 'by the female sex, body culture will combat and prevent the diseases and the weaknesses of the abdomen, and will thus rectify the terrible consequences of the centuries of the mistaken feeling of beauty from wearing the corset.'[25] Nudism would help solve the problem of women's sagging breasts.[26] Physically, women had much to gain from engaging in nudist activity.

Naked activity and in particular naked sports were vital both to Germany's rebirth and to women's bodies. '*Nacktsport* is the foundation for a better, purified moral disposition to grow and to make our *Volk* healthy, capable of achievement and also able to rise up,' explained one author.[27] Sports and other physical activities were better conducted in nakedness because doing so benefited the body as well as the mind.

Naked physical activity produced superior health effects on the body because of the air exchange between skin and air. 'The immediate sensation of air and water on the naked skin calls forth a healing influence on the entire nerve system and the composition of the blood,' noted one nudist. Naked sports, however, also produced aesthetic results, both in a physical sense among those who participated and in their ability to appreciate aesthetics.[28] Most important was the fact that *Nacktsport* helped women come to understand the body as a natural form, acceptable in its nakedness and something to be honored not gradually ruined through artificial or cosmetic means.

In naked activity, 'the female sex will accustom itself to the nakedness of the body, come to know and to regard the body in a healthy sense, to observe and to construct the body for its physical beauty.'[29] Naked activity would produce harmony for women, suggested Marianne Fleischhack.[30] Realizing that due to their positions, women of the 'middle "working" classes' would likely never have beautiful bodies, as their bodies lost 'the original form, [became] ugly and disharmonious,' one author noted that by engaging in naked activity one could certainly expect a success in preventing bodily ugliness.[31]

Making women's bodies healthy and strong was the critical first step for any transformation of women to occur, and unlike in the case of men it was the pre-

Figure 6.2 Nudists enjoyed themselves. Here nudist girls return from swimming. Image from *Lachendes Leben* Jahrgang VII, Heft 2. Courtesy of ANRL.

condition for all other changes, whether in women's intellectual abilities or in their social roles and positions. Ruy de Fontanel, one of the contributors to *Call to Women!* flatly declared that 'one must have the courage to say it, woman does not possess the gift of reorganization, of creation.' Moreover, he continued, there had never been a woman of genius, 'it does not exist,' he frankly noted.[32]

For Fontanel, there had never been any woman who had produced anything worthy of world historical importance, whether in art, literature or science. 'What woman's name has gone done in literature, has passed over all borders, has been pronounced from generation to generation with renewed amazement?' He wondered. 'What is the immortal work from women in the arts, in the sciences? Who thanks woman for one single discovery? Has she ever achieved anything great in music? Where are her masterpieces?'[33] Kästner himself wondered, 'whether women, because of their in-born qualities, will always need to be tutored by men.'[34] This situation was due in part to the realities of evolutionary biology that had made women physically smaller than men. Fontanel's comments should be seen, however, as criticisms of contemporary women, not women in general, and as such as criticisms of the society that had restricted women and hidden their bodies. Clearly, the implication was that the nudist woman would be much different.

Women were incapable of advanced thought or creativity because their bodies were weak, underdeveloped. To explain why women's bodies were not only smaller and weaker but also underdeveloped, Fontanel suggested, 'we must bring to mind Darwinian racial theory.'[35] In nature, he continued, everything had a purpose, and women's physical inferiority as well as the general inequality of the sexes stemmed ultimately from the need to raise and to educate children. It was thus at the dawn of human history that women developed their ability to sacrifice, their sense of loyalty and watchfulness over children. At the dawn of humanity, when all people lived in small groups of hunter-gatherers, men, Fontanel explained, steadily grew stronger to repel the vicious animals that threatened the tribe, whereas women, deprived of this brutal experience, grew weaker and guarded only the hearth.[36]

This strategy was successful as it allowed for a good deal of procreation. In addition to his interest in Darwinism, Fontanel was also a committed Lamarckian and believed the physical traits the sexes developed in their mutual defense roles were gradually passed on to their offspring, so that by the twentieth century all girls and women were weak, all boys and men were strong.[37] Moreover, guarding the hearth, rather than hunting and fighting, enabled women to cultivate their beauty. From a purely Darwinian standpoint, argued one nudist, men needed only strength to succeed in the quest to acquire a mate; women, as it was their destiny to become mothers, did not, and, not needing strength to attract mates, they focused their efforts on cultivating beautiful bodies to lure mates, something that as people moved into cities and began to degenerate required ever more artificial means to be maintained.[38] Over time, these early gender roles solidified and became the norm, and women's intellect, in concert with their physical strength, slowly atrophied.

A superior intellect could only reside in a physically powerful body. 'Here clearly rests the reason that women generally cannot equal men in their intellectual accomplishments, for a strong, healthy organism is the foundation upon which intellectual greatness can flourish and mature.'[39] Though the evolution of human society to base itself on money and commerce rather than brute strength had negated the importance of body strength to a certain degree, the real promise for women's development was to be found in the loss of the crippling medieval notion of body shame, which nudism was able to eliminate. Also important was the slow acceptance by women of the ideas of sports and activity, naked or otherwise.[40] Nudists were not Neanderthals, and in addition to the suggestion that women's mental inferiority rested on their general physical frailty, it was proposed that perhaps women of genius were absent in the historical record because they had for so long been denied access to clubs, organizations and opportunity in general.[41] Whatever the ultimate cause, weak bodies or exclusion from public life, nudism promised to rectify both.

For women, the nudist experience was not only an exercise in constructing strong, healthy, beautiful bodies and mental prowess, but also a means to return women to a psychologically more natural state, as it would cause them to lose their sense of body shame and accustom themselves once again to the sight of nakedness – their own, other women's and, importantly, men's.[42] Women, observed J.M. Seitz, wanted to be naked neither around men nor around each other.[43] Women's sexual organs were more centrally located and impossible to conceal, unlike men's, which could be easily overlooked, thus contributing to women's greater adherence to the notions of body shame and greater reticence to be naked.[44]

In the nudist experience, women, like everyone who tried it, would lose their feelings of body shame and disassociate the ideas of sex from nakedness and the body, but for women the experience of nakedness would also promote self-confidence in their sex and pride of their bodies. 'And the words: "Just a girl!" will never come over the lips of a free human,' proclaimed one nudist.[45] Nudist women would not skip motherhood to save their beauty.[46] Mothers would even pride themselves on their birthmarks.[47] The nudist woman was beautiful but not vain. Her looks served a higher purpose, namely building and reproducing the race.

Being naked was the duty of health, reminded Änne Franke, but for women, as they possessed a powerful sense of shyness towards nudity, the first step, namely removing clothes, was the most difficult.[48] Girls, unlike boys who might have years of opportunity in sports clubs to see a comrade changing clothes, or men who would confront nakedness upon joining the military, had little occasion to see others in various states of dress and undress. Contemporary society raised women to be more fearful of the experience of nakedness and far less inclined to attempt nudism, giving them no opportunities to be naked around others.[49] Nevertheless, assured one author, women would experience little emotional difficulty during their first *Luft-* or *Sonnenbad*, naked around so many others, as long as it was done among true believers in nudist ideology and not among anyone seeking some sort of sexual pleasure, whether actual or voyeuristic. 'Mutual nakedness of both sexes is a **matter of trust**' (bold in original),' he stated flatly.[50]

Observing nakedness, while helpful for everyone in overcoming their body prejudices and fear of nakedness, was especially powerful and important for women. In the first sense, looking at nakedness would enable women to become familiar with their own bodies, presumably causing them to want to desist from all practices that generated physical harm. 'It is very much desired,' noted one author, 'that [women] would show their bodies and would observe themselves, as they would certainly cease the many practices that disfigure their bodies.'[51]

Richard Ungewitter, for one, found much to admire in the body of a woman raised as a nudist, uninhibited and unafraid to show her naked body to the world. 'What a magisterial, self-aware, natural and free posture, well-proportioned, well-developed, healthy, tanned body this sixteen-year-old girl raised in nakedness since her youth shows.'[52] Nudist women possessed a number of qualities absent in their clothed counterparts; these qualities were of particular importance in building a strong race but also a strong sex, one quite unlike that of their mothers, as these new women, raised in nudism, would not shy away from either physical or intellectual challenges.

Nakedness and naked observation would also compel women to become more beautiful physically, as it made them healthier, and provided them with examples of others' bodies to imitate.[53] Though predisposed to be shier than men, likely an evolutionary trait to protect from men's advances at an early age, women needed to become accustomed to nakedness and mixed-gender circumstances.[54] Losing their body shame and reticence about nakedness, their own as well as others', would be tantamount to women rejoining the world of humans, enjoined one author.[55]

Naked sports and other naked activity, especially with men and women together, would generate a more relaxed atmosphere between the two groups, which was a precondition for improved gender relations and marriages. People generally, but women in particular, would find themselves at ease in mixed naked circumstances, as they would no longer need to strive for men's attention, and because everyone in such a situation would be fully naked the desire to eroticize through partial concealment of certain body parts would also wither away.[56]

Nudist Motherhood

Women were vital to the nudist movement, to its success and to the transformation of the German race and nation. 'Just as important as the development of the male body is the corresponding bodily education of the female sex,' declared one author mildly.[57] Women's bodies needed to become more physically fit and more robust in part because it would make them better suited to motherhood, something nudists invariably referred to as women's natural calling. The birthday celebration in the nudist future would continue to be a day for the individual to celebrate his or her own existence, but the celebrant would also give pause to thank the *Volk*, God and above all his or her mother for life. For the mother herself, a child's birthday would become a day of honor (*Ehrentag*).[58]

The nudist mother would produce much healthier offspring, bettering the race overall. 'How many hundred thousand newborn children would be rescued from death each year,' wondered Heinrich Pudor, 'if pregnant mothers, instead of wearing tight bands that cut deeply into the skin, instead of binding themselves with skirts, instead of wearing stockings up to their thighs, instead of wearing boots, left their bodies free and actively practiced nudism?'[59] The nudist park, agreed another, was clearly the best place for both mothers and expectant mothers.[60] Remarkably, nudism would make labor and delivery a pleasant experience, noted another, in contrast to the pain that ensued from following a doctor's advice, which was further evidence of Jewish influence in medicine.[61]

The nudist concept of beauty, rooted in ancient Greek aesthetic ideals 'was of absolute importance for the health of mothers and was a question of life for the race.'[62] The concept of beauty that nudist activity both emulated and created would subtly direct women to motherhood, and help them fulfill their racial missions. 'Thus would the compulsion [*Drang*] for physical beauty of our women and maidens, which anyway has its own racial worth, also fulfill higher duties,' explained Hans Surén in the Nazi reprint of his call to nudism.[63]

The assumption that the natural destiny of women was motherhood was not peculiar to *Nacktkultur* under the Nazis. Rather, it was characteristic of nudism throughout the first part of the twentieth century. Thus could Fritz Stube, a doctor, declare in 1925 on the pages of the nudist magazine *Lachendes Leben* that women were central to the survival of the species, fundamental to victory in the Darwinian survival of the fittest and solely responsible for the rebirth of the Fatherland. 'Therefore, you, German woman,' he called, 'strive for the goal; help with the reconstruction of the Fatherland through your health.'[64]

Biologically, the influence of women on the future generation was of near cosmic importance. For example, sex determination of fetuses was thought to be something women controlled, albeit on an unconscious level. A male child, for example, would acquire a feminine disposition, possibly even becoming a homosexual, while still in the womb if the mother secretly longed for a girl during the pregnancy.[65] The same was true of female fetuses – if a mother wished for a boy, they too would be affected with a homosexual or masculine disposition. Men, it was thought, had only coincidental influence on determining gender; for example, an active, healthy nudist man was thought able to make a boy, whilst a quiet, relaxed man would fertilize eggs to become girls, but other factors such as amount of time after menstruation that fertilization occurred could influence the process.[66] Women, in nudist ideology, had the power to determine the race's future through their ability to determine the nature of the next generation, including its overall racial purity.

It was every German's responsibility to become healthy. However, it was women's special duty to become so, as they were responsible for the reproduction of a healthy, nudist race. 'Every person should consider it to be vitally important to achieve health, beauty and fitness, but this is especially so for women, as a consequence of their physical and intellectual predisposition.'[67] The fate of the *Volk* rested in the uteri and on the shoulders of women to bear healthy children and to raise them naked. 'More sun! More light! Is the cry of our desperate age,' and pregnant women needed more ultraviolet light, exclaimed one.[68]

Women, in particular, in order to better fulfill their destinies and their duties as wives and mothers, needed to undergo a vigorous reconstitution and strengthening of the body – something that would require both physical activity and a reorientation away from superficial beauty concerns. 'For us women, it is our job to go back to plainness and simpleness, instead of always looking in fashion magazines.' This was especially true since for the nudist future a strong body was far more important than anything else; 'the body was more essential than the face,' concluded Margarete Bink-Ischeuschler.[69]

It was a woman's special destiny to marry and to produce children, and it was to achieve those ends that nudists encouraged women to prepare themselves and their bodies. 'In consideration of the most important question [*Lebensfrage*] of marriage, every maiden knows that the happiness of her life depends on health, beauty and fitness. Moreover, it is the requirements of motherhood, which suggest to a woman, especially, to cultivate these three qualities,' noted Margarete Bink-Ischeuschler.[70]

Some nudists, notably Richard Ungewitter, a man extreme in nearly all his views, believed that in order to save the *Volk* girls should be raised and educated explicitly in terms of their future roles as wives and mothers.[71] 'It is necessary that the female sex is raised for marriage, rather than as competitors of men for careers as is presently the case. The natural career for a woman is marriage, that can never be altered, if our *Volk* is not to die off.'[72] A woman defined, noted Clara Rubbe, was 'a spouse, a mother, a housewife, that is the definition of woman.'[73]

As mothers, women would regenerate the nation not only in purely biological ways but also symbolically, in more abstract ways. In a role that hearkened back to nudist ideas about the evolutionary origins of women's weaker bodies, nudism relied on women to teach the next generation its values and ideas, especially those of *Nacktkultur*. Men, exhausted from the never-ending struggle for existence in the harsh world of work, were unable to inculcate the proper ideas in the next generation; this work could only be achieved by mothers.[74] Furthermore, men were seldom involved directly in a child's life, as careers drew them away, and those who were, were derided as 'henpecked,' and 'pot-watchers.'[75] It was women who brought nudist values into daily living (*Alltag*), taught them to the children and generally kept them alive, viable, whereas men tended to dogmatize the movement.[76] Women had a better understanding of health and hygiene and were more capable of draining the moral swamps of the metropolis, claimed another.[77]

While capable of great intellectual feats, men, in an important contrast to women, had little to offer the state in practical terms, noted one author. Whereas men could only present the state with the ability to fight wars, women could and did provide it with motherhood, an altogether more important contribution than the barbarism of organized murder.[78] If it was the great assignment of women to develop themselves physically and to become active partly in order to achieve equal status and equal ability with men, it was also because women were uniquely capable of completing the transformation of German society.

Nudist ideology and nudist activity would make women both into better mothers of a new generation of children, raised according to the principles of naked living, and the symbolic mothers of a new society. If left ignorant of nudism, women would continue to ruin children by raising them incorrectly – something that undoubtedly explained the fact that an astonishing 67 percent of all school age children in Germany were sickly. 'Here there rests the guilt of the mother for extraordinary great damage due to improper raising,' explained one author.[79] A more assured woman produced better children.[80]

Introducing German women to nudist thought and winning them over to the nudist way of living virtually guaranteed that these women would become better mothers, and that their offspring would also be superior, racially and hygienically. The next generation could not be expected to learn about nudism, let alone understand its importance, if Germany's mothers were themselves forbidden from doing so, admonished one nudist.[81] The only way German society was ever going to be permanently improved was for children to be raised as nudists. This would only occur when women and mothers learned to accept their nakedness and their bodies, so that they could raise the next generation in the same way. Such mothers would introduce their children to the facts of life, sex and the body more readily and more thoroughly than their clothed counterparts, and their explanations in turn would enable future generations to appreciate and understand bodily nakedness. The occasion for these explanations would be the mothers' own nakedness.[82]

Nudist Woman

The nudist woman, sexually emancipated, chaste, naked, confident and self-aware, would gradually lead the nation to greater glories through her natural maternal instincts. 'The intellectually awakened, worldly experienced woman can raise her children better, can better captivate her husband, and as his comrade, his companion, can better his position in life.'[83] A smart, educated woman would naturally produce a similarly intelligent man, as women, although they lacked leadership positions in society, or even in the family, nonetheless successfully steered events from behind the scenes. 'We see in those cultures where a woman's development and experience in her intellectual capacities is taken away . . . the intelligence of men remains correspondingly retarded, and the whole culture suffers.' Without women to stimulate them, to push them onward intellectually, men themselves would gradually cease to be able to think, reflected one author.[84] It was within the family that German society would become nudist society and where the most important changes, led by women, would occur.[85]

The nudist call for women to join the nudist movement was as much a plea for the success of the movement as anything else. Without women, true aesthetics would never be realized, and the liberation of women from prudery, prejudice, heresy, misuse and marital dependence as well as the freedom to have 'their own sexual lives' was a precondition for all people to be able to return to their primordial states ('*urwüchsigen*').[86] Furthermore, as the social position of women was often indicative of the overall development of a culture, improving their status would naturally and logically improve the nation and the culture.

Ensuring that women maintained the same level of rights and status as men was the one sure means to cause the race to ascend higher levels of cultural and spiritual achievement.[87] Though virtually all nudists understood that women's participation in nudism was vital to the movement's victory, few expressed it as clearly as Kästner did: 'If we leave women behind, so will the entire movement become one-sided, and will not serve the higher goals that we have placed for ourselves: healthy bodily development, moral purity in thought and the furtherance of the sense of true beauty.'[88]

As part of the greater effort to draw women, especially bourgeois women, out of their lives of idleness and into a more active existence, nudists called for women to abandon their perfume and powder and to acquire strong bodies, and most of all to again become members of the greater national body. In developing their bodies physically, women, it was hoped, would develop greater independence and feelings of worth, not only as women but also as people. A woman 'must develop herself to become an energetic person, and to leave her gender unnoticed,' and her mantra should be 'I am a person, a link in the chain of human gender and have retained from nature the ability to determine my existence and my will,' explained one author. The twin paths to women's full emancipation were sports, which provided women 'a place in the sun,' and education, as women's best hope to become men's equals.[89] In the nudist vision of the future, an idle woman, like those to be found in Germany's prewar middle classes, had little relevance and no place.

Active, productive women were deemed by nudist ideologues to be more valuable to the race, and more deserving of acknowledgment and rights. Women were not born weak, though they quickly became so due to the idle lives to which German society relegated them, claimed one.[90] Recovering innate strength, especially physical strength, and becoming productive members of society, a notion that included motherhood, was an important characteristic in the nudist vision of women and the future.[91] A woman's strength did not subtract from her femininity in any way, rather the two were fused together. 'To win back this lost, forgotten strength must become the main duty of womanhood,' exclaimed one nudist. Even if science had shown men to be women's mental and physical superiors, reminded Clara Rubbe, in no way did that justify women becoming the servants of men.[92]

Nudism would set women free both from their sense of body shame and shyness of naked bodies and would also secure for them a measure of independence, no longer the decorated wives of men but strong bearers of the race. Much like her ancient Spartan ancestors, the nudist woman would be powerful physically and emotionally, capable of bearing equal responsibility with men.[93] In nudism, German women would be emancipated to motherhood; they would want to be mothers first, their 'natural occupation.'[94] *Nacktkultur*'s ideologues anticipated the nudist experience would transform contemporary women beyond recognition. The new, nudist woman would no longer be shy, gossipy, false but rather would be simple, plain, openhearted, fecund and their offspring numerous, strong and intelligent.[95] For the nudist, the ideal woman possessed a good body and good qualities. She would have,

> a good skin color, well-supplied with blood, a tight, powerfully shaped waist without a cushion of fat. As attributes for the woman we prize: loyalty, sweetness, gentleness, intelligence, independence and participation in the intellectual interests of men. A woman should be the comrade of a man, not the same as a man, but definitely of equal value, not a helpless creature that requires the protection of a man or cries for his help for every little thing. The ideal does naked sports, is steeled against the weather, [is a] sun-browned woman that not only stands intellectually close to a man, but also rows, plays tennis, climbs mountains and frolics about with him in Adam's costume. Such an ideal woman needs sport as much as a man does.[96]

Kästner ends his list of qualities with a final reminder of this sporty, naked, intelligent woman's most important quality, namely 'that only a strong, healthy woman can bear strong, children worthy and capable of life.'[97]

The ideology of *Nacktkultur* generally called for the emancipation of women, though to be sure this call was not a call for political emancipation, and certainly had little in common with feminism. However, as Ann Taylor Allen notes, in the German context a distinction between Anglo-American notions of feminism and the German women's movement must be drawn.[98] Political rights or political equality for women made little sense in the ideology of *Nacktkultur*, as it was a utopian movement that envisioned a transformation of Germany away from its present multi-fractured state into a kind of people's community reminiscent of the mythologized tribal past, where social, political, sexual and religious divisions did not exist. Women would be men's equals, though not because of a constitutional amendment or paragraph but because nudist activity made them physically strong, socially independent, productive, and because once their bodies were de-eroticized both sexes would learn to respect each other as a matter of course.

Nudist ideas of women's emancipation were an odd mixture of old and new, and can be partially explained by nudism's interest in the movement for sex reform. Alone among the many *Lebensreform* movements, *Nacktkultur* was deeply influenced by the ideas of the sex reform movement, which also called for a liberation of sex, sexual mores and sexual knowledge from the mores of the nineteenth century.[99] Sexologists and sex reformers, like nudists, preached the need for knowledge about sex and sexual functions, the importance of sexual pleasure, and both movements sought the sexual emancipation of women and the strengthening of the family unit.[100] Sexual emancipation for women, or for men for that matter, was not a call for sexual license, whether from sex reformers or from nudists, and though some women activists, notably the indefatigable Helene Stöcker of the Bund für Mutterschutz (League for Protection of Mothers), advocated free love, most did not, seeking rather the improvement of marital relations.[101]

Conclusion

Nudists believed the social effects of their movement would for generations ripple throughout the German race, and the nation would become a place where, freed from clothing and body prejudice, gender relations would be revolutionized, marriage partners equalized and children would mature gracefully and knowingly into adults. Intimate knowledge of the body based on its nakedness would be the catalyst for breeding a new German and a new Germany.

Creating the Germanic nudist utopia required foremost that Germans' bodies be made capable of actually generating that paradise. The desire for a 'noble, good and beautiful' mate was both perfectly understandable in and of itself from the nudist perspective, but it was also 'the fundament to the higher development of the human species.' Nudists knew from their understanding of Darwin's theories that the best would always find an equal partner; nudism was important in guaranteeing that the selection process did in fact function as it should.[102]

The promise of nudism was that the body would be transformed into the literal Aryan racial ideal – healthy, beautiful and a worthy bearer of the racial seed. Once healed and beautified, nudist ideologues assured, the naked body would dominate public space where it would become the focus of daily, social and national life, completing the conditions necessary to transform Germany into a strong, healthy nation peopled by a *Volk* that lived in organic harmony with each other and with nature and that was above all else racially pure.

–7–

Sex, Race and Nudism

The success of nudism, as well as the very practice of *Nacktkultur*, were predicated on Germans shedding their clothing and bathing nude in the light, air and sun together with others – activities that would bring them into direct visual contact with naked bodies, their own as well as those of other Germans. Nudist activity struck at the heart of many of European and German society's most basic concepts and longest-held taboos, namely that bodies were to be clothed, that their nakedness was sinful, useful in most cases only for sexual activity, and that exposing oneself, especially one's genitals, was an indecent, obscene and largely forbidden act.

Nudism transformed Germans and Germany by transforming not only the body, but also, equally importantly, by changing Germans' attitudes towards the body, and in the process dismantling centuries of prejudice, antipathy and fear of the body as well as the source of that hostility. In the nudist experience, the body would be stripped of its religious and social constraints and made into an object to be gazed upon and appreciated. Most importantly, the body would be stripped of its eroticism, enabling Germans to reform sex and gender. Nakedness, the form of nudism, was itself a powerful force – one that was necessary to complete the transformation of Germans into nudists and Germany into a nation of nudes.

The experience of mixed-gender nudism, however difficult it might seem to engage in, was the most important and the final step in the process of transforming one's own body into an ideal, beautiful form. In the process of mutual observation that compelled Germans to beautify their bodies, another more fundamental, albeit paradoxical, transformation would also occur. In the nudist paradox, nudism promoted marital and sexual unions of racially fit partners for the goal of breeding a racially pure *Volk* by engaging its participants in a powerful, non-voyeuristic process of constant observation and mutual evaluation that simultaneously de-eroticized the naked body and made it the basis of mate selection.

Being naked among so many other naked Germans was a vital experience in two key regards. First, by inspiring everyone to become beautiful, nakedness completed the transformation of the body, making it healthy and beautiful. Second, the experience of being naked in a group of naked Germans caused the body to lose all of its eroticism and sexual appeal. The ramifications of de-eroticizing the body are profound for Germans and the German race. Once made healthy and beautiful, once stripped of its meaning, the body becomes the basis for every decision Germans make about each other. The nudist body becomes the foundation for personal and racial regeneration. The body becomes the nation.

The Uses of Nakedness

As a force, nakedness was important for a number of reasons. Nakedness connected Germans to nature, and being naked returned one to a state of naturalness; it made the participant once again a part of the cosmos.[1] Nakedness helped one transcend the daily trivialities of life that nagged at body and person alike, miring both in unhappiness and misery. Naked play and exercise conducted under the warming sun, for example, produced 'adventurous people with lively, soulful bodies.'[2] Nakedness helped produce joy of the body for its owner, and the 'naked human is universally in joyful mood.'[3] Since wearing clothing produced suffering, body joy could only result from immersing the body in naked body culture.[4] 'The naked body,' announced one author, 'gives joy to living.'[5]

Living naked, affirmed Richard Ungewitter, brings forth a sense of wonderfulness, of liberation.[6] It had been proven, noted one nudist, that the Nordic was only happy when naked.[7] 'Here at the nudist park,' rhapsodized another, 'the soulful human body finds itself once again, here it rests and acts, laughs and mourns, here it lives beautifully and uncovered, just like the sons and daughters of a southern sun.'[8] Of course, 'one needed to have experienced the revitalizing influence of sun, air and water oneself to understand that it [nudism] is not about fanaticism or fanciful romanticism.'[9]

Nakedness means to survive in the harsh reality of Darwinistic struggle. 'What *Freikörperkultur* means is a way for the body, in sports, at play, in exercise, in air- and sunbathing, to recapture its physical and moral health that are so necessary for the struggle for existence [*Kampf ums Dasein*].'[10] Nakedness compelled men to want to be strong and graceful, and women to be beautiful and powerful, noted Hans Surén. These qualities would appeal to members of the opposite sex, increasing one's chances for mating, and that would also be passed along to the coming generation making it a better cohort overall.[11]

One of the most important effects of nakedness was its ability to create the desire of an individual to become physically more beautiful. Nakedness was a means to fulfill nudism's aesthetic goals.[12] Being naked awakened an aesthetic need both in oneself to become more beautiful and in the observer of nakedness, either one's own or that of another, to become more beautiful. 'Nakedness,' explained nudist Margarete Bink-Ischeuschler, 'leads to pride of the body, pride of the body leads to beauty, leads out of the degeneration of our *Volk* and to a racial ascendancy.'[13]

Looking at a naked body, nudists argued, awakened an aesthetic sense in the observer that was so powerful that it overwhelmed the fear, the prejudice and one's bodily 'miseducation,' which was an expression among nudists that referred to all social and religious principles that fostered a negative view of the body.[14] Through a variety of elements 'natural beauty became stamped by the mark of immorality and sin,' precipitating its total disappearance from human view.[15] 'Precisely because of the circumstance that nakedness discloses the miseducation of our civilized bodies, it awakens in us the aesthetic urge to make ourselves beautiful through physical exercise, sport and play.'[16] 'That is the miracle effect of nakedness,' explained nudist Ursula van Zyl, 'it is the means to acquire true beauty.'[17]

Viewing a naked body satisfied certain normal human needs and improved the race, suggested one magazine early in the century.[18] Gazing upon a nude and being observed while nude oneself made the body become beautiful by inspiring everyone to improve their physical appearances. In nudism, the 'body ideals became better,' and people responded by adjusting their bodies according to the new icons of health and beauty. Gradually, 'through physical development, people again became worthy of the honor of the body.'[19]

Nudism awakened the desire to make oneself beautiful because it allowed one to see both one's own faults as well as the physical beauty of others, thus providing an example to emulate. One could begin alone at home, and then join a group of other nudists, for example. 'The hygienic first step consists of observing oneself daily before the mirror while naked, but when possible in the company of others, in order for everyone to be able to point out each others' faults.'[20] 'Ideal nakedness,' explained one nudist, 'is founded on the desire to bathe the body in sun and air in community with others who are also so disposed to care for and cultivate [it], to be aware of its beauty and to acknowledge the beauty of others' bodies.'[21]

Viewing nudes and becoming beautiful applied to everyone equally. It was an activity and a process that benefited all Germans. Everyone, even the working classes with their limited space and reduced possibilities, could and should make time for an hour daily of critical inspection in front of the mirror while naked, to be followed by a sponge bath and breathing exercises, argued one author. Such activity would compel one to self-improvement and to become beautiful, he reasoned further.[22]

After accustoming oneself to the sight of one's own nakedness and becoming familiar with one's own body, explained Seitz, an individual was ready to proceed to the company of others, possibly in same-sex naked swimming. Later still, Seitz continued, one could make the final transition to mixed-gender nudism. This, he commented, was the most difficult step, and required both the greatest diligence and the most perseverance. One could prepare for that necessary and eventual reality, he added, by looking at the many photographs of the opposite sex that appeared in nudist publications, as that was their intended use.[23] Looking and being looked at while naked caused participants to do more than reinforce each other's desire to be beautiful, however. Mutual naked observation de-eroticized the body.

De-eroticizing the Body

De-eroticizing the body was a powerful – perhaps the most powerful – effect of being naked. The de-eroticized body separated notions of sex and sexuality from the body, causing it to be redefined as essentially un-erotic, as natural. De-eroticizing the body, however, was also an act pregnant with any number of other broader effects, including a reconfiguration of the sexual order that dominated and undergirded German society, and eventually even the hierarchical structure of German society itself. In the ideology of nudism, the de-eroticized body would quite literally become the basis for a new society characterized by mass social nakedness, egalitarianism, racial purity, national strength and high cultural achievement.

A German needed to be naked and to be able to view naked bodies, especially naked bodies of the opposite sex, as something 'natural and self-understood,' rather than as the source of sexual excitement and sexual pleasure, or as the locus of sin and moral corruption, or even as something to fear, to lust after or to fantasize about.[24] It was keeping body parts hidden from view that created so many other problems for the German and for German society, especially sexual problems. 'Through this secretiveness, fantasies are summoned forth that cause a driving intellect into reverie.' Furthermore, the individual who could not bear to view another's naked body, especially of the opposite sex, regardless of the reason, would not develop into a full person, could not produce nor even bear a culture. Such a person would be a 'follower, governed by the events of the general humdrum,' rather than a creative, intellectually rich and vibrant person.[25]

In the naked experience, all negativity towards the body, all sexuality and the problems produced by its suppression would fall away, like so many clothes. During the time that one was naked, feeling the warmth of the sun on one's skin and the presence of others' gaze on one's body, one could also feel a happiness, a sense of innocence, even naïveté returning. The nudist 'finds in those hours once again his or her childish, natural [*unbefangenes*] essence, and will have no time or space for other thoughts.'[26] Nakedness instilled in one a sense of respect for the body. 'As soon as the clothes fall,' explained one author known only as '*katholik*,' 'natural feeling and a sense of naturalness [*Unbefangenheit*] return to [the body].'[27]

All testimony from nudists, ideologues and participants notwithstanding, there was a tiny faction of nudists that believed nudist activity would lead to a stimulation of one's sexual desires, and that men and women should be separated at all times during the nudist experience. Werner Schulte, for example, believed that the increased air-exchange of a naked person would cause the inner secretions to increase, which in turn caused the sex secretions to increase, resulting in a sexually stimulated person. Such a series of responses needed to be strictly guarded against, though he offered no suggestions for how to do so.[28]

A second nudist who cautioned against mixed-gender nudism was Klara Muche. Muche, though a staunch advocate of nudism's health effects, also advised against mixed-gender nudism, believing only a small minority were actually so chaste as to be able to control their inflamed passions once at the nudist park.[29] Contributing to this point of view, moreover, was one of nudism's most well-known advocates, Hans Surén. Surén, despite all his comments to the contrary, suggested in his 1924 nudist work, *Der Mensch und die Sonne* (*Humans and the Sun*), that nudists could not demand mixed-gender nudism 'for we must be aware of the psyche and the individuality of everyone.'[30] Surén, whose later experiences suggest that he may have been a homosexual, may have made his comments less motivated by concern for people's feelings and more by his desire to see nude men and not nude women.[31] These voices were a significant minority.

A characteristic feature of nudism, however, was its ability to eliminate the association of both the body and nakedness with sexual activity. Once immersed in nakedness, Germans would soon realize, explained J.M. Seitz, that in nudism 'all people became again free, and all people [would] have the best protection and the best prophylactic against temptation.'[32] In his unpublished memoirs on the history of the nudist movement in Germany, Herman Wilke, a nudist for much of the twentieth century, observed that the desire to improve Germans morally in general and especially with regard to their attitudes towards sex was a basic tenet of the ideology, which was made explicit in the 1920s. Writing to the Landkreis Teltow, the Reichsbund für Körperkultur (RFK) stated that the 'goal of the *Freikörperkultur* movement rests in the attempt to establish a counterweight to the degeneration and demoralization of our *Volk* through a disciplined, natural [read: naked] morality and a truthful conceptualization of the things and proceedings of sexuality.'[33]

Nakedness enabled Germans to overcome their inhibitions and to cast aside their fears, prejudices and lusts with regard to the naked body, enabling them to develop fully as individuals, and as a strong *Volk*. The ability to see one's own or others' nakedness was the sign of an advanced person but 'not being able to see oneself, or avoiding the nakedness of others is proof in the highest measure of one's own worthlessness.'[34] Only nudism, because of its unique conception of nakedness as natural, shame – and sin-free, could resolve the sexual problems that beset Germany. 'It has been proven,' wrote Hans Surén, 'that an overexcited sensuality is often healed at one stroke by participation in nudism.'[35]

The naked body needed to be liberated from the lies that surrounded it and made pure and free through its own nakedness. The participant in nudist activity would feel his or her 'sensuality become calm, lose all physical, erotic and sexual desire, even the impure, vile aftertaste that as a tragic consequence of our deceitful morality continues to oppress and shame life.'[36] Nudism 'offers a naked life based on reason as well as an important hygienic advantage for our souls, in that it brings one to a greater purity through the observation of naked people and demolishes the sexual curiosity that creates so much trouble.'[37] The answer to Germany's sexual and moral morass was not the erection of greater barriers to seeing and knowing the naked body, but, counterintuitively, the promotion of the naked body.

In the naked experience, the participant would learn that the language of bodies often had little to say sexually, but could, if listened to carefully, guide one to a new discourse altogether – one of truer, deeper relationships and honesty in general. The nudist would learn to become free of both a false body image and its social, sexual and moral consequences.

Nudism taught participants to see beyond the sexual differences of the body, indeed even helped teach people to see beyond sex altogether.[38] 'It is quite self-understood that the naked person is respectable and attuned to his or her senses,' noted one.[39] German men and women would come to abandon their sexualized views of each other, which are reinforced and further excited by their clothing, and instead regard each other only with respect, unencumbered by secret sexual thoughts and desires. Mutual nakedness would 'awaken understanding and esteem of the opposite sex, and [cause] the ruinous sultry sexuality to disappear.'[40]

Even direct observation of the genitals, an activity that might under different circumstances evoke a variety of responses ranging from embarrassment and discomfort to sexual excitement for both observer and observed, was perfectly acceptable and even necessary in nudism. 'It is to be anticipated that the sexual organs of humans, whether of the male or the female, are never and can never be immoral, for they are important to life and have a higher duty to fulfill, that of reproduction.'[41] The genitals, it should be recalled, were those organs that had suffered the most under the non-nudist understanding of the body.[42]

Nudism had a sexually calming influence on its participants, in part, because it hid nothing from the curious, and allowed everyone to see whatever they wanted to see, indeed it allowed them to see what nature had designed them to want to see. 'Sexual excesses would be pulled up by their roots if the genders possessed a natural conception of each other,' argued one nudist.[43] 'Looking at an uncovered body of the opposite sex itself cripples any stifling of the budding physical development through an oppressive, sultry sensualness,' noted one.[44] Nudism and nakedness cooled the heat between half-clad youth, ended fantasy and even the need for fantasy, as it solved many of the mysteries surrounding the opposite sex before they could even be posed.[45] 'It is not the naked body as such that is the source of immorality, rather the sexual thoughts and fantasies that arise in the minds of people, when they cannot see the unencumbered naked body of the opposite sex.'[46]

Nudism and the Sex Drive

It was not only the fact that nudism provided the opportunity to see what the other half looked like that caused it to be a de-eroticizing influence, however. Nakedness 'has the task, and achieves it too, of killing desire to have sex [*Geilheit*].[47] Nakedness stripped the body of its ability to send a sexual message, and in so doing provided the occasion for people to discover the humanity and person that the body embodied, rather than only seeing an opportunity for sexual activity, either as a fantasy or in actuality.

Eliminating the desire to have sex or even to experience lustful or sexually laced thoughts was the essential consequence of nudism. Gazing at a naked figure in a natural setting produced sexually calming results in even the most unbelievable circumstances. Discussing the ability of nudism to relax the passions rather than inflame them, a letter-writer to the nudist magazine *Figaro* related his experiences as a prisoner of war in Siberia during the First World War and later the Russian Civil War. 'The atmosphere among these young, strong men was thunderously sexually charged.' Moreover he warned ominously, 'woe to the female creature, regardless of age, who fell into our hands.' After establishing the degree of potential sexual wildness and sexual depravation among the prisoners, the unnamed author surprises the reader with a description of a troop of men as relaxed, calm, almost incapable of sexual stimulation after returning from a swim at the beaches on the Sea of Japan in summer 1917. 'As they returned, they were so happily focused, and even the wildest and raunchiest among them were gripped by the deepest calm, sweetness, timorousness, and patience to everyone.'[48]

When pressed about their mood, the men explained that upon coming to the beach they spied 'a young Russian woman about twenty years old with her children.' The young woman and her children, like the prisoners, had arrived at the ocean to swim, however, she did not notice them. 'Without noticing the prisoners of war, the young, beautiful woman disrobed first herself then her children completely, and then took her children in her arms and entered the surf.' So overwhelmed by the image of the naked Russian woman and her children in nature were the prisoners of war that they, our witness reports, forgot themselves entirely, and lost all desire to act upon the sexual urges imprisoned within them. 'While watching her, not one of the hundred men,' explained the author, somewhat unbelievably, 'felt anything but the most respectable feelings and stirrings, not one risked even a spoken word, much less mentioned one of the otherwise daily obscenities.' The author's conclusion here is important. He writes, 'a naked woman who presents herself as innocent, free and natural is holy to every man.'[49]

The combination of nakedness and nature created purity of mind and deed. Nakedness relieved the need and the pain of sexual desire even for a group of men for whom the opportunity for sexual intercourse with women was an impossibility. Nakedness, whether merely observing it as in the case of the prisoners, or participating in it as Germans did, taught a basic lesson, namely that there was far more to people than their sexual attributes, and far more to oneself than sexual urges.

The naked experience forced people to move beyond their shortsighted sexual needs and observe that a human being, someone with emotions, needs and personality was before them, and not a set of sex organs for the observer's own voyeuristic gratification. In nudism, 'a person gets to know the other person, and finds to his or her embarrassment that a work of nature is standing before him or her, not an apparatus of sexual satisfaction.'[50] Nudism humanized people because it forced everyone to present themselves honestly to the world, and people engaged in nudism not to experience sexual gratification, or even the 'sexual temptation or social allures,' but instead to create tighter bonds with their fellow humans.[51]

Disarming the Masturbator

In *Nacktkultur* there was a cure for every sexual disease and every sexually generated problem, whether an overheated, barely controllable sexual stimulation, or solitary indulgence in the vice of masturbation. Quite frankly and quite assuredly, noted one nudist magazine, nudism prevented masturbation, even the desire to masturbate.[52] Richard Ungewitter, one of nudism's most outspoken authors and tireless advocates, devoted considerable space in his works to the discussion of masturbation, and the impact of *Nacktkultur* on the masturbator.

Nakedness was the only cure for masturbation, he wrote, as 'nakedness is calming on the sensual drive.' Sleeping naked, without sheets or covers, with open windows, a morning bath without sponges or soap, vegetarianism and of course vigorous naked activity were all important aspects of stopping or preventing masturbation, he noted.[53] His readers wrote to him often telling of their own suggestions and offering their thanks in the drive to end their onanism.

In his books he published numerous letters from confessed masturbators, all of whom heaped praise on him and on nudism for having cured them of their habit. Presumably all men, the authors of the letters were students, teachers, engineers, a retired military captain, Lutheran pastors, gymnastics instructors, a seminarist and a government official [*Regierungssupernumerar*]; at least one was from a member of the youth movement, the Wandervögel, and there were also a number from soldiers written from the field during the First World War, who apparently carried his books in their knapsacks.[54] These letter-writers all found solace from their sex drive and inclination to masturbate in the many nude photos in Ungewitter's books.

The reports presented by the grateful authors of readers' letters to Ungewitter touched a number of common themes, chiefly that in nakedness they found satisfaction for their desire to see a naked body, but no eroticism. Some reported finding a new understanding of the holiness of the body, or renewed desire to fight eroticism, and, remarkably, one even managed to convince both his wife and his mother-in-law to become nudists, thus satisfying his own lifelong desire to see naked women.[55]

By demonstrating that nakedness and naked activity were not erotic, nudism was able to promote family harmony. In one family, the father and the servant girl,

Anna, practiced nudism, but the mother and son did not. The son confessed in his letter that whenever he saw Anna's nakedness he would immediately need to masturbate, but that after participating in nudism himself, together with Anna and his father, he no longer needed to masturbate. Happily, and to everyone's joy, he and Anna later married.[56] Other writers informed of their new understanding of race. Most, however, relayed their newfound sense of relaxation, and told of how much better they felt and lived as a result of gazing at the nude photos in his works.[57]

Viewing the Naked

Being naked and being seen while naked as well as seeing nakedness of others, not only de-eroticized the body but also satisfied certain natural human needs, which held the promise of improving and deepening, even equalizing Germans' relationships. There was a natural longing within every human to see others naked, and this was a desire, according to Hans Surén, that was perfectly normal and the source of much soul-bound worrying during the years of puberty.[58] 'In the subconsciousness of everyone,' explained another, 'there rests a desire to see one's friend, one's comrade and one's lover naked.'[59] This desire to see one's circle of friends and acquaintances naked, if ignored, oppressed or otherwise left unacknowledged and unfulfilled, likely due to Jews and other 'racially alien and ecclesiastical influences,'[60] could often produce 'fantasy for which the half-clothed was a dangerous seedbed.' Whereas 'total nakedness could wipe away all dumb fantasy with a laughing naturalness and give back a happy and pure sense.'[61] The longing to see others in their nakedness, reminded Hans Surén, had nothing to do with sexual urges.[62]

Relationships and friendships among Germans, whether sexual or non-sexual had suffered greatly under the regime of clothing and body enmity, nudists argued. Only in the naked experience could friendships and other relationships be truly established. People had a desire to see their friends and acquaintances as they actually looked, 'unflatteringly, not made up and not covered up.'[63] Being naked allowed individuals to come to know each other without the pressure of sex. It showed the 'sexually unclouded recognition of the spiritual and intellectual value of our fellow humans.'[64]

Such a view would foster true friendships, since the act of revealing oneself was akin to bearing one's soul. 'It was a symbol of openness, to show one's naked self to another. It is as if in removing one's clothes, one removes the armor from the soul: look here, here I am, and so should you love me and attend me,' explained one author.[65] Relationships formed in clothed society could never blossom into the deep, trusting relationships fashioned at the nudist park, as clothes were little more than packaging that concealed a poor product, and nakedness by contrast displayed a beautiful one.[66]

Through nudism, people would learn to become masters of their thoughts and desires, especially those involving sexual matters, rather than be controlled by them, as was presently the case. The sex drives were rechanneled and expressed in a pure, non-sexually stimulating, non-sexually gratifying manner in nudism, thus leading the nudist to 'master the urges.'[67] One author explained that in the naked experience, 'the will is steeled and humans are raised to self control and perseverance,' and lifetimes devoted to fantasy, masturbation and sexual puzzlement would thus be avoided.[68] Nakedness at the nudist park, explained one author, was so natural, so pure, that even for a couple deeply in love it would be impossible to act on their emotions and desires. 'It is just impossible that two people together in a larger community would let on about their relationship to one another [*von ihren Beziehungen zueinander etwas laut werden lassen*],' explained one author.[69]

'Nudism,' explained Therese Mühlhause-Vogeler somewhat idealistically, 'is thus suited to create a new foundation for the relationships between the sexes, and to prevent so much unhappiness that is born of sexual surprises.'[70] One manner of preventing the unhappy relationships that appeared to nudists to characterize German society was to raise the young as nudists, so that the mysteries of their bodies and of each others' bodies, especially those of the opposite sex, would never develop.

Every human, nudists insisted, possessed a need, a desire, to see a friend, a lover, an acquaintance or even a total stranger as that person truly was, without the artifice and false pretenses of clothing. Suppressing this desire only resulted in recourse to a life of fantasies, and schoolyard half-truths about the body and sexuality, compounding the preexisting ignorance and negative attitudes towards the body.[71] Intimate knowledge of the body based on its nakedness would be the catalyst for breeding a new German and a new Germany. Ultimately, the body was made naked and de-eroticized specifically to promote sexual activity among Germans, as nakedness calmed sexual excitement, satisfied the all too natural human need to observe nakedness and afforded the best opportunity to find the most suitable partner with whom to improve the race.

The Century of Sex

European society at the dawn of the twentieth century was consumed with sex and sexuality. Intellectually, the new century began with the unprecedented declaration that sex was at the center of the human psyche and general psychological development. First Freud, and later others, revolutionized psychology with their union of sex and the psyche – at one stroke scandalizing contemporary society and founding modern psychoanalysis.

Nationalists made sex and sexuality an integral part of the modern religion of the nation, channeling its energy and its drive for their own uses, national integration and national glory.[72] Long-standing worries about the quality of the race, concern about which groups were having sex and with whom all deepened and became more explicit among eugenicists and racial hygienists, but also among politicians, doctors and biologists.[73] Although eventually becoming a matter of state interest and policy, at the turn of the century sex entered the political arena only in conjunction with women's issues, especially with the rise of feminism.[74] Practiced privately for millennia, sex was suddenly an important and enduring force in European society and politics.

The fin-de-siècle fascination with sex was neither a popular whim nor a scientific fad, however. Interest in sex expanded and intensified over the course of the twentieth century. Virtually every aspect of European life became infused with and transformed by the growing interest in sex that marked the final years of the nineteenth and opening years of the twentieth century. Sex lurked at the heart of bourgeois fears about the profligate and fecund underclass, dogged socialists' efforts to curtail lower-class misery, reinforced moralists' concerns about growing vice and immorality, became the subject of scientific study with a companion reform endeavor, known as sex reform. Sex was responsible for the downright horror expressed by church officials and other conservatives about abortion and other birth control methods. Sex riveted popular attention. Sex scandals fueled the sales of the boulevard press, and sent no small number of men to their deaths on the dueling grounds.[75]

The Europe-wide interest in sex was no less marked in Germany, where the sexual milieu of the day profoundly and deeply influenced the emerging ideology of *Nacktkultur*. Although its roots extended back into a number of different nineteenth-century intellectual and popular traditions, *Nacktkultur* was very much a product of the twentieth century. Nowhere is this more evident than in the centrality of sex to the ideology of nudism, especially in the realization of the nudist vision. 'The fate of a culture,' one nudist author explained, 'is necessarily that of its sexual activity.'[76]

Ultimately, making Germany into a nudist racial paradise would occur through sex – by Germans producing and reproducing healthy, beautiful, racially pure children, who themselves would beget equally beautiful and healthy children, and who would continue the process ad infinitum, until the *Volk* was thus remade. Sex was the primary motivation for and ideological climax of *Nacktkultur*.

Like many concerned with issues of race and the national population in the late nineteenth and early twentieth centuries nudist ideologues turned to the twin sciences of eugenics and racial hygiene for permanent solutions to the perceived degeneration around them.[77]

Reproduction according to the principles set forth in the theories of modern genetics, themselves recently formulated by Gregor Mendel, tempered with the popular understanding of Darwin's theories of evolution as the 'survival of the fittest' (expressed in German as the much harsher 'struggle for existence' or *Kampf ums Dasein*) offered a measure of hope to those individuals and groups like Germany's nudists who believed their race had entered its final stages and needed to be regenerated or face extinction.[78] For nudists, any attempt to renew the race would fail unless it based itself on the principles of nudism. 'National renewal, Nordification and improving the character and nature of Germans either psycho-technically, morally or through racial hygiene and eugenics is not in the least possible without *körperkultur* [sic],' explained one author.[79] In the nudist experience, the national stock would be purified and the coming utopia would be peopled through breeding. Above all, *Nacktkultur* would guarantee German victory in the birth contest.

The general orientation of *Nacktkultur* towards creating the conditions for the healthy to breed is reflected in the eventual name of the National Socialist nudist organization, the Bund für Leibeszucht (BfL). The term *Leibeszucht*, which has no direct translation into English, is a combination of the words *Leib*, which means body, and *Zucht*, which carries a number of biological and zoological meanings, all related to breeding, or rearing and cultivation of a race or stock. In a figurative sense, however, *Zucht* also means education, training, drill, discipline, modesty and propriety, all of which were tenets of *Nacktkultur*. As a term, *Leibeszucht* transmitted the core messages of nudism: body discipline, body awareness, physical education and physical development, morality and self-control all as part of the larger endeavor of cultivating both individual and racial bodies.

Nacktkultur was an ideology that anticipated an evolutionary transformation of German society into a nudist racial paradise. In the nudist view, modern Germans had become simply too corrupted both physically and with regard to their understanding of the body by either disease or racially foreign influences to be able to establish the utopia overnight. Nudist theorists hoped and expected that the victory of their movement would encourage Germans to procreate in large numbers. Sex was central to the realization of the nudist dream.

Among nudists the principles of breeding and proper mate selection were well established. The task remained to bring those same ideas to the broader population, who it was believed would then embrace nudism and use principles of eugenics to guide their relationships. 'One should always bear in mind,' reminded Hans Surén, 'that from small nudist circles the new German nation [*Germanentum*] will grow.'[80] In nudism the basis for racial regeneration through reproduction of fit, robust, Germanic offspring would occur in the union of two Germans who after careful consideration would select each other for the lifelong union of marriage. The nudist idea of marriage was not necessarily the same as the one practiced by so many Germans of the day; rather it was the product of intense reform of both the body and ideas of sex. The nudist marital union incorporated a number of important concepts from the *Lebensreform* milieu, in particular, sex reform.

Sex Reform and the Companionate Marriage

The nudist conception of marriage was influenced in equal parts by eugenic concerns and the sex reform movement, which sought, in part, to reform marriage in order to create greater possibility for marital and social happiness. In the nudist experience, the institution of marriage would be reformed to ensure the race's vitality. A union of two healthy, beautiful, nudist Germans was ultimately intended to produce children of quality for the race. The same gaze that was so necessary and so powerful in de-eroticizing the body was now instrumental in locating and selecting one's ideal partner for mating and marriage.

As nudists surveyed their society they were appalled at what they saw, especially with regard to sexual matters and sexual ethics, which they believed were rooted ultimately in German society's general unfamiliarity with and outright disdain for the body and its functions, however normal and necessary. One of the guiding principles of nudism, however, was the belief that the body was something good and holy, a positive force, that if properly considered and observed would effect powerful and fundamental changes in German society, reconcile social divisions, promote morality, heal or if begun early enough in one's life, totally prevent all problems that stemmed from sex and sexual matters.

Like education reform, clothing reform, vegetarianism, housing and land reform, sex reform was related to the broader *Lebensreform* movement, though only nudism appears to have had any serious affiliation with or interest in sex reform.[81] Generally, sex reformers believed that knowledge, rather than ignorance, of sex, sexuality and sexual function, including the mechanics of reproduction, was the best solution to the perennial problems produced by sex: accidental pregnancy, disease, the stigma of illegitimacy, among others. Sexual knowledge, sexual freedom and sexual pleasure were the cornerstones of the sex reform movement, and these ideas appealed to a wide variety of other groups and ideologies, including intellectuals, socialists and communists, some feminists and most nudists, though not always for the same reasons.

Sex reformers, nudists included, wanted to better the modern human condition generally by providing people with the necessary knowledge and the means for greater sexual pleasure and satisfaction, especially by helping them establish control over their own fertility. These were seemingly modest goals that nonetheless challenged and threatened most aspects of contemporary society and politics, as well as views on morality. Although the interest in sex and sexology was a pan-European phenomenon, sex reform was dominated by central Europeans, chiefly German and Austrian doctors. Sex reform was both an emancipating and a liberating force.

On a practical level, the goal of the sex reform movement was to improve humans' lives by reordering first the sexual and later the social and political worlds. Sex reform functioned on an individual level by providing information and even technology and services on a range of topics such as birth control, including abortion, the need for and acceptability of sexual pleasure during intercourse, and the naturalness of sexual differences, chiefly homosexuality. Sex reformers hoped to better society by seeking to eliminate sex-based social inequalities, whether located within the traditional German patriarchal family, in marriage custom or in the unequal regulation of vices such as prostitution that punished women, but not their male customers. Sex reform emphasized the careful selection of a marriage partner, for reasons that concerned one's own happiness but also the nation's eugenic health.

The Use of the De-eroticized Body

Among nudists, marriage was considered the foundation for building the *Volk*, and nudist reform intentions centered on the twin ideas of the love-match and of producing racially fit offspring.[82] A child raised to adulthood in nudist culture was not only healthy from a lifetime of being naked and in the sun, but was also apt to make a better choice of marriage partner than a non-nudist. 'Only in nudism,' continued another, 'can one find the best types, and become acquainted with [another's] constitution and true qualities.'[83]

Although the purpose of marriage was 'the completion of one of the reasons for existence, namely having and raising valuable children,' the partners in the marriage should also be happy and in love with one another.[84] A marriage founded on mutual love was recommended by nudists as the best, with the caveat that both lovers were racially fit equals.[85] The nudist marriage, like all relationships formed in the nudist experience, would be a union of equals, where women's influence and role were equal to men's. In nudism, sex reform was applied to marriage in order to build stronger unions between Germans for the purpose of securing a viable future for the race.

Contemporary marriages, arranged or otherwise, as well as the entire German marriage pattern were condemned by nudists, who generally believed that such marriages would be replaced by harmonious unions between individuals deeply in love with one another.[86] Contemporary marriages were denounced as being little more than money transactions, motivated not by mutual love and respect but by business and money. One nudist, sounding like the Marxist he probably was, denounced the entire middle-class marriage strategy that dictated that one marry the right girl from the right class. He especially criticized the notion that one's value was determined by one's class membership, rather than by other, more sensible criteria. Ultimately, he concluded, middle-class wives were little more than prostitutes, since like prostitutes they used sex to secure a means for living though to be sure in the case of the wives it was with the same man.[87]

One of the most consequential and fundamental problems with modern marriages, from the nudist standpoint, was the fact that they were often based on uninformed decisions, which was indicative of the overall lack of honesty between partners. This was a dishonesty rooted above all in the concealed body. By making the body highly visible, and by placing the naked body at the center of the decision of whether to marry, nudism promised to make every relationship a happy, honest one.

The lack of honesty in marriages was evident from the earliest moments of courtship or acquaintanceship of the potential spouses, typically conducted while wearing clothing, and continued unabated throughout the relationship. The importance of honesty in relationships could not be overestimated. Once one acquired one's own sense of joy from nudism, it would exert a positive influence on one's relations to others, especially those with the opposite sex. The new understanding of living gained in nudism would give 'insight into the importance of clarity in relationships; it would mean marriage on a foundation of love, truth and attention,' exclaimed one enthusiastic nudist.[88] For nudists, honesty in a relationship began at the most basic level, by knowing one's own body as well as that of everyone else. Nudism not only allowed for no secrets to be kept about one's body, but it also required that one's nakedness be visually accessible to everyone as the precondition for building a happy, healthy marriage and an honest, moral society.

In nudist parlance, contemporary German marriages were contracted under the lie of clothing and could not be expected to produce anything but negative results.[89] Under the system of mate selection and choosing a marriage partner dominated by clothes, those with the best tailors, not those with the best bodies, were marrying.[90] Clothing, nudists explained, was like a kind of packaging, which concealed or altered the form of the person beneath, so that the true form was always hidden from or distorted for the suitor; this could lead to considerable disappointment on the wedding night, assured one nudist.[91]

The body would become the main criterion for mate selection, and this process was made possible only in mass social nakedness. In nudism, 'the naked human body is a vehicle for choosing and of natural selection,' explained another.[92] Hans Surén endorsed this idea as well, noting that naked youth was likely to make more appropriate decisions about marriage and the race. Allowing the young to view each other naked in a natural setting, such as a forest, would enable them 'to see their bodies and to recognize what among Germans was characteristically beautiful or ugly.'[93] Women and girls should have full knowledge of men and men's bodies prior to the marriage because it provided the basis for a sounder, happier marriage, as at the very least, awareness of men's bodies by women and girls from an early age would prevent them from ignorantly entering the marriages and being 'mistreated and taken by surprise by the "well-experienced" young husband.'[94]

By being around each other while naked, Germans would be able to determine who the better lifelong mate would be – a decision that carried profound implications. In nudism, 'not only would the health of the individual be improved,' announced one proponent, 'but this movement also has an importance for racial hygiene.'[95] In making the decision about whom to marry, the nudist was influenced above all by physical characteristics. 'One sees in the naked human whether he or she is physically harmonious or unbalanced,' and youth would become acquainted with the naked bodies of others as they truly appeared, complete with failures, mistakes or beauty, thus enabling a superior decision to be made.[96] In naked selection, all knowledge of one's potential partner was on the body and it was obvious.

Looking for a partner for marriage or mating at the nudist park increased the likelihood that people would find their ideal partners, at least in physical terms, and was something that would improve the race beyond measure as well as ensure happy marriages. 'Mate selection according to one's wishes about the body will follow, and can, so to speak, be a good natural selection [*Zuchtwahl*], the most essential element for bettering the race,' commented one author. An unpleasant discovery about the body of one's new spouse was often only first made after the wedding itself, when it was too late to do anything about it, and often condemned the marriage partners to misery. In nudism, 'the many unpleasant surprises and bitterest disappointments with regard to the body, often the cause of unhappy marriages, are prevented.'[97] Nudist practice provided the occasion for participants to observe and to take note of every physical feature of everyone else. In nudism, ideologues maintained, spouses would only be selected after mutual, visual, naked inspection had occurred.

In bourgeois society, nudists complained, the body was all too often ignored or overlooked when couples married, as viewing the naked body before the wedding was considered an immoral act. Choosing one's lifelong mating partner in the nudist experience offered the advantage of guaranteeing happiness, or at least preventing unhappiness in the marriage, and was thus a far better way of establishing a relationship. 'Mate selection,' explained one, 'would be placed on a healthier foundation if it rested on truth of the body.' Moreover, a number 'of disappointments would be spared.'[98]

A surprising and unpleasant revelation on the wedding night or honeymoon was no way to build a happy marriage. The reality that some Germans found themselves trapped in an unhappy marriage or with an unhealthy partner would be obviated by nudism.[99] Mutual naked marriage or partner selection was important because it helped dismantle middle-class controls over the body, over love and over sexuality, potentially enabling lovers from any background or social status to marry once in love.

Intimate knowledge of the body of one's partner was essential prior to the marriage, both for personal happiness and to ensure the high racial quality of any children. The question of racial hygiene in selecting a marriage partner, assured one nudist, would assume 'an enormous importance.'[100] Nudist practice would enable the 'bettering of the German race by promoting marriages between blonde-haired, blue-eyed types.'[101] Nudism provided the circumstances and the knowledge needed for Germans to make better decisions in choosing their partners for marriages. In nudism, 'one would learn how to better estimate the value of a healthy, well-formed, athletically trained body.'[102] 'Only in nudism,' explained one nudist, 'can one find the ideal types, and come to know [another's] constitution and true qualities.'[103] At the very least, demanded one author, all engaged couples 'should appear before each other naked for their entire lives before the union, so that all physical defects can be recognized,' and the marriage possibly avoided.[104]

Awareness and knowledge of other's bodies, especially of marriage partners, was important not only for identifying physical defects but also for other equally important racial reasons. Bodily ignorance of one's lifelong mating partner could lead to further racial degeneration, if, for example, one partner suffered from syphilis or other venereal diseases. In nudism, those infected with any kind of disease that produced external sores would be unable to conceal their condition, and would thus be marked as poor partners for marriage. Cleverly and deceptively hidden by clothing, 'a small, weak, possibly tubercular girl, complained one author, could easily present herself as a healthy, fully developed woman in order to trick a man into marrying her.'[105] Nudists' ideas about marriage were motivated largely by their racism, especially their racial anti-Semitism and by their understanding of sex and reproduction.

Mutual naked observation from earliest childhood through adulthood and old age was demanded by one author to prevent 'sexual mistakes' from being kept secret between partners, and possibly poisoning the race.[106] While important, sexual mistakes and venereal infections were not the only reasons nudist ideologues demanded mutual naked observation by all Germans, especially potential marriage partners. Nakedness promoted honesty between people, and prevented any trickery or deceit, and thus had crucial racial consequences. Given the constant, unavoidable viewing of participants at the nudist park and the racial anti-Semitism that permeated *Nacktkultur*, one is tempted to conclude that nudism was also a means of identifying otherwise well-assimilated Jews.

Circumcision is not customary among gentile Germans, and in the nudist experience Jewish males at least would be unable to conceal from view their circumcised penises. From the nudist standpoint, these circumcisions would identify them as individuals with whom to avoid sexual relations.

Some evidence does exist to suggest that nudism was a means to distinguish Jews in German society, who because of their appearance or behavior might not have been readily identifiable as such. The concern for being identified, however mistakenly, as a Jew at the nudist park was a real one. For example, in an exchange

Figure 7.1 Body training or having fun? Image from *Lachendes Leben* Jahrgang VIII, Heft 5. Courtesy of ANRL.

of letters between two Germans that appeared in an advice column in the nudist magazine *Lachendes Leben*, the question of circumcision for medical reasons and its possible consequences was debated. One letter-writer was asking for advice about a surgery that he was considering to relieve his discomfort when obtaining an erection, due to a constricted foreskin.[107] So great was his pain and discomfort that it had begun to affect his sex life and his marriage. His immediate concern was that he might lose sensation in his penis, and thus reduce sexual pleasure during intercourse because of the operation. The response he received, however, did not offer him any answers about his sex life, but it did raise another point for him to consider.

In the next issue, a reader responded recommending against the surgery in the strongest terms, though for reasons of appearance, not sensation. He himself, the respondent admitted, had had a similar surgery for a similar condition some years before, and now as a result was afraid to participate in nudist activity lest he be mistaken as Jewish. 'In the operation,' he recalled, 'my member was disfigured in that manner, so that now I don't dare take the chance to participate at any meeting, as I fear that someone may assume because of my "circumcision," that I am Semitic, which I really am not.'[108] This is not to say that circumcision among gentiles was unheard of, but it was comparatively rare. A quick review of the photographs in any nudist publication reveals that virtually no males were circumcised; the most notable exception is Hans Surén, whose circumcision is unavoidably evident in a number of photographs. However, given his later status as a Nazi and his rank of major in the SS it is relatively safe to assume that Surén was not Jewish. At the very least, this episode suggests that even in nudism appearances still mattered a little.

In order to ensure that marriages were grounded in honesty, a key to their success, to spouses' mutual happiness and the proper development of any children, nudist proponents demanded that no marriage occur before both parties had occasion to view each other naked. Using nudism to help one find and to guarantee that a potential marriage partner was both healthy and racially acceptable was perfectly welcome practice, and was in essence one reason among many for *Nacktkultur*'s very existence. In the nudist state, such a selection process would become commonplace, believed one author. 'For the unmarried, the role of naked sports when selecting one's mate is of far-reaching importance, for those who wish to marry cannot be careful enough when choosing,' said Wilhelm Kästner.[109]

In nudism, such a system of blindly marrying someone without full knowledge of their physical appearance and racial qualities would not exist as nudists inescapably possessed intimate knowledge of their own as well as others' bodies.[110] Such a practice might also create a number of more deeply passionate and love-filled marriages, when a man or woman, for example, caught sight of a 'Venus or Apollo' suddenly appearing from underneath the now discarded clothing.[111]

According to nudist ideology, mass social nakedness would guarantee that only the most suitable partners found and mated with one another. Nudism forced people to be seen as they truly were, without the artifices – or shielding – of clothing. 'In selecting a marriage partner, especial value will be placed on healthy and well-formed bodies, since both sexes will see each other naked, free of disguises,' explained one nudist.[112] The vision of nudist courtship and mating was relatively simple and was driven above all else by the observation and evaluation by all Germans of each others' healthy, beautiful bodies, themselves the products of nudist activity. *Nacktkultur* created the circumstances and provided the means to construct physically as well as sexually aware, confident and healthy individuals, whose new physical form and sense of natural nakedness would allow them to unite with the opposite sex as equals for the purpose of creating a superior generation of Germans. The 'care of the self' in nudism existed only to better the race through marriage of racially fit equals and eugenic breeding, not to complete the cultivation of the self. The nudist union can in this sense be understood as a departure from the marital pattern discerned by Foucault.[113]

The naked viewing of potential marriage partners was considered by nudists to be instrumental both in the success of the marriage overall and in the racial improvement of the *Volk*. It loosely followed the ancient Germanic custom of naked partners falling in love and reproducing in large numbers.[114] This aspect of nudism, with its explicit racial implications and functions, appealed greatly to the National Socialists when they came to power, and it became altogether more pronounced during the regime.

In 1934, for example, Walther Darré, the Reichsbauernführer, presented a speech to a group of farmers' wives that recalled that the custom among ancient Germanic tribes (a designation that included Finns and Swedes) had been for men and women to be intimately familiar with their own and each others' naked bodies; this knowledge was in fact the source of their strength. Darré, like so many others in the top Nazi leadership, called on Germans, in this case the farmers of Germany, to revive that tradition, shed their clothes and be naked in order to strengthen the *Volk*.[115]

Hans Surén, a Nazi, a nudist and a member of the SS, was one of nudism's most vocal proponents in the 1930s, and certainly its most well-integrated member into the Nazi regime. Throughout the 1930s he propagated many of the same ideas that had long been part of *Nacktkultur*, though with greater authority and in the context of a government that openly supported his efforts and nudist ideas. 'It was the holy duty of Nordic nudism,' he wrote, 'to revive this symbol' of the naked body 'at play, in sports and washing,' as pure, chaste and as how the Germanic forefathers lived. 'We must lose our shyness of our own bodies, and return Germanic pride to them,' he called in another effort to promote the nudist-Nazi ideals. 'There lives a longing in both men and women for the view of the naked beauty of the other sex,' he recalled, and in Germans this was 'our nature and expression of our pure Aryanness.' This naked mutual viewing, of course, had no sexual aspects or implications, 'unlike with some other races.'[116] Again Darré wrote, 'One must take great care with the Nordic race, that the two genders get to know each other as they were created.'[117]

Fully aware of each others' bodies and uninfluenced by the pressures of sex, whether of their own inclination to have intercourse or seduced by the allure of hidden, mysterious body parts that enhanced temptation and flirtation, naked Germans would unite based around the principles of founding a large family, and their relationships would be rooted in honesty, especially body honesty. 'Only the fittest, strongest men and women will find each other in the desire to have children. No one should hide their imperfections and defects with clothing.'[118] Many such couples would be formed, all of which would produce quality, racially robust children that would eventually repopulate Germany. In addition to the fact that 'the body thrives in the sun, it loses its sexual vice, it retains its uncorrupted, beautiful form as the "likeness of God", and also satisfies the desire for beauty,' one of the many reasons that people practiced nudism was that it brought 'young men and young women to happy, pure marriages that produced healthy, beautiful, racially worthy children through its process of mutual selection.'[119]

The offspring from any nudist union would be healthy, just as the nudists themselves were, since, reminded one nudist, '*körperkultur* [sic] results in the duty to be healthy.'[120] The child raised to adulthood in nudism, whose body glowed with health and elegance, could not be expected to 'select someone inferior to him or herself in order to reproduce.'[121] Perhaps most importantly, according to nudist proponents, the marriage based in nudism and resulting from nudist activity would improve the race, as it 'will also be a healthy form of "natural selection", so to speak, an essential precondition for improving the race.'[122] Marriages themselves, nudists maintained, needed to be better composed in order to be able to produce and to raise the kind of children needed to complete the regeneration of the race and nation. The consideration of racial hygiene during the process of choosing a mate, reminded one author, was of 'enormous importance.'[123]

Marriages were themselves only properly conceived in the nudist experience, for personal as well as racial reasons. 'Among devotees of nudism, the beautiful will always join with the beautiful, and from that union – assuming they both lead natural-oriented lives – beautiful children will be produced. And beauty is health, for disease can never be beautiful,' assured one.[124] Germans could lay the foundation for the coming nudist state by ensuring that the next generation was better conceived and better prepared for a life of nakedness than they themselves had been, and here nudism was expected to play the pivotal role. The next generation should be raised fully aware and fully knowledgeable of the body and its functions, and nakedness was 'the education to truth.'[125] 'Communal *Nacktkultur* was therefore a necessity for the hygiene of love, the precondition for the cultivation of sexuality. For sexual education [nudism] is even more important than straightforward explanations,' exclaimed one author.[126]

As modern as it was reactionary, nudist ideology combined the two most important directions in twentieth-century sex, eugenics and sex reform, into a single, workable utopian movement of the body that would produce not only a pure Germanic *Volk*, but more importantly, would also make Germany into a society of joyous, confident individuals who willingly entered marital unions based solely on the knowledge of each others' naked bodies and motivated only by mutual love. In the naked experience, uninfluenced by the headiness of erotic temptation and unconfused by any sexual urge, as masters of their bodies and desires, intimately aware of everyone's naked body, its beauty, health and even its flaws and imperfections, Germans would first be able to get to know each other properly, then become truly acquainted and ultimately fall in love and marry. 'Exactly during mate selection,' explained Therese Mühlhause-Vogeler, 'nudism performs its greatest duty; for nowhere else is a person freer of disappointing misconceptions, be they conscious or unconscious, as in nakedness.'[127]

However radical in its appearance or shocking in its approach, *Nacktkultur* was no revolutionary movement. It did not seek to overthrow the centrality of the family as the basic organizational unit of the German nation, but instead sought to strengthen it through a restructuring that at once made women men's equals yet nevertheless assigned them to the role of motherhood. Within the framework of the family, German gender relations would be transformed, men and women would be equal in all things and the companionate marriage would be the order of the day, though its purpose nevertheless remained that of producing the next generation and raising it according to the principles of *Nacktkultur*. 'The Nordic race,' reminded one author, 'owes its very existence to breeding laws.'[128] Nevertheless, in the nudist experience and within the nudist marriage, women would gain some measure of equality with men, as they would graduate from passive to active participant in the selection process. Women would not only have agency in finding a mate, but would also be able to exercise that agency to a greater degree within the marriage itself, especially with regard to sexual and reproductive matters.

Breeding a better race, one that was rooted in nature and racial purity, depended in large part on the ability of Germans to locate and to identify their ideal mates according to the principles of racial hygiene and nudism. 'An individual should determine if a potential partner has qualities to give his or her children that are worthwhile for the social body,' exclaimed one nudist.[129] Finding the right marriage partner was crucial to breeding an improved German race and nation, and in many ways *Nacktkultur* culminated in mate selection. The nudist marriage, however, was more than a vehicle for bringing offspring into the world – it was also the foundation for the coming racial paradise and a microcosm of equality and harmony in all aspects of Germans' social, marital and sexual relations with one another. The nudist marriage was to be an extension of the relationships developed in the nudist park, where boys and girls, men and women forged lifelong friendships and marital unions based on mutual respect, love and truth, and which were devoid of sexual craving, erotic titillation or concerns over financial or social status.

The Nudist Marriage

Germans' marriages, like all of their relationships, would be restructured by nudist activity in such a way that all parties stood on a more equal footing with one another. In the nudist marriage, women shared equal value with men in all regards, and no longer would the husband lord over his wife as was traditionally the caricature. 'The man is no more the master over the passive, obedient wife, rather the experience, the devotion is determined by each partner and is voluntary.' Even sexual relations among nudists would be made by mutual consent rather than by one partner alone. 'And the man will no longer determine the frequency of the experience – even in the marriage – but rather the wife, independent master of her own body, will give herself when love draws her to, and will resist the desires of the husband, when during the time that devotion to her sensibilities demands it.'[130]

In the matter of sexual relations between the sexes, nudism generally called for a reform that provided for greater freedom of sexual activity than that which they believed governed their parents' generation. Although nudist ideologues decried the idea of free-love as a Jewish plot to undermine the strength and heritage of the Aryan race, the idea of sex before marriage was not opposed.

Sexual relations between two Germans who loved one another truly and deeply, not who found one another in a momentary tryst that involved the exchange of money, was acceptable. 'It is not to be understood why intercourse before marriage, properly speaking, should disgrace the man or the maiden,' wondered one anonymous author.[131] Sex, especially premarital sex, far from being an immoral act that caused one to suffer from society's reproaches was understood in nudism as an expression of love, and as a departure from the failed moral codes of the past.

Robert Laurer, *enfant terrible* of Weimar nudism, characterized the generation before him as having condemned sexual expression and activity even within marriage, yet at the same time it tacitly acknowledged even approved of men's infidelity, either with prostitutes or with mistresses. This double morality, he suggested, could and would be solved by the adoption of the nudist ethic. 'The youth of today, the generation that will lead the twentieth century, is readily and energetically prepared to supplant the double morality with a "simple" [one], which grants women the same right as the man, even in pleasures.'[132] The experiment of encouraging abstinence was a failure, Laurer continued, and premarital sex with one's beloved was an acceptable measure to control the spread of venereal disease, and unlike prostitution did not involve the purchase of another's body. Finally, he noted, marriage in the economic atmosphere of the day (the early 1930s) was an expense beyond most couples' means.[133] Like so much else in nudism, the endorsement of monogamous premarital sex was made because it bettered people's lives in the present, not in the distant afterworld.

Nudist unions, in contrast to those in clothed society, would be based on love as well as mutual selection. Having grown accustomed to the sight and presence of naked men, women would know better what to look for in a spouse, and would base their decisions accordingly. At the nudist park, 'partner selection according to physical desires – by both parties – will result.'[134] Potential partners would be far more suited to one another, at least in terms of physical well-being and beauty.

Meetings and relations between the sexes would be marked not by flirtation, coquetry or sexual undertones as was presently the case, nudists argued, as 'coquetry and flirtation were simply impossible' in nakedness and nature.[135] Instead, 'joint meetings between naked athletes will occur, where males and females will work in mutual respect, camaraderie.'[136] Once naked, suggested one nudist, the tactic common to women of altering the body artificially to catch another's eye, as with a corset for example, would cease.[137] The nudist marriage would be a union of two Germans whose mutual nakedness established them as equals in the identification of marriage partners, in the following courtship and ultimately within the relationship.

In the nudist experience, the arranged or negotiated marriage would disappear, and this was a trend at least one nudist believed had already begun. Men no longer desired, he believed, women who were not active, sporty, physically fit, intelligent and, most importantly, their companions in life. 'I believe,' he wrote, 'that marriages where men and women have learned to value one another as good friends, and who have joined in a life-union, will command the day.'[138] The steady disappearance of the arranged marriage in favor of the companionate marriage was not least because nudism fostered more genuine interaction between individuals, and greater respect for the opposite sex. Nudist activity encouraged a sense of community and cooperation with one's fellow German that clothed or contemporary society had been unable to achieve, as it was built on the fundamental misrepresentation of the person that clothing produced. The nudist marriage, observed one author, unlike that of most Germans, ignored superficial or artificial qualities, such as money, title or dowry, and instead based itself on what she termed the human qualities, 'kindness, intelligence, health.'[139]

Conclusion

While the goal of nudism was the total transformation of the German national, social and racial body into a nudist utopia, the agent of that change, and the focus of nudist effort, was the individual body. The ability of nudism to heal the nation and to breed the race occurred as the direct result of two distinct, yet interrelated effects of the nudist experience. The first effect was produced in the *Luft-* and *Sonnenbad* and made the body physically healthy and beautiful, a living example of the Hellenic-Germanic aesthetic ideal and the hearty, visually appealing bearer of the racial seed. The second effect produced in the nudist experience, however, was purely sexual.

Mass nakedness for the German nation was not only a goal of *Nacktkultur* but was also the means to achieve broader nudist goals of creating a racially homogeneous, socially united, politically powerful Germany. Observing naked bodies was a vital component of the nudist experience as it changed the meaning of the body, especially the personal body, transformed it, stripped it, redefined it, made it into an ideal form – the celebrated *Vorbild*, naked, chaste and un-erotic – in order to make it into Germany's agent of national and racial improvement. Creating a new understanding of the body was a task that would be largely accomplished by separating, especially, the ideas of sex and sexuality from the body and nakedness.

Although important to the mental and physical health of a German, nakedness

Sex, Race and Nudism • 159

Figure 7.2 A less idealized image of sun worship. German nudists sunning themselves. Image from *Lachendes Leben* Jahrgang VII, Heft 9. Courtesy of ANRL.

was above all else an ideal form useful for making the body into an ideal form, which in one of its socially, sexually and ideologically most powerful and most important functions is exactly what it did. The ideal body itself then became the basis for the new German society – free, unashamed, beautiful, naked, chaste and yet also sexually enthralling. In this community of nudes, based on egalitarianism rather than hierarchy, a new society would develop that did not recognize social, gender or class distinctions.

In the desexualized world of nudist activity, people would come to treat each other more kindly and regard each other more tenderly. Nakedness taught 'an honest, chivalrous esteem of the genders for one another. Free of all sexuality – which, by the way, has nothing in common with nakedness,' and men and women would form deep, soulful friendships and marriages, noted one author.[140] One long-term goal of nudism was 'the familiarization of the genders to a comradely, unencumbered relationship to one another through education to personal freedom, as well as the ennoblement of the understanding of sexual proceedings and of the relations between the sexes.'[141]

Sun- and airbathing healed body and mind, and promoted a natural understanding of sex. Nudism produced not only a healthy body but also 'a healthy sexuality and therefore a personal, moral stimulation and a happy new generation.'[142] Mass social nakedness facilitated a general de-eroticization of society.[143] Ultimately, the relationships begun in nudism would become the basis for lifelong partnerships, and a new, better Germany.

Epilogue

Nudism quickly reemerged in the aftermath of the Second World War as Germans began to rebuild their nation and their society. In early 1947, for example, nudist Hermann Wündrich inquired of the city of Hamburg about the possibility of again participating in nudism. Wündrich was informed by the city that the nudist organization Liga für freie Lebensgestaltung had been given permission by the military government to reconstitute itself, and was in fact attached to the newly reestablished Verband für Leibesübungen.[1] Other nudist clubs and organizations were eventually refounded throughout West Germany. In 1949, Karwilli Damm together with the members of the Darmstadt-based group Orplid helped found the Deutscher Bund für Freikörperkultur (now the Deutscher Verband für Freikörperkultur or DFK), thus realizing the dream of creating a 'trans-zonal' nudist organization that had been circulating since at least 1947.[2] British and American military occupation forces apparently saw little harm in allowing Germans to organize around the principles of nudism and to practice nakedness.

As nudists rebuilt their shattered organizations the unity of nudist organizations that the Nazi state had imposed quickly gave way to the more traditional localism reminiscent of the *Nacktkultur* of the pre-1933 era. The DFK, like nudism itself, continues to thrive; however, it is only one of very many nudist organizations that currently exist in Germany. Nudism is alive and well in Germany, and many Germans continue to be socially and publicly naked today, either as members of organized clubs or more often as weekend beachgoers seeking to even out a tan or simply to enjoy the sensation of sun and surf on the naked skin.* In this regard, there is little difference between contemporary Germans and those who were naked fifty or one hundred years ago.

Nudism quickly reemerged as an element of German public life. It remains important in Germany to this day, albeit with significant and fundamental differences to its pre-Second World War form – differences that point to a larger transformation of Germany itself in the post-1945 era, and which suggest perhaps a *Stunde Null* (Zero Hour) of mentalities, if not of other social and political trends, did occur. The nudism of today, is markedly different from that of an earlier era,

---

*The German tourist wishing to be naked while on foreign vacation can select from any number of travel books that specifically address the opportunities for nakedness abroad.

and while the history of nudism in the post-Second World War Germanies waits to be written (the advent of the birth control pill, the sexual revolution and the student revolts would have to play a decisive role in shaping more recent views of nudism and the body) some important points about contemporary nudism can be advanced, which suggest important continuities and discontinuities in German history after 1945.[3]

Nudism as it is practiced in the post-Second World War era and today is fundamentally different from the nudism of the first half of the twentieth century. What is undoubtedly different about today's nudism is its gradual transformation from a highly ideological belief in the human body as the agent of national and racial regeneration to a free-time activity one engages in while on vacation or on the weekend, rather than being part of an effort to create a new configuration of life, to borrow the title of one of *Nacktkultur*'s tracts from the 1920s. Nudism is today something far less lived and much more to be consumed, if consumption is the right word. Nudism is now very much a part of the story of post-Second World War German prosperity, tourism, consumerism and especially leisure time.

In its postwar manifestation as a free-time leisure activity, contemporary nudism hearkens back to those nudists who flooded East Prussia's lakes and Swabia's rivers on religious holidays and weekends, to the consternation of the local pastors and priests. Organized nudists tended to respect the fact that they would likely be considered disturbing to their non-nudist contemporaries, and whatever their feelings about clothed society organized nudists often made some effort to conceal their nakedness behind fences or in forests. The unorganized or weekend nudist, only naked in nature on certain occasions and not necessarily out of some deep ideological conviction, by contrast, typically did not take precautions to prevent scandals. One result of this casual attitude towards nudism as leisure-time activity is that nudism is now as widely and publicly practiced as many nudists once hoped and dreamed. Public parks and public beaches in Germany overflow with nakedness on sunny days, to no one's apparent concern.

There is nevertheless something quite different about contemporary nudism. Most obvious, I think, is that it is largely devoid of its earlier ideology, especially the racial aspects; no nudist today is likely to articulate the kind of underlying beliefs in the power of the body to regenerate the nation and to purify the *Volk* through nakedness, just as all but the most far-right extremist German would rarely give voice to such ideas.[4] Nor did the de-ideologization of nudism occur due to anyone's particular efforts. No voice from the era of refoundation in the late 1940s and early 1950s ever spoke up for the need to confront nudism's role or affiliation with the recent past, and to my knowledge no such confrontation with the past ever occurred among nudists, just as it did not in West German society at large. It is likely that the bankruptcy of ideologies of race, eugenics, and promises of national ascendancy did not need to be explained to the survivors of Hitler's regime and Allied conquest.

A second important aspect of the de-ideologization of nudism that occurred is the idea of reform. Nudism emerged at about the same time and as a part of the broader *Lebensreform* milieu of the 1890s and early 1900s. Reform was always one of the key aspects of nudism. Nudist attitudes towards food, clothing, marriage, sex and other aspects of life were formed by the Life-reformers, who, like the nudists, hoped to transform Germans and Germany by changing personal attitudes, behaviors and activities away from self-destructive ones, such as meat, alcohol or tobacco consumption or marrying the wrong girl for the right reasons. Life-reformers and nudists advocated vegetarianism, temperance and the sexually gratifying love-match to achieve their vision of healthy, happy Germans.

Nudists hoped to reform the physical form of the body, and they hoped to reform its meaning from one derived from Christianity, in which it was largely understood to be negative or sinful, to one that was healthy, straightforward and appreciative of the body's functions and beauty; in this they were largely successful. In the post-1945 era, the body suggests not so much illness or sin as it does health, fitness and beauty. The idea of reforming life has all but disappeared from nudist rhetoric, much as life-reformers themselves have disappeared, even as many of their ideas became adapted into the mainstream.

In another sense, too, contemporary nudism bears little resemblance to its early predecessor. Alongside race, the second ideological pillar in the nudist edifice was the belief that nature was somehow better. In nudism, artificial additions to the body, such as clothing but also medicines, so-called racially alien religious doctrines and modernity in general, all worked as unnatural elements that slowly destroyed Germans and Germany. Nature, it was declared by many at the turn of the century, could reverse the effects of cities and cure the personal body as well as the metaphoric national or racial body. Moreover, and perhaps more importantly, the social reform of Germany could only take place in the natural world beyond the somehow racially inimical cityscapes of capitalism, where socialism, Americanism and alcoholism, to name only a few ills, all lurked. In early nudism in particular, metropolises, harmful though they were, were not to be abandoned for the countryside. Nature was not urbanism's antipode, but its antidote.

There undoubtedly remains deeply embedded in German consciousness a fundamental belief in the goodness of nature and 'natural' goods over other kinds, witness the public agitation spawned by any suggestion of importing so-called genetically modified (GM) foods from the United States, for example. A string of stores known in German as *Reformhäuser*, or reform houses, which purvey all manner of 'natural' goods can be found in virtually every major German city (another triumph of the Life-reformers), and homeopathic medicines and therapies enjoy a certain amount of official recognition. The advantages and realities of living in a thickly populated urban center are still likely to elicit ambiguous responses from Germans. Many on weekends continue to abandon their concrete jungles for the greenery of the outlying districts for long walks and sojourns in nature, and this is a habit that hearkens back to the early back-to-nature impulse of a previous century. Like their *fin-de-siècle* forebears, few modern Germans ever actually abandon their city lives for residence in nature. Nature is a place to visit, to dream about, not to live in. The nature of nature, however, has been altered.

The idea of nature as a better place or healing force has itself been forced to undergo certain revisions as science has steadily undermined the dreamy-eyed, romantic belief that all in nature is without question better for people. Clearly, the nudist fantasy that sunshine could first kill and even prevent bacterial infections would find few believers today. If nudism ever prevented any cases of tuberculosis, it likely had more to do with removing people from damp and dank housing, a benefit of their movement that nudists recognized, than it did with a vigorous air-exchange between the inner organs and the outside world whereby poisons were secreted through the skin, as nudists also believed. The development and mass availability of antibiotics has unquestionably done far more to cure diseases than sunlight ever would. More broadly, the late-twentieth century realization that too much sun is harmful, even cancerous, certainly marks an important reversal in appreciation of the sun and tanning.[5] In no small way, contemporary nudism has survived its own ideological past.

German nudism is now entering its second century. It has outlived both the Age of Victorianism, 'classical modernity' and modernity and continues to thrive even in the postmodern age. Nudism and the idea of nakedness have survived a century of profound social, political, economic, cultural change and devastation, as well as powerful political-ideological movements, which in their quest for totality of the nation, of the public, of the individual and even of the mythical *Volk* were unable to or, more importantly, unwilling to bring about an end to nudism. Nudism is no more an individual response, a kind of escape, from political repression such as existed under the Kaiser's regime, than it is a response to widespread freedom and a liberal, democratic, permissive social-political order such as existed in the Weimar Republic.

There does not appear to be any discernable relationship between political freedom or repression and the desire to exhibit one's naked body before others. Moreover, the one regime that potentially could have prevented anyone from practicing nudism in nature or in public, for any number of reasons whether ideological, political or moral, did not do so. The Nazis banned nudism, almost as an allergic reaction to its perceived relationship to the social and political environment of the despised Weimar Republic. Ultimately, however, the National Socialists allowed and promoted nudism; they understood it was neither decadent nor immoral, but rather an activity performed in service of the individual and the nation, to the benefit of both.

To be sure, leading Nazis such as Agricultural Minister Walther Darré, SS Chief Heinrich Himmler, Surgeon General Dr Wagner, Minister of the Interior Rudolf

Heß, Nazi Germany's national athletic director von Tschammer und Osten, and the head of the Office of Racial Policy Dr Groß found other compelling reasons to support nudism. Its similarity to Nazism's own racial policies, views and ambitions undoubtedly appealed to all of them, as likely did its ideology of the body, body cultivation, strength and beauty. Dr Groß, moreover, recognized that nudism could be a useful ally in the coming Nazi struggle against organized religion. More importantly, Groß also realized the basic problem that he 'could not on the one hand promote racial and pro-natalist policies and on the other hand defame and slander the human body as something that should under all circumstances be concealed.'[6] Nazism and nudism shared considerable ideological common ground; both had deep roots in popular culture and radical ideologies dating at the very least from the turn of the twentieth century.

Originating in the late nineteenth-century Wilhelmine reform milieu, nudism and other Life-Reform endeavors, including the much-vaunted youth movement, based themselves on the belief in rerooting modern life somewhere in the natural world, in the unspoiled environment. It is no coincidence that this is the era that saw the birth of the environmental movement.[7] Many of these Life-Reform groups offered themselves as models and alternatives to the prevailing economic and social system that simultaneously produced so much wealth and so much misery, as well as dangerous alternatives to capitalism, especially socialism.

Wanting far more to soften the rough edges of capitalism than to discard it altogether, nudists and other Life-reformers, as their name implies, sought to reform life, and in so doing to reshape the nation. In a sense, the Green Party is both the heir and the political incarnation of such impulses. Reform of life would precede and in fact would cause reform of the nation, of the race. While the Wilhelmine reform milieu may have had substantial support, even occasional leadership, from university educated elites, it was far more the non-university trained, non-elites who argued for, practiced and were the foot soldiers of Life-Reform.[8]

The great difference, of course, between today's Greens and other politically oriented reformers, and nudists and other Life-reformers is that the latter rejected any idea of reform through politics. Reform of the nation in nudism in particular was specifically formulated to occur without any instance of the state's involvement. Nudist reform of the nation and the *Volk* was above all else personal reform. To build a better, healthier, stronger, more powerful, more successful, racially and socially homogeneous, united Germany was entirely predicated on first constructing oneself in that manner. The state never played any role.

While it would be disingenuous to argue that nudism existed independently and ignorantly of broader political forces, it did see itself as a means to escape the internecine and self-destructive nature of political struggle by preaching an ideology of the nation, national wholeness and racial purity rooted in the individual person and, literally, in that person's body. In nudism, national unity, harmony and class cohesion would be achieved not by parliamentary decree or popular vote, or by the rise and success of political mass movements or even by the elimination through murder of millions of non-Germanic outsiders, but instead by the transcendental and near-mystical communal experience of nakedness. In the ideology of *Nacktkultur*, the nation was an organic extension of the person, and with little bloodshed, nudist society would grow organically from the new body transformed by nakedness in nature and from the new bodies nudist partners literally created with each other.

As a social movement, nudism stretches across the twentieth century, and the traditional historical turning points in German history, nearly all taken from the world of high politics, 1914–18, 1933, 1945 and 1989, become altogether less important. The World Wars did not bring an end to this social custom, such as they did both to governments and to so much else that characterized the historical Germany, such as militarism or to a certain extent even nationalism. Importantly, nudism not only survived a variety of very different regimes – reactionary monarchy, liberal democracy and Nazism – but it actually thrived under all three. Part of the reason for this can be found in the appeal of the ideas of Life-Reform mentioned above, which, like nudism, also found a level of support in Nazism, and included to our eyes such bizarre juxtapositions as Hermann Göring protecting animals from experimentation, anti-smoking campaigns, not unlike our own, to protect the nation's health, and even a pronounced reluctance by Nazis to interfere in the daily lives of Germans by forcing them to stop their nudism altogether.[9]

In nudism, the individual's body would be healed, beautified and the next generation bred all without any interference or help from the state or through political means. Indeed, nudism solved the social problem in ways politics could not. For those who reviled industry because it incapacitated workers' intellects and prevented them from participating in culture, a near universal assessment among believers in nudism, nudist ideologues offered that *Nacktkultur* 'cultivates the machine-person [*Maschine Mensch*],' helped them to learn, built strength, fostered ability and relaxed.[10] Nudists argued that machine-based modern work was, by definition, dehumanizing.[11] Workers suffered from loss of joy due to their work, and in the opinion of many nudists were slowly drawn to socialism through their desperation.

In order to rehumanize work and to orient the worker away from radical political solutions, at least one nudist asserted in all seriousness that *Nacktkultur* be brought to the factory, for morale and health. 'Simply throwing off one's clothes brings us joy of work, health, joy of existence,' commented Hans Surén. Surén further suggested that workers and industry would benefit equally from a naked workforce.[12] 'Working naked always produces a happy and joyous mood, because it reminds us of our Germanic ancestors, for whom every healthy person carries a longing,' he explained.[13]

Surén held that the naked worker was a happy worker, and a happy worker was a more productive worker.[14] Working naked, he thought, would compel workers to wash themselves more often than they washed their dirty clothes, thus bestowing on them greater health. In any event, working naked would refocus workers' 'will and strength' away from 'divisive politics' towards 'the simple questions of health and inurement [*Abhärtung*],' he explained.[15] Surén envisioned that naked work would be suitable for broad sections of industry. 'There are many factories [*Werke*] and workshops, aside from commerce [*Verkehr*], where one could work very felicitously nude and barefoot.'[16]

Furthermore, nudism, if practiced for its ideological reasons, was a way for individual Germans to become national and racial saviors. If, as nudists understood it, society was decadent, immoral, hypocritical, given over to licentiousness and the pursuit of luxury, then when it finally collapsed there would be a core group of pure Germans, the nudists, to rebuild it. Like the ancient Germans about whom they fantasized and whose lifestyle they sought consciously to reconstruct through studied imitation, modern German nudists were naked and chaste, self-disciplined, strong and fit, both racially and physically.

Important for personal, racial and national regeneration was the sense of wholeness that nudism recreated. The modern machine age replaced the harmonious balance of body, mind and spirit with the new 'trinity of human, machine and organization.'[17] People, lamented one author, now only had value as machines, and their careers were their identities.[18] The debate about the perils of the machine age, its tempo and its effects of hollowing Germans' souls, limiting their leisure time and governing their lives lasted well into the Nazi era, with no clear solution.[19] The most devastating extremes of industrial labor manifested themselves in Taylorism, which contributed to the intellectual death of the worker – the first step in the ultimate destruction of the body. 'Nerves and bodies need peace, and if the mind remains troubled with work, it disturbs the body's efforts to make up for the energies expended during the day, and depreciates the level of health,' explained the nudist Therese Mühlhause-Vogeler.[20]

While focusing primarily on the body as the means to regenerate tired workers and degenerate Germans, nudism benefited minds and spirits too. One author reminded his readers that, 'only those who were healthy in body, mind and spirit could accomplish the tasks set forth by the present struggle of life!' Nudists argued that a healthy body was a precondition for a healthy intellect and complete soul, and because 'body culture was body refinement,' *Nacktkultur* was able to accomplish this task so necessary for living in the hectic modern world. Nudism conceived of people as wholes, and it would enable people to recover from their machine-induced physical and mental fatigue, because it 'comprehends people in their totality and culminates in community [*Gemeinschaft*].'[21]

Nudists, like their imagined ancient forebears, were close to nature, uncorrupted by either the Christian religion or by the infiltration and influence of Jews. Nudists were furthermore incorruptible in the face of temptation from sex, luxury, lucre or easy living, and could not succumb to biological pathogens. The apotheosis of health, paragons of beauty and visible, living incarnations of the noble, naked ancient Germans, nudists were set to rebuild and to repopulate Germany.

Though for different reasons, nudism and the idea of the naked body continue to be important in German society to this day, as anyone who visits Germany today invariably notices when confronting for the first time in their lives nude or semi-nude lunchtime sunbathers in city parks, most famously Munich's English Garden, or when flipping on the television during primetime.[22] In 2002, for example, over 300 nudists were set to rally in support of greater nudist freedoms in the capital Berlin.[23] It is not just a case that German society is more tolerant of public nakedness, which it undoubtedly is, especially when compared with the United States. The naked body and the idea of the naked body are both very much a part of German society, of the modern German nation.

Notes

Introduction: The Decline of the Germans

1. Dr Robert Werner Schulte, *Körper-Kultur: Versuch einer Philosophie der Leibesübungen* (Verlag Ernst Rheinhardt, 1928), pp. 38–9.
2. Fritz Stern, *Kulturpessimismus als politische Gefahr: Eine Analyse nationaler Ideologie in Deutschland* (Alfred Scherz Verlag, 1963); Klaus Bergmann, *Agrarromantik und Großstadtfeindschaft* (Verlag Anton Hain, 1970). Much good work has been done on this and some examples include the Pan-German League, the best study of which is Roger Chickering, *We Men Who Feel Most German: A Cultural Study of the Pan-German League, 1886–1914* (George Allen and Unwin, 1984). Also helpful is Geoff Eley's, *Reshaping the German Right: Radical Nationalism and Political Change after Bismarck* (University of Michigan Press, 1980).
3. George Mosse, *The Crisis of German Ideology: Intellectual Origins of the Third Reich* (New York: Grosset & Dunlap, 1964).
4. Rainer Lächele, 'Protestantismus und *völkische* Religion im deutschen Kaiserreich'; '"Das heilge Feuer", eine katholische Zeitschrift, 1913–1931', in Uwe Puschner, Walter Sachmitz and Justus H. Ulbricht, eds, *Handbuch zur völkischen Bewegung, 1871–1918* (K.G. Saur, 1996), pp. 150–68; on later attempts, see also Doris Bergen, *Twisted Cross: The German Christian Movement in the Third Reich* (University of North Carolina Press, 1996).
5. Magnus Weidemann, 'Neudeutscher Idealismus,' in *Die Freude*, Heft 1, p. 7.
6. Ibid., p. 6.
7. Richard Ungewitter, *Kultur und Nacktheit: Eine Forderung* (Verlag Richard Ungewitter, 1911), p. 41.
8. Wilhelm Kästner, *Nacktsport* (Verlag W. Kästner [1911]), p. 1.
9. Hans Vahle, *Zielskisse der Freikörperkultur: Ein Leitfaden für Leibeszucht und gesundes Leben* (Polverlag, 1932).
10. *Lebensreform* was the subject of an extensive recent exhibition at Darmstadt, accompanied by a nearly 1,200 page collection of essays. Kai Buchholz, Rita Latocha, Hilke Peckmann, Klaus Wolbert, eds, *Die Lebensreform: Entwürfe zur Neugestaltung von Leben und Kunst um 1900*, 2 vols (Verlag Häuser,

2001). On the exhibition see, *Frankfurter Allgemeine Zeitung*, 'So sollst du leben!' (Frankfurt am Main) 13 November 2001. See also, Kevin Repp, *Reformers, Critics and the Paths of German Modernity: Anti-Politics and the Search for Alternatives, 1890–1914* (Harvard University Press, 2000); Diethart Kerbs and Jürgen Reulcke, eds, *Handbuch der deutschen Reformbewegungen, 1880–1933* (Peter Hammer Verlag, 1998); Wolfgang Krabbe, *Gesellschaftsveränderung durch Lebensreform: Strukturmerkmale einer sozialreformerischen Bewegung in Deutschland der Industrialisierungsperiode* (Vandenhoeck and Rupprecht, 1974); Florentine Fritzen, 'Gesünder Leben: Die Lebensreformbewegung und deutsche Gesellschaft, 1900–2000' (Frankfurt am Main, forthcoming).

11. Hans Surén, *Mensch und Sonne: Arisch-olympischer Geist* (Verlag Scherl, 1936), pp. 92–4.
12. Dr von Hauff, *Das Freibad*, Heft 4 (1931), p. 77.
13. K. Besser, 'Schamgefühl und Körperkultur,' in *Der Leib Urania*, Heft 2 (1926), p. 93.
14. Dr med. K. Reissner, 'Die hygienische Notwendigkeit,' in Manfred Berg, ed., *Die Wahrheit um den Körper: Ein Aufruf zur Selbstbesinnung!* (Karl Haug Verlag, 1927), p. 30.
15. Adolf Weide, *Verjüngung absolut* (Selbstverlag des Verfassers, 1929), p. 22.
16. Kurt Reichert, *Vom Leibeszucht und Leibesschönheit: Bilder aus dem Leben des Bundes für Leibeszucht* (Verlag Deutsche Leibeszucht, 1940), n.p.
17. Dr Bernhard Schulze, 'Rechtfertigung,' in Charly Sträßer, ed., *Jugendgelände: Ein Buch von neuen Menschen* (Der Greifenverlag zur Rudolstadt, 1926), p. 93.
18. Dr Max Seber, 'Die kulturellen Grundlagen,' in Berg *Wahrheit*, p. 23.
19. Surén, *Mensch*, pp. 162–3.
20. Renatus, 'Körper und Geist,' in *Die Freude*, Heft 12 (1925), pp. 528–35.
21. Reissner, 'Die hygienische Notwendigkeit,' p. 30.
22. Hans Surén, *Der Mensch und die Sonne* (Dieck and Co., 1924), pp. 11–12.
23. Surén, *Der Mensch*, p. 12.
24. J.M. Seitz, *Die Nacktkulturbewegung: Ein Buch für Wissende und Unwissende* (Verlag der Schönheit, 1923), p. 23.
25. Besser, 'Schamgefühl und Körperkultur,' p. 93.
26. Walter Heitsch, *Freikörperkultur-Lebensfreude* (Robert Laurer Verlag), 1925, p. 7.
27. Vahle, *Zielskizze*, p. 5.
28. Vahle, *Zielskizze*, p. 6.
29. Weide, *Verjüngung absolut*, pp. 22–3.
30. H.W. Behm, *Reigen der Keuschheit* (Robert Laurer Verlag, 1928), p. 23.
31. Vahle, *Zielskisse*, p. 5.

32. Renatus, 'Körper und Geist,' pp. 528–35.
33. Joanna Bourke, *Dismembering the Male: Men's Bodies, Britain and the Great War* (University of Chicago Press, 1996).
34. For some examples see Marc Bloch, *The Royal Touch: Sacred Monarchy and Scrofula in England and France*, translated by J.E. Anderson (Routledge & Kegan Paul, 1973); Uli Linke, *German Bodies, Race and Representation After Hitler* (Routledge, 1999) George Mosse, *The Image of Man: The Creation of Modern Masculinity* (Oxford University Press, 1996); Catherine Gallagher and Thomas Laqueur, eds, *The Making of the Modern Body: Sexuality and Society in the Nineteenth Century* (University of California Press, 1987); Eric Naiman, *Sex in Public: Early Soviet Ideology: The Incarnation of Early Soviet Ideology* (Princeton University Press, 1997); David G. Horn, *Social Bodies: Science, Reproduction, and Italian Modernity* (Princeton University Press, 1994); for a broader historical perspective, see Philippe Ariès and Georges Duby, eds, *A History of Private Life,* translated by Arthur Goldhammer, vols 1–5 (Belknap Press, 1987–1991).
35. Linke, *German Bodies*; Mosse, *The Image of Man*.
36. Thomas Laqueur, *Making Sex: Body and Gender from the Greeks to Freud* (Harvard University Press, 1990); Linke, *German Bodies*; Cornelie Usbourne, *The Politics of the Body in Weimar Germany: Women's Reproductive Rights and Duties* (University of Michigan Press, 1992); Atina Grossmann, *Reforming Sex: The German Movement for Birth Control and Abortion Reform, 1920–1950* (Oxford University Press, 1995); for a quick study on the struggle between science and individuals for body, see Michel Foucault, *The History of Sexuality: An Introduction*, translated by Robert Hurley (Vintage Books, 1990).
37. Naiman, *Sex in Public*.
38. Kathleen Canning, 'The Body as Method? Reflections on the Place of the Body in Gender History,' in *Gender & History* 11 (November 1999), pp. 500–13.
39. Laqueur, *Making Sex*; Foucault, *History of Sexuality*; Peter Gay, *The Bourgeois Experience: Victoria to Freud*, vol. 1, *Education of the Senses* (Oxford University Press, 1984), and vol. 2, *The Tender Passion* (Oxford University Press, 1986); and George Mosse, *Nationalism and Sexuality: Respectability and Abnormal Sexuality in Modern Europe* (Howard Fertig, 1985).
40. Berg, *Wahrheit*, p. 3. On sport culture, see Horst Überhorst, *Vergangen nicht vergessen: Sportkultur im deutschen Osten und im Südentland von den Anfängen bis 1945* (Droste Verlag, 1992); on Olympics, politics and bodies see, Thomas Alkemeyer, *Körper, Kult und Politik: Von der 'Muskelreligion' Pierre de Coubertins zur Inzenierung von Macht in den Olympischen Spielen von 1936* (Campus Verlag, 1996).

41. Michael Hau, *The Cult of Health and Beauty in Germany: A Social History, 1890–1930* (University of Chicago, 2003); Paul Weindling, *Health, Race and German Politics Between National Unification and Nazism, 1870–1945* (Cambridge University Press, 1989); Chad Ross, 'Building a Better Body: Nudism, Society, Race and the German Nation, 1890–1950,' Ph.D. diss., University of Missouri, 2003, especially chapter 1.
42. Berg, *Wahrheit*, p. 3; Eric Hobsbawm, *The Age of Empire: 1875–1914* (Vintage Books, 1987), pp. 206–7 offers a brief description; Peter Gay, *The Tender Passion*, especially chapter 2; Ann Goldberg, *Sex, Religion and the Making of Modern Madness: The Eberbach Asylum and German Society, 1815–1849* (Oxford University Press, 1999) is a good, recent study, see especially pages 85–189.
43. Franz Kinskofer, 'Das Ethos der Nacktheit,' in Berg, *Wahrheit*, p. 5.
44. The question of how fundamental the idea of wholeness was to nudism as either a structural or a critical formulation is left ambiguous by Michael Grisko, 'Freikörperkultur und Lebenswelt- Eine Einleitung,' in Michael Grisko, ed., *Freikörperkultur und Lebenswelt: Studien zur Vor – und Frühgeschichte der Freikörperkultur in Deutschland* (Kassel University Press, 1999), p. 9.
45. Therese Mühlhause-Vogeler, *Freie Lebensgestaltung: Ein Beitrag zur Neuformung des Lebens-Stiles* (Robert Laurer Verlag, 1926), p. 5.
46. Anonymous, *Freiheit dem Leibe!: Eine zeitgemäße Studie zur Förderung der Lichtbewegung Eltern und Erziehern dargeboten* (Dieck and Co. Verlag, 1927), p. 10.
47. Mosse, *Nationalism and Sexuality*, pp. 48–58.
48. Weide, *Verjüngung absolut*, p. 26.
49. Seber, 'Die kulturellen Grundlagen,' p. 23.
50. Renatus, 'Körper und Geist,' pp. 528–35.
51. Kinskofer, 'Das Ethos der Nacktheit,' p. 7.
52. Reissner, 'Die hygienische Notwendigkeit,' p. 30.
53. Vahle, *Zielskisse*, p. 8.
54. Magnus Weidemann, *Wege zur Freude: Gesammelte Aufsätze und Bilder* (Robert Laurer Verlag, 1926), pp. 73–74.
55. Surén, *Der Mensch*, p. 3.
56. Seitz, *Ein Buch*, p. 23.
57. Schulte, *Leibesübungen*, p. 45.
58. Magnus Weidemann, *Deutsches Baden: Ein Führer zur Freude, Schönheit und Gesundheit* (Robert Laurer Verlag, 1926), p. 21.
59. Heitsch, *Lebensfreude*, p. 17.
60. Seitz, *Ein Buch*, 1925, p. 9.
61. Vahle, *Zielskisse*, p. 10.

62. *Figaro*, 'Das Bild,' Heft 1 (1928), p. 48.
63. Mühlhause-Vogeler, *Freie Lebensgestaltung*, p. 16.
64. Alfred Kurella, 'Körperseele/Drei Briefe,' in *Der Leib Urania*, Heft 1 (1924), pp. 32–3.
65. Krabbe, *Gesellschaftsveränderung*; John A. Williams, 'Giving Nature a Higher Purpose: Back-To-Nature Movements in Weimar Germany, 1918–1933,' Ph.D. diss., University of Michigan, 1996.
66. Giselher Spitzer, *Der deutsche Naturismus: Idee und Entwicklung einer volkserzieherischen Bewegung im Schnittfeld von Lebensreform, Sport und Politik* (Verlag Ingrid Czwalina, 1983).
67. Georg Pfitzer, *Der Naturismus in Deutschland, Österreich und die Schweiz*, Band 1 (Richard Danehl's Verlag, 1964); Karl Toepfer, *Empire of Ecstasy: Nudity and Movement in Weimar German Body Culture, 1910–1935* (University of California Press, 1997).
68. Toepfer, *Empire*; Wilfried van der Will, 'The Body and the Body Politic as Symptom and Metaphor in the Transition of German Culture to National Socialism,' in Brandon Taylor and Wilfried van der Will, eds, *The Nazification of Art: Art, Design, Music, Architecture and Film in the Third Reich* (Winchester Press, 1990), pp. 14–52; Michael Andritzky and Thomas Rautenberg, eds, *'Wir sind nackt und nennen uns "Du" . . .': Von Lichtfreunden und Sonnenkämpfern, eine Geschichte der Freikörperkultur* (Annabas Verlag Günther Kämpf KG, 1989).
69. Ulf Ziegler, *Nackt unter Nackten: Utopien der Nacktkultur, 1906–1942* (Verlag Dirk Nishen, 1990).
70. Oliver König, *Nacktheit: Soziale Normierung und Moral* (Westdeutscher Verlag, 1990).
71. Surén, *Der Mensch*, p. 54.
72. Therese Mühlhause-Vogeler, 'Neues Leben durch Freikörperkultur,' in *Lachendes Leben*, Heft 12 (1930), p. 2.
73. Jefferson Selth's bibliography, *Alternative Lifestyles: A Guide to Research Collections on Intentional Communities, Nudism and Sexual Freedom* (Greenwood Press, 1985), for example, includes the practice of nudism with those who participated in sexual experimentation, swinging and such; this is an inclusion many nudists would object to as it perpetuates a sexual stereotype many in the movement seek to avoid.

Chapter 1 Nudism and Nudists

1. BA-B R1501/110964, 'Das Badewesen 1 January 1907–31 December 1918.'
2. To give just a few examples, Christopher Isherwood, *Goodbye to Berlin* (Hogarth Press, 1940); Graf Harry Kessler, *Tagebücher 1918–1937*, edited by

Wolfgang Pfeiffer-Belli (Im Insel-Verlag, 1961); Otto Friederich, *Before the Deluge: A Portrait of Berlin in the 1920s* (HarperCollins, 1995); and a very important study, Peter Jelavich, *Berlin Cabaret* (Harvard University Press, 1993).
3. Dr Hans Vahle, *Zielskisse der Freikörperkultur: Ein Leitfaden für Leibeszucht und gesundes Leben* (Polverlag, 1932), p. 10.
4. Charly Sträßer, 'Neutzeitliche Freikörperkultur,' in *Sonniges-Land*, Heft 7 (1931), p. 77.
5. Charly Sträßer, 'Der neue Kurs,' in *Das Freibad*, Heft 5 (1931), p. 81.
6. For the record, Pudor did always claim that nudism was his idea first, and he accused Ungewitter of stealing it to make a fortune. It is highly likely that Ungewitter did in fact establish the first nudist organization to have branches in every part of Germany, first as the Loge des aufsteigenden Lebens, later the Treubund für a. L. On the accusation and the 'evidence' see, Dr Heinrich Pudor, Anhang in *Nacktkultur, Zweites Bändchen: Kleid und Geschlecht; Bein und Becken* (H. Pudor Verlag, 1906).
7. The name change occurred just after or during the waning days of the First World War. Ungewitter does not explain why he chose to change the name. The *Treubund* rather than the *Loge* appears in the 1920 edition of *Nackt: Eine kritische Studie* (Verlag Richard Ungewitter, 1909), which was published originally in 1909; it does not appear in the 1911 edition.
8. Ungewitter, *Nackt*, p. 113.
9. Seitz, *Ein Buch*, p. 130.
10. No Author, '25 Jahre Freikörperkultur,' in *Das Freibad*, Heft 6 (1929), p. 102; M.A. Brünner, 'Nacktsport-Vereinigungen einst und jetzt,' in *Das Freibad*, Heft 4 (1931), pp. 61–2.
11. No Author, '25 Jahre Freikörperkultur,' in *Das Freibad*, Heft 6, pp. 102–3.
12. Ibid., pp. 61–2.
13. Brünner, 'Nacktsport-Vereinigungen einst und jetzt,' pp. 62–4. See also Seitz, *Ein Buch*, pp. 127–30.
14. Wilhelm Kästner, *Kampf der Lichtfreunde gegen die Dunkelmänner* (Verlag W. Kästner 1910), pp. 8 and 84.
15. No Author, '25 Jahre Freikörperkultur,' p. 103.
16. Brünner, 'Nacktsport-Vereinigungen einst und jetzt,' p. 64.
17. No Author, '25 Jahre Freikörperkultur,' p. 103.
18. Hugo Peters, ed., *Revolution und Nacktkultur* (Verlag der Schönheit, 1919), p. 11; Seitz, *Ein Buch*, p. 131; on the latter date, see, Sträßer, 'Der neue Kurs,' p. 81.
19. Dr Heinrich Pudor, *Katechismus der Nackt-Kultur: Leitfaden für Sonnenbäder und Nacktpflege* (H. Pudor Verlag, 1906), pp. 23–31. Gröttrup called it a *Volksbewegung*, literally a People's movement. Bernhard Gröttrup,

'Ich-die Idee-und Herr Laurer: Erinnerungen-Mehr Ueberzeugungstrue zu unseren Idealen-Mehr Mißtrauen gegen die Geschaftlhuber in der Bewegung,' in *Figaro*, Heft 22 (1929), pp. 820–1.
20. Fritz Dittmar, 'Der große Tag,' in *Das Freibad*, Heft 3 (1931), pp. 44 and 50.
21. Seitz, *Ein Buch*; Erich Maria Remarque, *Im Westen Nichts Neues* (Propyläenverlag, 1929), supports this.
22. Richard Ungewitter, *Nacktheit und Aufstieg: Ziele zur Erneuerung des deutschen Volkes* (Verlag Richard Ungewitter, 1920), p. 48.
23. KaE, A2 1220 'Sittenpolizei. Nacktkultur. anstössige Kleidung usw. Allgemeines, 1925–1944,' Abscrift from Bischof Keppler 15 July 1925.
24. *Gemeindelexicon für den Freistaat Preußen, Band I Provinz Ostpreußen* 'Verlag des Preußischen Statischen Landesamts, 1931'.
25. EZA-B 7 Nr 3813 answers to Rundfrage 27 August 1932.
26. Walter Heitsch, *Freikörperkultur Lebensfreude: Ein Führer zu Freude, Schönheit und Gesundheit* (Robert Laurer Verlag, 1932), p. 8.
27. Heitsch, *Freikörperkultur*, 1932, pp. 8–9.
28. EZA-B 7 Nr 3813 answers to Rundfrage, 17 February 1932.
29. Ibid., 1 February 1932.
30. Ibid., 30 January 1932.
31. Ibid., 30 January 1932.
32. Ibid., 27 August 1932.
33. Magnus Weidemann, *Deutsches Baden: Ein Führer zur Freude, Schönheit und Gesundheit* (Robert Laurer Verlag, 1926), p. 25.
34. *Sonnenland*, Heft 1 (1930); *Figaro*, Heft 14 (1928), p. 452; *Figaro*, 'Freikörperkultur-Strand im Seebad Heringsdorf,' Heft 10 [1930], pp. 365–6.
35. Heitsch, *Freikörperkultur*, 1932, p. 9.
36. J.M. Seitz, *Die Nacktkulturbewegung: Ein Buch für Wissende und Unwissende* (Verlag der Schönheit, 1925), p. 106; Seitz, Ein Buch, p. 135.
37. On Fuchs see, Seitz, *Ein Buch*, 1925, p. 106; all else Seitz, *Ein Buch*, pp. 133–4; Hans Surén, *Der Mensch und die Sonne* (Dieck and Co., 1924), pp. 76–7.
38. Walter Heitsch, *Freikörperkultur-Lebensfreude* (Robert Laurer Verlag, 1925), p. 9. Toepfer *Empire of Ecstasy: Nudity and Movement in Weimar German Body Culture, 1910–1935* (University of California Press, 1997*)*, gives a good list, though it is not clear if all listed are nudist magazines or just those that feature naked photos.
39. BLHA Rep 30 Berlin C Title 121, Nr 17130, Prüfstelle Berlin für Schund und Schmutzschriften, 10 April 1928, p. 1.
40. BLHA Rep 30 Berlin C Title 121, Nr 17050, Prüfstelle Berlin für Schund und Schmutzschriften, 22 May 1928.
41. Ibid.

42. Felix Holländer, *Wege zu Kraft und Schönheit*, film book for *Wege zu Kraft und Schönheit: Ein Film über modernen Körperkultur in sechs Teilen*, directed by Wilhelm Prager ([n.p.'n.d.]).
43. Heitsch, *Freikörperkultur*, p. 5; on *Sonnenkinder* see *Der Leib Urania* Heft 9 (1925), p. 285. Ungewitter regarded *Sonnenkinder* as the crown jewel of nudist propaganda. In Richard Ungewitter *Nacktheit und Moral: Wege zur Rettung des deutschen Volkes* (Verlag Richard Ungewitter, 1925), pp. 9–10.
44. No Author, 'Kritik an dem Bericht über den Internationalen Kongreß der Freikörperkultur in Dornzhausen im August Heft des *Freibad*,' in *Das Freibad*, Heft 11 (1930), p. 215.
45. Fred Look, 'Wie denken Sie über die Nacktkultur?', in *Figaro*, Heft 1 (1933), pp. 10–12.
46. Seitz, *Ein Buch*, pp. 139–40; Heitsch, *Lebensfreude*, pp. 34–5.
47. Heitsch *Lebensfreude*, p. 34.
48. Seitz, *Ein Buch*, p. 6.
49. Seitz, *Ein Buch*, 1925, pp. 107–8.
50. Heitsch, *Freikörperkultur*, 1932, p. 39.
51. Vahle, *Zielskisse*, pp. 35–6; Heitsch, *Freikörperkultur*, 1932, p. 39–48; A.E. Beck, 'Zusammenschluß is not! Ein Arbeitsausschuß deutscher Freikörperkultur-Verbände,' in *Sonnenland*, Heft 2 (1930), pp. 1–2; No Author, 'Die Einheitsfront marschiert!' in *Sonnenland*, Heft 2 (1931), p. 33.
52. A. Kirner, 'Der große Plan für die Münchener Freikörperkulturverbände,' in *Das Freibad*, Heft 4 (1930), p. 78.
53. Seitz, *Ein Buch*, pp. 135–6.
54. Brünner, 'Nacktsport-Vereinigungen einst und jetzt,' p. 70.
55. Ibid., p. 64. See also Seitz, *Ein Buch*, pp. 131–2.
56. Seitz, *Ein Buch*, pp. 130–1.
57. Charly Sträßer, ed., *Jugendgelände: Ein Buch von neuen Menschen* (Der Greifenverlag zur Rudolstadt, 1926), pp. 51–3.
58. Ibid., p. 69.
59. Heitsch, *Lebensfreude*, p. 35.
60. Therese Mühlhause-Vogeler, 'Robert Laurer: Der Werber für die Idee der Freikörperkultur,' in *Lachendes Leben*, Heft 10 (1932), pp. 12–13; p. 16.
61. Magnus Weidemann, 'Wichtige Mitteilungen der Schriftenleitung,' in *Die Freude*, Hefte 4–5 (1923), pp. 73–5.
62. Bernhard Hagedorn, 'Tagebuch des *Figaro*,' in *Figaro*, Heft 24 (1931), 1925; Hagedorn, 'Tagebuch des *Figaro*: Tagung der Körperkulturschule Adolf Koch (23 bis 25 November im Preußischen Heerenhaus),' in *Figaro*, Heft 24 (1929), p. 895.
63. No Author, 'Ein Wort zur Aufklärung: Robert Laurer, dem "Geistesgestörten," zur Antwort,' in *Figaro*, Heft 3 (1929), p. 85.

64. Ibid., pp. 85–6.
65. Anton Putz zum Adlersthum, 'Der Weg zum Helotentum in der Freikörperkulturbewegung: Ein trubes Kapitel aus der Geschichte der Bewegung,' in *Figaro*, Heft 17 (1929), pp. 616–22.
66. Bernhard Gröttrup, 'Ich-die Idee-und Herr Laurer,' pp. 819–20; Bernhard Hagedorn, 'Tagebuch des *Figaro*,' in *Figaro*, Heft 1 (1930), pp. 5–6; Bernhard Gröttrup, 'Wiedermal: Herr Laurer,' in *Figaro*, Heft 16 (1931), p. 610; Charly Sträßer, in *Das Freibad*, Heft 7 (1931), pp. 129–30.
67. LaSH Abt. 260 Nr 19594.
68. SSAL PP-V 4475.
69. StaH #136–2/81.
70. Ulrich Linse, 'Sonnenmenschen Unter der Swastika: Die FKK-Bewegung im Dritten Reich,' in Michael Grisko, ed., *Freikörperkultur und Lebenswelt: Studien zur Vor- und Frühgeschichte der Freikörperkultur in Deutschland* (Kassel University Press, 1999), pp. 239–79.
71. SSAL PP-V 4475.
72. BA-B NS Personal file on Richard Ungewitter, Nr 2101 Box 1301 File 14.
73. Pudor's autobiography, *Mein Leben: Kampf gegen die Juda für die arische Rasse* (Dr Heinrich Pudor Verlag, 1939), is an excellent source of information for him.
74. BA-B NS Personal file on Hans Surén Nr 2100 Box 0401 File 06.
75. In *Mario und der Zauberer*, the narrator's little girl changes clothes on an Italian beach, to the consternation of the Italians, whose reaction then dismays the narrator. Thomas Mann, *Two Stories: Unordnung und frühes Leid & Mario und der Zauberer*, edited by William Witte (Rinehart and Company, 1959), p. 59. In Grass's masterpiece, *Die Blechtrommel*, Greff, the grocer, chastises little Oskar for looking at his books that contain photos of naked, well-oiled boys on beaches. Günter Grass, *Die Blechtrommel* (Luchterhand Verlag, 1974), pp. 97–8; Hans Fallada in *Kleiner Mann, was nun?* (Aufbau Verlag, 1994) has the longest and best discussion. Christopher Isherwood's *Goodbye to Berlin*, however, fails to even mention any kind of nudism, which does not mean it was not part of Berlin society while he was there, but he did spend time in affluent as well as working-class areas. Moreover, during his visit to the island of Rueggen in the Baltic, an island like Berlin, known for its nudism, he again mentions nothing. This is curious. Did only Germans take an interest, untoward or prurient, in public nakedness in the Weimar period?

Chapter 2 Pastors, Priests, Nazis and Police: The Moral and Political Campaigns against *Nacktkultur*

1. BLHA Rep 30 Berlin C Title 121, Nr 17050, Prüfstelle Berlin für Schund und Schmutzschriften, 22 May 1928.
2. Adolf Weide, *Verjüngung absolut* (Selbstverlag des Verfassers, 1929) pp. 1–2.
3. Ibid.
4. Ibid., pp. 53–6.
5. Ibid., pp. 16–17.
6. HsaD G 15 Groß-Gerau R 60.
7. Ibid.
8. Ibid.
9. Ibid.
10. Ibid.
11. Jungmann's phrasing, reproduced here, was so vague that in October his superiors had to request clarification of by which 'signs' he determined the man had been 'morally excited,' HsaD G 15 Groß-Gerau R 60.
12. Ibid.
13. Ibid.
14. Adolf Koch, 'Die kulturpolitischen Hintergrunde,' in *Das Freibad*, Heft 8 (1931), p. 136; Richard Ungewitter, *Nacktheit und Moral: Wege zur Rettung des deutschen Volkes* (Verlag Richard Ungewitter, 1925), pp. 14–19.
15. Charly Sträßer, 'Ein Kardinal und acht Bischöfe,' in *Das Freibad*, Heft 10 (1931), pp. 168–70.
16. Dr Hans Graaz, *Nacktkörperkultur* (Verlag der Syndikalist, 1927), pp. 20–1.
17. August Knobling, 'Fkk-Politik von Morgen,' in *Das Freibad*, Heft 11 (1931), pp. 186–9.
18. EZA-B 7 Nr 3810 and 7 Nr 4086 quoted in Mitteilungen of the Arbeitsgemeinschaft für Volksgesundung, e.V. from 25 August 1927.
19. EZA-B 7 Nr 4086 Mitteilungen 25 August 1927.
20. EZA-B 7 Nr 3810 and 7 Nr 4086 Mitteilungen 25 August 1927.
21. Walter Heitsch, *Freikörperkultur Lebensfreude: Ein Führer zu Freude, Schönheit und Gesundheit* (Robert Laurer Verlag, 1932), p. 8.
22. Heitsch, *Freikörperkultur*, 1932, pp. 8–9.
23. No Author, 'Sieg der Freikörperkultur?', in *Das Freibad*, Heft 9 (1929), pp. 161–2.
24. EZA-B 7 Nr 3813 answers to Rundfrage, 30 January 1932.
25. EZA-B 7 Nr 3813 news clipping from *Große Anfrage* Number 8, Berlin 15 June 1932.
26. EZA-B 7 Nr 3813 Mitteilungen for the Arbeitsgemeinschaft für Volksgesundung, e.V. from 9. March 1933. See also *Figaro*, 'Tagebuch des *Figaro*:

Der Zwickel im deutschen Blätterwald,' Heft 21 (1932), pp. 805–7, which reprinted a number of press reactions from all over Germany and from all parties. They universally mocked and derided Dr Bracht for his anachronistic and reactionary, not too mention cruel to the poor and unemployed, rule governing the wearing of bathing costumes. See also, No Author, 'Bracht gegen die Körperkulturschule Adolf Koch!', in *Figaro*, Heft 21 (1932), pp. 809–10; *Figaro*, Heft 17 (1932), p. 766. Hans Vahle also notes that public nakedness is forbidden only in Prussia, in *Zielskisse der Freikörperkultur: Ein Leitfaden für Leibeszucht und gesundes Leben* (Polverlag, 1932), pp. 27–8.

27. Ixmann, 'Die Zwickelkontrolle,' in *Lachendes Leben*, Heft 12 (1933), p. 16.
28. Fred Reith, 'Freikörperkulturprozeß in Danzig,' in *Das Freibad*, Heft 6 (1930), pp. 101–2; Bernhard Hagedorn, 'Tagebuch des *Figaro*: Polizei und Nacktkultur,' in *Figaro*, Heft 9 (1932), pp. 325–6.
29. No Author, 'Freikörperkultur – die Hauptsorge der Polizei,' in *Figaro*, Heft 24 (1932), p. 925.
30. Dr Warneyer, 'Ist Betätigung des Nacktsports ein Ehescheidungsgrund?', in *Figaro*, Heft 10 (1929), pp. 369–71.
31. EZA-B 7 Nr 3812 excerpt from *Vorwärts*, 2 February 1931.
32. Warneyer, 'Betätigung,' pp. 369–71.
33. EZA-B 7 Nr 3809, 'Die öffentliche Sittlichkeit und die Verschärfung der Strafbestimmungen bei Vergehen gegen dieselbe, May 1925–December 1926.' Letter from Deutscher e.V. Leherinnen in Barmen to Generalsynode der evangelischen Landeskirche Preußens in Berlin from 29 November 1925.
34. EZA-B 7 Nr 3810 Mitteilungen of the Arbeitsgemeinschaft für Volksgesundung, e.V. from 25 August 1927.
35. EZA-B 7 Nr 3811 'Die öffentliche Sittlichkeit und die Verschärfung der Strafbestimmungen bei Vergehen gegen die dieselbe, January 1928–April 1929' and 7–4087.
36. EZA-B 7 Nr 3810 and 7 Nr 4086 Mitteilungen of the Arbeitsgemeinschaft für Volksgesundung, e.V. from 25 August 1927.
37. EZA-B 7 Nr 3811 'Die öffentliche Sittlichkeit und die Verschärfung der Strafbestimmungen bei Vergehen gegen die dieselbe, January 1928–April 1929' and 7–4087 'Die Arbeitsgemeinschaft für Volksgesundung, e.V., August 1928–December 1929,' Mitteilungen of the Arbeitsgemeinschaft für Volksgesundung, e.V. from 15 August 1928.
38. Ibid.
39. EZA-B 7 Nr 3810 and 7 Nr 4086 Mitteilungen 25 August 1927.
40. EZA-B 7 Nr 3810 and Nr 4086 Mitteilungen of the Arbeitsgemeinschaft für Volksgesundung, e.V. from 25 August 1927.
41. EZA-B 1/A2/164 Mitteilungen für Leiter von Ortsgruppen des Weißen Krezes.

42. EZA-B 1/A2/162 'Sittlichkeitsbestrebungen. Bekämpfung der Geschlechtskrankheiten von August 1908 bis 1920.'
43. EZA-B 7 Nr 3808 'Die öffentliche Sittlichkeit und die Verschärfung der Strafbestimmungen bei Vergehen gegen die dieselbe, January 1920–April 1925.'
44. Peter Jelavich, *Berlin Cabaret* (Harvard University Press, 1993).
45. Richard Ungewitter, *Nacktheit und Aufstieg: Ziele zur Erneuerung des deutschen Volkes* (Verlag Richard Ungewitter, 1920), pp. 1–2.
46. Richard Ungewitter, *Nacktheit und Kultur: Neue Forderung* (Verlag von Richard Ungewitter, 1913), p. 1.
47. Richard Ungewitter, *Kultur und Nacktheit: Eine Forderung* (Verlag Richard Ungewitter, 1911), pp. 5–8.
48. Ungewitter, *Nacktheit und Kultur*, pp. III-15.
49. Michael C. Hurley, 'A Comparative Study of the Legal Response to Public, Social Nudity in the United States and West Germany,' unpublished paper, Saint Louis School of Law: 1983, p. 39. This distinction between non-sexual and sexual nudity, although acknowledged in principle, is fundamentally absent from American jurisprudence in practice. One student of law suggests that German courts have been more 'reluctant to imbue popular prejudice with the force of law.' This argument is only believable if one ignores the very real and deadly consequences of the enshrinement into law of popular prejudices against Jews, Gypsies, communists to name only a very few groups, during the 1930s.
50. EZA-B 7 Nr 4086 'Die Volksgemeinschaft zur Wahrung, von Anstand und guter Sitte, July 1920–July 1928,' #9. See also Mitteilungen 15 July, 1927, #13.
51. EZA-B 7 Nr 3841 Sittlichkeit 1888–1918.
52. EZA-B 1/A2/164 memo to Protestant Church committee from 1925 March 1925.
53. EZA-B 7 Nr 4086 'Die Volksgemeinschaft zur Wahrung, von Anstand und guter Sitte, July 1920–July 1928,' pp. 1–2.
54. EZA-B 7 Nr 4086 #30.
55. EZA-B 7 Nr 4087 15 October 1928.
56. Ibid.
57. BLHA Rep 30 Berlin C Polizeipresidium Title 121 Nr 16990.
58. BLHA Rep 30 Berlin C Polizeipresidium Title 121 Nr 16945.
59. EZA-B 7 Nr 3813 Fritz Weigt, 'Hat das Gesetz gegen die Schund und Schmutzliteratur bisher versagt?'
60. BLHA Rep 30 Berlin C Title 121, Nrs 17040, 17001.
61. BLHA Rep 30 Berlin C Title 121, Nr 17130, Prüfstelle Berlin für Schund und Schmutzschriften, 10 April 1928, p. 1.
62. Ibid.

63. Ibid., p. 2.
64. BLHA Rep 30 Berlin C Title 121, Nr 17040, Niederschrift, 8 May 1928, p. 36.
65. BLHA Rep 30 Berlin C Title 121, Nr 17050, Prüfstelle Berlin für Schund und Schmutzschriften, 22 May 1928.
66. BLHA Rep 30 Berlin C Title 121, Nr 17130, Oberprüfstelle Leipzig für Schund und Schmutzschriften, 22 August 1928, Niederschrift, pp. 6–8.
67. Ulrich Linse, 'Sonnenmenschen Unter der Swastika: Die FKK-Bewegung im Dritten Reich,' in Michael Grisko, ed., *Freikörperkultur und Lebenswelt Studien zur Vor – und Frühgeschichte der Freikörperkultur in Deutschland* (Kassel University Press, 1999), pp. 239–79.
68. StaH 136–2/81 Abschrift. On Frick see, SSAL PP-V 4475 'Vereinigung für neuzeitliche und gesunde Lebensgestaltung, ab 1935 Bund für Leibeszucht e.V., Sitz Leipzig, 1931–1943' Abschrift: Bekämpfung der Nacktkulturbewegung.
69. StaH 136–2/81 Abschrift.
70. Ibid.
71. Ibid.
72. Ibid.
73. StaH 614–1/11 'Mitgliedschaft im Reichsverband für Freikörperkultur, Sitz Berlin, 1932–1933,' Sonderrundschreiben Nr 3b/33 from 10 March 1933.
74. StaH 614–1/12 'Mitgliedschaft im the Kampfring für völkische Körperkultur, Sitz Berlin, 1933,' Rundschreiben 1/33, 15 May 1933.
75. NSHaH 403 Memorandum from Karl Bückmann from 8 January 1934.
76. BA-B R1501 Nr 126337 letter from Karl Bückmann to Heß, Dr Lammers, Dr Wagner and Minister Darré from 27 Februar 1934.
77. TSAG Thüringisches Kreisamt Schleiz Nr 329, fol 88. Memo from Thuringian Ministry of Interior to Polizeiverwaltungen from 17 January 1934.
78. IFB File 150–200 letter to Karwilli Damm from Deutscher Bund für Körperkultur from 8 August 1940.
79. BA-B, R1501 Nr 126337, 'Stellungnahme zur Freikörperkultur vom 22. Februar 1934.'
80. NSHaH Hann 180 Lün. III.XVI Nr 396. Report to Preuss. Minister des Innern from 4 May 1933.
81. NSHaH Hann 180 Lün. III.XVI Nr 396. Numerous reports, telegrams.
82. NSHaH Hann 180 Lün. III.XVI Nr 396. Report from Landkreis Harburg to Regierungspräsident in Lüneburg from 14 July 1935.
83. StaH 614–1/11 Fritz Schorn 'Bericht über einen Besuch bei der Polizeibehörde' from 27 November 1933. In an earlier version of his report to the Kampfring, Schorn says that he was told that membership in the 'Arbeitersportkartell was beside the point, for the *Nacktkultur* league as such has been

banned.' 23 November 1933 in 'Bericht über Verhandlungen bei der Polizeibehörde.'
84. StaH 614–1/12. Both of these reports also appear in StaH 614–1/1. StaH 136–2/81 Entwurf of 31 August 1937.
85. NrWHSA Regierung Aachen 23719 decree from Reichs – und Preußisches Minister des Innern from 8 July 1935.
86. Homosexuality appears to have been understood by the Nazis to mean men only; lesbians were not recognized and persecuted as homosexuals. On this see, Claudia Schoppmann, 'National Socialist Policies Towards Female Homosexuality,' translated by Elizabeth Harvey in Lynn Abrams and Elizabeth Harvey, *Gender Relations in German History: Power, Agency and Experience from the Sixteenth Century to the Twentieth Century* (Duke University Press, 1997), pp. 177–86. For persecution of homosexuals in the Third Reich, an important introduction is Geoffrey Giles, 'The Institutionalization of Homosexual Panic in the Third Reich,' in Robert Gelately and Nathan Stoltzfus, eds, *Social Outsiders in Nazi Germany* (Princeton University Press, 2001), pp. 233–50.
87. The other three were Schönburger Jugendgeländebund, the Verein für Lebensreform, and the Communist Party's Wochendverein Sonne. This cited from SSAL PP-V 4457 'Freikörperkulturbund in Leipzig, e.V. 1926–1940.'
88. As late as 1940 the BfL was still being reminded by the city of Leipzig that its members could not be nude while swimming in its own grounds. SSAL PP-V 4475 letter from Stadt Leipzig to BfL from 8 January 1940.
89. SSAL PP-V 4492 Gestapo report from 22 April 1937; Aufstellung from Georg Fischer from 1933.
90. StaH 614–1/1 'Allgemeine Verwaltungsgelegenheiten 1921–1933,' Abschrift from Kamfpring für völkische Freikörperkultur, Bezirk Groß-Hamburg from 14 Novermber 1933.
91. Heß's position is quoted in BA-B R1501 Nr 126337, 'Stellungnahme zur Freikörperkultur vom 22. Februar 1934,' p. 5.
92. BLHA Rep 30 Berlin C Title 148B 'Vereine' Nr 782, pp. 5–6; pp. 10–11.
93. On his role see Robert Proctor, *Racial Hygiene: Medicine Under the Nazis* (Harvard University Press, 1988). For quote see LaSH Abt. 260 Nr 19594.
94. LaSH Abt. 260 Nr 19594.
95. von Tschammer und Osten was appointed to his position in April 1933. BA-B Schneider, '*Reichssportführer* Tschammer und Osten' Zeitungsdienst Berlin 26 March 1943 gives the appointment date as 28 April 1933. Hans Borowik on the other hand gives the date as 29 April 1933 in BA-B Zeitungsdienst.
96. BA-B R1501 Nr 126337, 'Stellungnahme zur Freikörperkultur vom 22. Februar 1934,' p. 5.

97. Ibid.
98. The request to local police was issued on 9 March 1937 for BLS and Liso. For BLS see SSAL PP-V 4492 letter from Dresden Gestapo to Leipzig Gestapo, for Liso see SSAL PP-V 4494, 4378 letter from Dresden Gestapo to Leipzig Gestapo.
99. For BLS see SSAL PP-V 4492 report from Leipzig Gestapo to Dresden Gestapo from 22 April 1937; for Liso see report from Leipzig Gestapo to Dresden Gestapo from 29 April 1937.
100. NSHaH Hann. 180 Lün. III.XVI Nr 396 'Bekämpfung der Nacktkulturbewegung, 1933–1935,' report to Regierungspräsident in Lüneburg from 10 July 1939, p. 87
101. BA-Be NS 19 1152 report to Reichsführer SS persönlicher Stab, 25 May 1939.
102. NSHaH Hann. 180 Lün. III.XVI Nr 396 from 3 June 1939.
103. Ibid.
104. BA-B NS 19 1152 report to Reichsführer SS persönlicher Stab, 25 May 1939.
105. Ibid.
106. Ibid. Unfortunately this file ends here, and no clue is given as to why Himmler wanted to view the film, to his reaction upon seeing it or even if he actually viewed it.
107. StaH 136-2/81 letter from Hamburg representation in Berlin to Senator Richter from 4 March 1938.
108. SSAL PP-V 4475 request from SD to Leipzig Gestapo from 14 January 1943.
109. This impression is especially strong in Michael Andritzky and Thomas Rautenberg, eds, *'Wir sind nackt und nennen uns "Du" ...': Von Lichtfreunden und Sonnenkämpfern, eine Geschichte der Freikörperkultur* (Annabas Verlag Günther Kämpf KG, 1989); other works include: Elena-Maria Calvo, 'Die Nacktkultur-Bewegung – historische Entwicklung und ideologische Grundlagen,' unpublished thesis, Universität Tübingen, 1981; Fabian Krüger, 'Die Lebensreform-Bewegung und Naturismus in Göttingen: Die wechselvolle Entwicklung der organisierten Freikörperkultur in der Weimarer Zeit und im Nationalsozialismus,' unpublished thesis (Universität Göttingen: 1999; Georg Pfitzer, *Der Naturismus in Deutschland, Österreich und die Schweiz*, Band 1 (Richard Danehl's Verlag, 1964); Dorothee Ritter, 'Der deutsche Verband für Freikörperkultur als Anschlussorganisation des deutschen Sportbundes,' unpublished thesis, Universität Tübingen, 1986; G. Spitzer, *Der deutsche Naturismus: Idee und Entwicklung einer volkserzieherischen Bewegung im Schnittfeld von Lebensreform, Sport und Politik* (Verlag Ingrid Czwalim, 1983); Simone Tavenrath, *So wundervoll*

sonnengebräunt: kleine Kulturgeschichte des Sonnenbadens (Jonas Verlag, 2000); Ulf Ziegler, *Nackt unter Nackten: Utopien der Nacktkultur, 1906–1942* (Verlag Dirk Nishen, 1990); Hermann Zinn, 'Die deutsche Freikörperkultur als soziale Bewegung,' unpublished thesis, Berlin, 1967.

110. Arnd Krüger, 'Zwischen Sex und Zuchtwahl. Nudismus und Naturismus in Deutschland und Amerika,' in Norbert Finzsch and Hermann Wellenrenther, eds, *Liberalitas: Festschrift für Erich Angermann zum 65. Geburtstag* (Franz Steiner Verlag, 1992), pp. 343–65.
111. W. Krabbe, *Gesellschaftsveränderung durch Lebensreform: Strukturmerkmale einer sozialreformerischen Bewegung in Deutschland der Industrialisierungsperiode* (Vandenhoeck & Rupprecht, 1974).
112. John A. Williams, 'Giving Nature a Higher Purpose: Back-To-Nature Movements in Weimar Germany, 1918–1933,' Ph.D. diss., University of Michigan, 1996, p. 12; pp. 28–56.
113. Wolfgang Pahncke, ed., *Geschichte der Körperkultur: Eine Auswahlbibliographie deutschsprachiger Veröffentlichungen* (Veröffentlichungen der Bibliothek der deutschen Hochschule für Körperkultur, 1967).
114. Gabriele Oettel, 'Freikörperkulturbewegung und Sexualerziehung,' unpublished thesis Universität Münster, 1972; Karl Toepfer, *Empire of Ecstasy: Nudity and Movement in Weimar German Body Culture, 1910–1935* (University of California Press, 1997), see especially pages 30–47, which feature the quotation and his discussion of nudism independently of dance.
115. Michael Grisko, 'Freikörperkultur und Lebenswelt – Eine Einleitung,' in Michael Grisko, ed., *Freikörperkultur und Lebenswelt: Studien zur Vor – und Frühgeschichte der Freikörperkultur in Deutschland* (Kassel University Press, 1999), p. 9.
116. *Die Freikörperkulturbewegung über sich selbst*, a publication of the Deutscher Bund für Freikörperkultur, e.V. (DFK) ([n.p.-n.d.]); see also Karwilli Damm, 'No Title,' *in Adolf Koch: Erinnerungen an einen Menschenfreund*, edited by Irmgard Koch ([n.p.-n.d.]). Another good example is the obituary of Hans Surén by fellow nudist Karwilli Damm in *Fkk: Organ der deutschen Freikörperkultur* (Drückeres J. Hoffman and Co., 1972), p. 110.
117. HsaD G 15 Groß-Gerau R 60, author unknown, 'Nacktkultur in Bayern,' reported in *Hessischer Volksfreund* Nr 43, 30 October 1928.
118. The Koch incident was quite well publicized and well known throughout nudist circles. Reports of it appear in Jay Gay, *On Going Naked* (Garden City Press, 1932), p. 61; Frances and Mason Merrill, *Among the Nudists: The Sincere Experiences of a Young American Couple in the Nudist Centers of Europe* (Garden City Press, 1931), pp. 146–8; in historiography: 'Die Nacktkultur-Bewegung,' p. 38; Bernhard Herrmann, *Arbeiterschaft, Naturheilkunde und der Verband der Volksgesundheit, 1880–1918* (Peter

Lang, 1990), p. 114; Ritter, 'Der deutsche Verband für Freikörperkultur,' p. 39; Toepfer, *Empire*, pp. 35–6; Zinn, 'Die deutsche Freikörperkultur,' p. 29.
119. BA-B R1501 Nr 126337, 'Stellungnahme zur Freikörperkultur vom 22 Februar 1934,' p. 4.
120. Ibid.
121. Koch, 'Die kulturpolitischen Hintergrunde,' pp. 135–6.
122. No Author, in *Deutsch Hellas*, Heft 12, Serie 1 ([n.d.]), p. 190.
123. Ungewitter, *Moral*, p. 86.
124. Examples include the Verein Deutscher Lichtfreunde, situated in Lübeck, LASH Abt. 260 Nr 19594, 'Freikörper – Nacktkulturbewegung: Licht – und Luftbad des Vereins Deutscher Lichtfreunde in Cleverbrück, 1933–1936'; J.M. Seitz, *Die Nacktkulturbewegung: Ein Buch für Wissende und Unwissende* (Verlag der Schönheit, 1925), p. 114.
125. Ungewitter began carrying the swastika as his own emblem as early as 1911, see his magazine *Mitteilungen*. On his reaction to Koch's trouble see Ungewitter, *Moral*, pp. 84–5.
126. Ibid., p. 85.
127. Adolf Koch, 'Gymnastiksystem oder freie Körperbildung,' in *Der Leib Urania*, Heft 1 (1925), p. 32.
128. Hermann, *Arbeiterschaft*, pp. 113–14. In Walter, Denecke and Regin, *Sozialistische Gesundheits – und Lebensreformverbände* (Verlag J.H.W. Dietz, 1991) one gains an altogether different view of Koch's relationship with the VVg; one that is marked less by cooperation and more by coercion. As an umbrella organization it contained groups favoring homeopathy, nutrition and housing reform, among other things.
129. Ibid., p. 46; quote on pp. 77–8.
130. Dr Hans Graaz, 'Der Kulturmensch und die Körperkultur,' in *Der Leib Urania*, Heft 3 (1926), pp. 125–7.
131. Ibid.
132. Elita Simon, 'Das nationale Wohl in den Händen der Frau,' in *Hellas*, Serie 1, Heft 6 ([1907]), p. 93.
133. Graaz, 'Der Kulturmensch und die Körperkultur,' pp. 125–7.
134. This is shown very nicely Williams, 'Giving Nature a Higher Purpose,' pp. 51–2.
135. Alfred Kelly, *The Descent of Darwin: The Popularization of Darwinism in Germany 1860–1914* (University of North Carolina Press, 1981), p. 8.
136. *Volksgemeinschaft* can be a tricky term to translate, largely due to the connotations of the term *Volk*, which by itself means 'people' or 'race.' A *Volksgemeinschaft* can be and often is translated as a 'people's' or a 'national community,' but under the National Socialists the term acquired a racial

connotation, and it thus becomes better to speak of a 'racial community' or 'racial state.' I am forced to agree with Verhey, from whose book I benefited greatly on this concept, that a good etymological investigation of the word is needed. For some literature on various *Volksgemeinschaften* in German history see Michael Burleigh and Wolfgang Wippermann, *The Racial State: Germany 1933–1945* (Cambridge University Press, 1991); Jost Hermand, *Old Dreams of a New Reich: Volkisch Utopias and National Socialism*, translated by Paul Levesque and Stefan Soldovieri (Indiana University Press, 1992); Ian Kershaw *Hitler: 1889–1936 Hubris* (Norton, 1998) has a good discussion of what Hitler envisioned in the term; on its intellectual origins see George Mosse, *The Crisis of German Ideology: Intellectual Origins of the Third Reich* (Grosset & Dunlap, 1964); Hannu Salmi, *Imagined Germany: Richard Wagner's National Utopia* (Peter Lang, 1999); Jeffrey Verhey, *The Spirit of 1914: Militarism, Myth and Mobilization in Germany* (Cambridge University Press, 2000).

137. Verhey, *The Spirit of 1914*, for quote see p. 213.
138. Ibid.; see also, Peter Fritzsche, *Germans into Nazis* (Harvard University Press, 1998).
139. Peter Fisher, *Fantasy and Politics: Visions of the Future in the Weimar Republic* (University of Wisconsin Press, 1991).
140. Magnus Weidemann, *Wege zur Freude. Gesammelte Aufsätze und Bilder* (Robert Laurer Verlag, 1926), p. 32.
141. Robert Laurer, in *Die Freude*, Heft 3 (1923), p. 64.
142. Wolfgang Reichstein, 'Freikörperkultur und Volksgemeinschaft,' in *Deutsche Fkk*, Heft 2 (1933), p. 21.
143. Herman Schmidt, 'Grundsätzliches und Erfahrungen über den Zusammenhang von Freikörperkultur und Gemeinschaftsleben,' in *Der Leib Urania*, Serie 3, Heft 10 (1927), pp. 347–50.
144. Reichstein, 'Freikörperkultur und Volksgemeinschaft,' p. 21.
145. Walther Brauns, *Den Freien der Welt! Bilder aus der Lebensgestaltung neuer Menschen* (Robert Laurer Verlag, 1926), p. 7.
146. Hugo Peters, ed., *Revolution und Nacktkultur* (Verlag der Schönheit, 1919), p. 14.
147. Magnus Weidemann, 'Zum Geleit!', in *Licht-Land*, Folge 1 ([n.d.]), pp. 1–4.
148. Wilhelm Kästner, *Kampf der Lichtfreunde gegen die Dunkelmänner* (Verlag W. Kästner [1910]), p. 11.
149. Walter Heitsch, *Freikörperkultur-Lebensfreude* (Robert Laurer Verlag, 1925), p. 35.
150. Adolf Weide, *Verjüngung absolut*, p. 13.
151. Seitz, *Die Nucktkulturbewegung: Ein Buch für Wissende und Unwissende* (Verlag der Schönheit, 1923), p. 152.

152. Hans Surén, *Mensch und Sonne: Arisch-olympischer Geist* (Verlag Scherl, 1936), p. 116.
153. Seitz, *Ein Buch*, pp. 132–9.
154. C. Almenroeder, 'Minister Darré über die Freikörperkultur,' in *Deutsche-Fkk*, Heft 3 (August, 1933), p. 39.

Chapter 3 Nudism and Medicine

1. For the definitive work on the *Naturheil* movement for the Wilhelmine era, see Cornelia Regin, *Selbsthilfe und Gesundheitspolitik: Die Naturheilbewegung im Kaiserreich, 1889–1914* (Franz Steiner Verlag, 1995).
2. Paul Weindling, *Health, Race and German Politics Between National Unification and Nazism, 1871–1945* (Cambridge University Press, 1989), p. 16; pp. 20–5; see also G. Stollberg, 'Die Naturheilvereine im Deutschen Kaiserreich,' *Archiv für Sozialgeschichte* 28 (1988), pp. 287–305.
3. Ute Frevert, 'The Civilizing Tendency of Hygiene: Working-Class Women under Medical Control in Imperial Germany,' in John C. Fout, ed., *German Women in the Nineteenth Century, a Social History* (Holmes and Meier, 1984), pp. 320–38.
4. Weindling, *Health, Race and German Politics*, pp. 22–4.
5. Richard Ungewitter, *Kultur und Nacktheit: Eine Forderung* (Verlag Richard Ungewitter, 1911), pp. 119–20.
6. Emil Peters, *Menschen in der Sonne: Die Heilkraft des Luft- und Sonnenbades, rationelle Körperpflege durch Luft, Licht und Sonne* (Volkskraft Verlag, [1913]), pp. 22–3.
7. Ungewitter, *Kultur und Nacktheit*, pp. 101–2.
8. Wolfgang Krabbe, 'Naturheilbewegung,' in Diethart Kerbs and Jürgen Reulcke, eds, *Handbuch der deutschen Reformbewegungen, 1880–1933* (Peter Hammer Verlag, 1998), p. 77.
9. Ungewitter, *Kultur und Nacktheit*, p. 82.
10. Richard Ungewitter, *Nackt: Eine kritische Studie* (Verlag Richard Ungewitter, 1909), p. 99.
11. Krabbe, 'Naturheilbewegung,' p. 77.
12. Ibid.
13. On this general discussion see, Karl E. Rothschuh, *Naturheilbewegung, Reformbewegung, Alternativbewegung* (Hippokrates Verlag, 1983), pp. 101–2.
14. Ibid., p. 13; p. 15.
15. Walter Heitsch, *Freikörperkultur-Lebensfreude* (Robert Laurer Verlag, 1925), p. 7.
16. BA-B R1501/110963, 'Das Bäderwesen 22 September 1887–31 December 1906.'

17. Hans Surén, *Mensch und Sonne: Arisch-olympischer Geist* (Verlag Scherl, 1936), pp. 22–3.
18. J.M. Seitz, *Die Nacktkulturbewegung: Ein Buch für Wissende und Unwissende* (Verlag der Schönheit, 1923), p. 65.
19. Dr Heinrich Pudor, *Nacktkultur, Erstes Bändchen: Allgemeines;Fußkultur*, third edition (H. Pudor Verlag, 1906), p. 17.
20. Anne Harrington, *Reenchanted Science: Holism in German Culture from Wilhelm II to Hitler* (Princeton University Press, 1996).
21. Richard Ungewitter, *Nacktheit und Moral: Wege zur Rettung des deutschen Volkes* (Verlag Richard Ungewitter, 1925), p. 73.
22. Ungewitter, *Nackt*, pp. 104–5.
23. Ungewitter, *Kultur und Nacktheit*, pp. 104–5.
24. Dr Hans Vahle, *Zielskisse der Freikörperkultur: Ein Leitfaden für Leibeszucht und gesundes Leben* (Polverlag, 1932), p. 38.
25. Ibid., pp. 8–9.
26. Surén, *Mensch*, p. 18.
27. Ungewitter, *Nackt*, pp. 101–2.
28. Weindling, *Health, Race and German Politics*, p. 16.
29. Richard J. Evans, *Death in Hamburg: Society and Politics in the Cholera Years, 1830–1910* (Clarendon Press, 1987).
30. Ungewitter, *Nackt*, p. 100.
31. Ungewitter, *Kultur und Nacktheit*, p. 101.
32. Ungewitter, *Nackt*, p. 100.
33. Dr med. K. Reissner, 'Die hygenische Notwendigkeit,' in Manfred Berg, ed., *Die Wahrheit um den Körper: Ein Aufruf zur Selbstbesinnung!* (Karl Haug Verlag, 1927), p. 29.
34. Ungewitter, *Nackt*, p. 103.
35. Ungewitter, *Kultur und Nacktheit*, p. 84.
36. Ibid., pp. 105–6.
37. Ungewitter, *Moral*, p. 105.
38. Peters, *Menschen*, p. 62.
39. Ungewitter, *Kultur und Nacktheit*, p. 103
40. Peters, *Menschen*, p. 23.
41. Ibid.
42. Richard Ungewitter, *Nacktheit und Kultur: Neue Forderung* (Verlag von Richard Ungewitter, 1913), p. 73.
43. Ungewitter, *Kultur und Nacktheit*, p. 100.
44. Ungewitter, *Moral*, p. 102.
45. Dr Strassmann, 'Der Wert des Lichtbades vom wissenschaftlichen Standpunkt,' in Wilhelm Kästner, ed., *Nacktsport* (Verlag W. Kästner, [1911]), pp. 5–6.

46. Adolf Weide, *Verjüngung absolut* (Selbstverlag des Verfassers, 1929), p. 65.
47. Hans Wolfgang Behm, *Reigen der Keuschheit* (Robert Laurer Verlag, 1928), pp. 57–9.
48. BA-B NS/5/VI Nr 4776 *Ultraviolette Strahlen und der menschliche Körper* ([n.p.-n.d]). Hans Surén acknowledged this trend as well, noting that Dr A. Bier was recommending sunlight for tuberculosis treatment. See Hans Surén, *Der Mensch und die Sonne* (Dieck and Co., 1924), p. 23.
49. Dr Hans Graaz, *Nacktkörperkultur*. Beiträge zum Sexualproblem, Heft 10, Herausgegeben von Dr Felix A. Theilhaber (Verlag der Syndikalist, 1927), pp. 16–17.
50. Vahle, *Zielskisse*, p. 11.
51. Richard Ungewitter, *Nacktheit und Aufstieg: Ziele zur Erneuerung des deutschen Volkes* (Verlag Richard Ungewitter, 1920), p. 32.
52. Dr Robert Werner Schulte, *Körper-Kultur: Versuch einer Philosophie der Leibesübungen* (Verlag Ernst Rheinhardt, 1928), p. 10.
53. Weide, *Verjüngung absolut*, p. 48.
54. Ibid., p. 11.
55. Ibid., pp. 48–9.
56. BA-B R 1501 Nr 126337, Stellungnahme zur *Freikörperkultur* from Reichsportführer to Reichministerium des Innern, pp. 3–6.
57. BA-BR 1501 Nr 110961 'Unser Ziel,' p. 8.
58. Frevert in 'The Civilizing Tendency of Hygiene' notes that from the 1840s forward the efforts of the medical community focused on generating a greater awareness of hygiene and cleanliness in order to improve health overall, but especially among the lower classes; see pages 323–9. Similarly, Ulla Gosmann, 'Der reinliche Körper,' in Regine Löneke and Ira Spieker, eds, *Reinliche Leiber – Schmutzige Geschäfte: Körperhygiene und Reinlichkeitsvorstellungen in zwei Jahrhunderten* (Wallstein Verlag, 1996) argues that bodily cleanliness was the general theme of nineteenth-century medicalization efforts among the masses. A number of historians have done research on health and hygiene in Germany in the pre-1945 era. For its implications for National Socialist thought and policy see among others, Frevert, 'The Civilizing Tendency of Hygiene'; Weindling, *Health, Race and German Politics* is the most thorough. Also important are Robert Proctor, *Racial Hygiene: Medicine Under the Nazis* (Harvard University Press, 1988) and *The Nazi War on Cancer* (Princeton University Press, 1999); Gosmann, 'Der reinliche Körper'; and finally Ann Schultz and Stefan Gostomczyk show in a local study the policy of cleanliness in action in '"Arbeiter gehören unter die Brause": Öffentliche Brause-und Wannenbäder in Hannover,' in Adelheid von Saldern, ed., *Wochenend und schöner Schein: Freizeit und modernes Leben in den Zwanziger Jahren, das Beispiel Hannover* (Elefanten Press, 1991).

59. This is Paul Weindling's phrase. See Weindling, *Health, Race and German Politics*, pp. 409–10. For a more recent study see Michael Hau, *The Cult of Health and Beauty in Germany: A Social History* (University of Chicago Press, 2003).
60. Weindling, *Health, Race and German Politics*, p. 230; Hau, *Cult*, pp. 107–9 is more thorough; BA-B R 1501/109413 'Reichsgesundheitswoche 1 February 1926–31 May 1926,' p. 148.
61. BA-B R1501 Nr 109412, 'Memo from Prussian Economics Minister, 26 October 1925'; BA-B R1501 Nr 109413 'Reichsgesundheitswoche 1 February 1926–31 May 1926,' p. 28. Similarly, BA-B R1501 Nr 109412; BA-B R1501 Nr 109413 'Reichsgesundheitswoche 1 February 1926–31 May 1926'; BA-B R1501 Nr 109413 'Reichsgesundheitswoche 1 February 1926–31 May 1926'; BA-B R1501 Nr 109412, *Aufruf zur Gesundheitswoche*, p. 21.
62. Popularizing and educating ideas about race were important functions of such exhibitions. See Atina Grossmann, *Reforming Sex: The German Movement for Birth Control and Abortion Reform, 1920–1950* (Oxford University Press, 1995); Michael Hau, *Cult*; and Cornelie Usbourne, *The Politics of the Body in Weimar Germany: Women's Reproductive Rights and Duties* (University of Michigan Press, 1992).
63. BA-B NS/5/VI Nr 4815 'Für Volksgesundheit,' *N.S.K.* Nr 227 28 September 1938.
64. BA-B NS/5/VI Nr 4780 'Dr Gerhard Wagners Wollen.'
65. BA-B NS/5/VI Nr 4780 'Volksgesundheit und Lebensführung' *Deutsches Ärzteblatt* Numbers 29–30, 68 Jahrgang. Berlin, 16, 23 July 1938.
66. BA-B NS/5/VI Nr 4780 'Dr Gerhard Wagners Wollen.'
67. BA-B NS/5/VI Nr 4781 Dr Hördemann 'Zehn Gebote gesunder Lebensführung,' *N.S.K.* Nr 119, 13 August 1939, p. 19.; BA-B NS/5/VI Nr 4776 *Ultraviolette Strahlen und der menschliche Körper*, n.p.-n.d.; BA-B NS/5/VI Nr 4779 Fr Gahl, 'Gesund durch Licht, Luft, Wasser,' *Der Mittlerdeutsche* Nr 50, 20 February 1937.
68. BA-B NS/5/VI Nr 4781 Dr Hördemann 'Zehn Gebote gesunder Lebensführung,' *N.S.K.* Nr 119, 13 August 1939, p. 18.
69. BA-B NS/5/VI Nr 4781, p. 18.
70. Ibid.
71. BA-B R 8034 Nr 462 Hans Surén 'Deutsche Gymnastik,' from the Reichsnährstand Archiv.
72. Ibid.
73. HSSt E 151/53 Bü 186 Memorandum from Gewerbeschulrat K. Maier to Württemburg Innministerium Abt. X, Stuttgart from 17. March, 1941.
74. Ibid.

75. Ibid.
76. BA-B NS/5/VI Nr 4815 'Für Volksgesundheit bestens gesorgt,' *N.S.K.* Nr 227 28 September 1938.
77. BA-B NS/5/VI Nr 4780 'Verbeugen ist besser als Heilen!: Kampf an der Natur erhält Gesund' [c. 1938].
78. Ibid.

Chapter 4 The Healthy Body

1. Ulla Gosmann, 'Der reinliche Körper,' in Regine Löneke and Ira Spieker, eds *Reinliche Leiber- Schmutzige Geschäfte: Körperhygiene und Reinlichkeitsvorstellungen in zwei Jahrhunderten* (Wallstein Verlag, 1996), pp. 89–90.
2. Dr Max Grunewald, 'Hygenische Körperpflege,' in *Das Freibad*, Heft 3 (1929), p. 41.
3. Hans Behm, *Reigen der Keuschheit* (Robert Laurer Verlag, 1928), p. 52. For a quick overview of the differences between *Zivilisation* and *Kultur* in the German context, see Jeffrey Herf, *Reactionary Modernism: Technology, Culture and Politics in Weimar and the Third Reich* (Cambridge University Press, 1984), p. 16.
4. Behm, *Reigen*, p. 52.
5. Dr Heinrich Pudor, *Nacktkultur, drittes Bändchen: Die Probleme des Lebens und der Zeugung* (H. Pudor Verlag, 1907), p. 18.
6. Behm, *Reigen*, p. 49.
7. Dr Hans Graaz, *Nacktkörperkultur*. Beitringe zum Sexualproblem, Heft 10; Herausgegeben von Dr Felix A. Theilhaber (Verlag der Syndikalist, 1927), pp. 13–14.
8. Pudor, *Nacktkultur, drittes Bändchen*, p. 18.
9. On the functions of skin as a gland see, Dr Graaz, 'Wesen der wichtigsten, besten, unbekannte Wirkung des Luft und Sonnenbades,' in Anonymous *Lichthunger-Lichtheil: Die Lebenskrafte der Luft und Sonne, dargestellt von sechszehn Autoren* (Verlag Lebenskunst-Heilkunst, 1924), pp. 19–22.
10. Dr med. K. Reissner, 'Die hygenische Notwendigkeit,' in Manfred Berg, ed., *Die Wahrheit um denkörper: Ein Aufruf zur Selbstbesinnung!* (Karl Haug Verlag, 1927), p. 32.
11. Behm, *Reigen*, p. 52.
12. Hans H. Reinsch, 'Die Sonne als Heilfaktor,' in *Das Freibad*, Heft 1 (1929), p. 1.
13. Anon, 'Warum nackt?', in Wilhelm Kästner *Kampf der Lichtfreunde gegen die Dunkelmänner* (Verlag W. Kästner [1910]), p. 20.
14. Emil Peters, *Menschen in der Sonne: Die Heilkraft des Luft- und*

Sonnenbades, rationelle Körperpflege durch Luft, Licht und Sonne (Volkskraft Verlag [1913]), p. 43.
15. Dr Heinrich Pudor, *Katechismus der Nackt-Kultur: Leitfaden für Sonnenbäder und Nacktpflege* (H. Pudor Verlag, 1906), pp. 10–11.
16. Walter Heitsch, *Freikörperkultur-Lebensfreude* (Robert Laurer Verlag, 1925), pp. 13–14.
17. Behm, *Reigen*, p. 52.
18. Pudor, *Katechismus*, p. 9.
19. Dr Konrad Küster, 'Die Wichtigkeit der Haut,' in Kästner, *Kampf*, pp. 42–3.
20. Pudor, *Katechismus*, pp. 11–12.
21. Küster 'Die Wichtigkeit der Haut,' in Kästner, *Kampf*, pp. 42–3.
22. Richard Ungewitter, *Kultur und Nacktheit: Eine Forderung* (Verlag Richard Ungewitter, 1911), p. 83.
23. Pudor, *Katechismus*, pp. 9–10.
24. Ibid.
25. Reissner, 'Die hygenische Notwendigkeit,' pp. 30–2.
26. Dr med. E. Buchholz, 'Das Luftbad für Herzkranke,' in *Lichthunger*, pp. 37–41.
27. Dr med. Kantorowicz, 'Die allegeneinen Wirkungen des Lichtluftbades,' in *Lichthunger*, p. 14.
28. Anon, 'Warum nackt?', in Kästner, *Kampf*, p. 20.
29. Graaz, 'Wesen der wichtigsten,' p. 18.
30. Peters, *Menschen*, p. 3.
31. J.M. Seitz, *Die Nacktkulturbewegung: Ein Buch für Wissende und Unwissende* (Verlag der Schönheit, 1923), pp. 66–7.
32. Reinsch, 'Die Sonne als Heilfaktor,' p. 1.
33. Seitz, *Ein Buch*, pp. 66–7. For a historical investigation of the origins of the *Sonnenbad* see Rothschuh, *Naturheilbewegung, Reformbewegung, Alternativbewegung* (Hippokrates Verlag, 1983), p. 75; pp. 90–2.
34. Seitz, *Ein Buch*, pp. 66–7.
35. Hans Surén, *Der Mensch und die Sonne* (Dieck and Co., 1924), p. 59.
36. Rothschuh, *Naturheilbewegung*, p. 75.
37. Adolf Weide, *Verjüngung absolut* (Selbstverlag des Verfassers, 1929), pp. 7–12.
38. Peters, *Menschen*, p. 59.
39. Behm, *Reigen*, pp. 57–9.
40. Seitz, *Ein Buch*, pp. 67–9.
41. Dr med. Georg Luda, 'Der Einfluß des Sonnenlichtes auf die Zirkulation und verschiedene Krankheiten,' in Kästner, *Kampf*, pp. 38–42.
42. Peters, *Menschen*, p. 62.
43. Dr Strassmann, 'Der Wert des Lichtbades vom wissenschaftlichen

Standpunkt,' in Wilhelm Kästner, *Nacktsport* (Verlag W. Kästner [1911]), pp. 4–5.
44. Ibid., p. 84.
45. Ibid., p. 61.
46. Graaz, 'Wesen der wichtigsten,' p. 23.
47. Strassmann, 'Der Wert des Lichtbades,' pp. 4–5
48. Kantorowicz, 'Die allegemeinen Wirkungen des Lichtluftbades,' pp. 11–16.
49. Ungewitter, *Kultur und Nacktheit*, p. 99.
50. Richard Ungewitter, *Nacktheit und Aufstieg: Ziele zur Erneuerung des deutschen Volkes* (Verlag Richard Ungewitter, 1920), pp. 31–2.
51. Peters, *Menschen*, p. 62; p. 82.
52. Surén, *Der Mensch*, p. 26.
53. Weide, *Verjüngung absolut*, p. 6.
54. Peters, *Menschen*, p. 82.
55. Surén, *Der Mensch*, p. 38. See also Emil Peters who cautioned those with heart conditions to consult their physicians prior to any *Lichtbad* activity. Peters, *Menschen*, p. 74.
56. *Figaro*, 'Ärztliche Ratschläge für das Sonnenbad,' Heft 11 (1927).
57. Surén, *Der Mensch*, pp. 25–6.
58. Heitsch, *Lebensfreude*, p. 16.
59. Peters, *Menschen*, pp. 80–2; see also Richard Ungewitter, *Nacktheit und Kultur: Nene Forderung* (Verlag von Richard Ungewitter, 1913*)*, pp. 90–1.
60. *Figaro*, 'Ärztliche Ratschläge für das Sonnenbad.'
61. *Lachendes Leben*, Heft 2 (1927).
62. Surén, *Der Mensch*, p. 38.
63. Seitz, *Ein Buch*, pp. 73–4. See also Surén, *Der Mensch*, pp. 19–20.
64. Weide, *Verjüngung absolut*, pp. 4–5.
65. Surén, *Der Mensch*, pp. 38–41.
66. *Figaro*, 'Ärztliche Ratschläge für das Sonnenbad'; see also Surén, *Der Mensch*, pp. 38–41.
67. Surén, *Der Mensch*, pp. 38–41.
68. On these ideas see, *Figaro*, 'Ärztliche Ratschläge für das Sonnenbad.'
69. Ibid.
70. Seitz, *Ein Buch*, p. 71; see also Surén, *Der Mensch*, p. 41.
71. *Figaro*, 'Ärztliche Ratschläge für das Sonnenbad.'
72. Seitz, *Ein Buch*, pp. 73–4.
73. Surén, *Der Mensch*, p. 41.
74. Pudor, *Katechismus*, pp. 34–5.
75. No author, 'Das Luftbad in der Kindererziehung,' in *Der Leib Urania*, Heft 8 (1926), p. 255.
76. Peters, *Menschen*, p. 79.

77. Ibid., p.54.
78. Hans Vahle, *Zielskizze der Freikörperkultur: Ein Leitfaden für Leibeszucht und gesundes Leben* (Polverlag, 1932), p. 13.
79. On these ideas see, Rothschuh, *Naturheilbewegung*, pp. 92–5.
80. Ungewitter, *Kultur und Nacktheit*, p. 85.
81. P. Schirrmeister, 'Wie legen wir Luftbader an?', in *Lichthunger*, pp. 60–4.
82. Richard Ungewitter, *Nackt: Eine kritische Studie* (Verlag Richard Ungewitter, 1909), p. 106.
83. Ungewitter, *Aufstieg*, pp. 66–7.
84. Dr Buchholz, 'Das Luftbad für Herzkranke,' pp. 35–6.
85. Ungewitter, *Nacktheit und Kultur*, pp. 90–1.
86. Peters, *Menschen*, p. 44.
87. Seitz, *Ein Buch*, pp. 73–4.
88. Dr Buchholz 'Das Luftbad für Herzkranke,' 35–9.
89. Dr med. Fr Schönberger, 'Winke für die Benutzung des Luft – und Sonnenbades,' in *Lichthunger*, pp. 24–6; see also Seitz, *Ein Buch*, pp. 73–4.
90. Surén, *Der Mensch*, p. 38.
91. Dr Fehlhauer, 'Luftbad und Nervenleidende,' in *Lichthunger*, pp. 43–4.
92. Pudor, *Katechismus*, p. 36.
93. Ibid.
94. Seitz, *Ein Buch*, pp. 73–4.
95. Schönberger 'Winke für die Benutzung,' pp. 24–6.
96. Hans Surén, 'Gesundheitliche Ratschläge für das Verhalten im Licht-, Luft-, und Sonnenbad,' in Surén, *Der Mensch*, p. 38.
97. Schönberger, 'Winke für die Benutzung,' pp. 26–7.
98. Surén, 'Gesundheitliche Ratschläge,' p. 38.
99. Fehlhauer, 'Luftbad und Nervenleide,' pp. 41–3.
100. Peters, *Menschen*, p. 43.
101. Schönberger, 'Winke für die Benutzung,' pp. 26–7.
102. Weide, *Verjüngung absolut*, pp. 46–7; p. 26.
103. Pudor, *Katechismus*, p. 36.
104. Seitz, *Ein Buch*, pp. 65–6.
105. Peters, *Menschen*, pp. 47–53.
106. Ibid., pp. 27–30.
107. Ibid., p. 53.
108. K. Finckh, 'Wie ich mich abhärtete,' in *Lichthunger*, pp. 50–4.
109. Peters, *Menschen*, p. 54.
110. Carl Buttenstedt, 'Was fehlt uns der Gesundheitpflege?', in Kästner, *Kampf*, p. 35.
111. Kantorowicz, 'Die allegeneinen Wirkungen des Lichtlnftbades,' p. 11.
112. Peters, *Menschen*, pp. 63–4.

113. Dr Buchholz, 'Das Luftbad für Herzkranke,' p. 39.
114. K. Finckh, 'Wie ich mich abhärtete,' pp. 50–4.
115. Peters, *Menschen*, pp. 33–41.
116. Ungewitter, *Kultur und Nacktheit*, p. 85.
117. Prof. Kreuzberg, 'Ein Erfolg des Luftbades,' in *Lichthunger*, pp. 48–50.
118. Graaz, 'Der Großstädter und das Luft- und Sonnenbad,' in *Lichthunger*, pp. 57–9; Ungewitter, *Kultur und Nacktheit*, p. 85.
119. Klara Muche, 'Luftbad und Sittlichkeit,' in *Lichthunger*, p. 47.

Chapter 5 The Beautiful Body

1. Franz Weschke, 'Erziehung zum Schönheitserkennen,' in *Licht-Luft-Leben* supplement to *Die Schönheit*, Heft 6 ([1919]), p. 81.
2. Anton Putz zum Adlersthum, 'Schönheit und praktische Nacktkultur,' in *Lachendes Leben*, Heft 5 (1927), p. 12.
3. Hans Vahle, *Zielskisse der Freikörperkultur: Ein Leitfaden für Leibeszucht und gesundes Leben* (Polverlag, 1932), p. 7.
4. Fritz Thies quoted in Walter Heitsch, *Freikörperkultur-Lebensfreude* (Robert Laurer Verlag, 1925), p. 11.
5. Hubert Rieck, 'Nacktheit als Kulturankläger,' in *Das Freibad*, Heft 6 (1931), p. 108.
6. James C. Albisetti, *Secondary School Reform in Imperial Germany* (Princeton University Press, 1983), pp. 16–35.
7. Suzanne Marchand, *Down From Olympus: Archeology and Philhellenism in Germany, 1750–1970* (Princeton University Press, 1996), especially pages 341–75. On its usefulness for the twentieth century, see Albisetti, *Secondary School*, pp. 3–15; pp. 59–118.
8. Marchand, *Down From Olympus*, pp. 7–16; see also Josef Chytry, *The Aesthetic State: A Quest in Modern German Thought* (University of California Press, 1989), pp. 11–37.
9. Hannu Salmi, *Imagined Germany: Richard Wagner's National Utopia* (Peter Lang, 1999), pp. 69–76.
10. Chytry, *The Aesthetic State*.
11. Professor Lux, 'Moral and Nacktheit,' in *Deutsch Hellas*, Serie 2, Heft 1 (n.d.-[1908]), p. 4.
12. Emil Peters, *Menschen in der Sonne: Die Heilkraft des Luft – und Sonnenbades, rationelle Körperpflege durch Luft, Licht und Sonne* (Volkskraft Verlag [1913]), p. 7.
13. Georg Fuhrmann, 'Wege zur wirtschaftliche Freiheit,' in *Hellas*, seriel, Heft 2 ([1907]), pp. 2–4.
14. Dr Hans Fuchs, 'Die Körperkultur in der Antike und Gegenwart,' in *Das*

Freibad, Heft 7 (1929), p. 69.
15. Dr Heinrich Pudor, *Nacktheit: Erstes Bändchen, Allgemeines; Fußkultur*, third edition (H. Pudor Verlag, 1906), p. 14.
16. Marchand, *Down From Olympus*, pp. 1–3.
17. Ernst Klotz, 'Das Geheimnis der griechischen Schönheit,' in *Die Schönheit*, Heft 6 ([1911]), p. 245.
18. Fuchs, 'Die Körperkultur in der Antike und Gegenwart,' p. 70; see also Wilm Burghardt, *Körperbejahung und Ethik* (Dr Gerhard Isert Verlag, n.d. [1936]), pp. 32–4.
19. Burghardt, *Körperbejahung*, pp. 32–4.
20. Fuchs, 'Die Körperkultur in der Antike und Gegenwart,' p. 70.
21. Peters, *Menschen*, p. 17.
22. Walther Brauns, *Den Freien der Welt! Bilder aus der Lebensgestaltung neuer Menschen* (Robert Laurer Verlag, 1926), p. 58.
23. Hans Surén, *Der Mensch und die Sonne* (Dieck and Co., 1924), pp. 87–8, quotation on p. 88.
24. Hans Surén, *Mensch und Sonne: Arisch-olympischer Geist* (Verlag Scherl, 1936), p. 144.
25. Brauns, *Freien*, pp. 58–71.
26. Heitsch, *Lebensfreude*, pp. 43–5.
27. Georg Fuhrmann, 'Wege zur wirtschaftliche Freiheit,' *Hellas*, Serie 1, Heft 2 ([1907]), pp. 2–4.
28. Dr Küster, 'Nackt-Photographien,' in Wilhelm Kästner, *Kampf der Lichtfreunde gegen die Dunkelmänner* (Verlag W. Kästner [1910]), p. 14.
29. Pudor, *Nacktkultur, Erstes Bändchen*, p. 14.
30. Burghardt, *Körperbejahung*, p. 32.
31. Fuhrmann, 'Wege zur wirtschaftliche Freiheit,' pp. 2–4.
32. Vahle, *Zielskizze*, p. 8.
33. Burghardt, *Körperbejahung*, p. 32.
34. J.M. Seitz, *Die Nacktkulturbewegung: Ein Buch für Wissende und Unwissende* (Verlag der Schönheit, 1923), pp. 95–6.
35. Emil Peters, *Menschen*, p. 17.
36. Ibid., p. 64.
37. Fuchs, 'Die Körperkultur in der Antike und Gegenwart,' p. 69.
38. Joachim Günther, 'Antike und moderne Körperkultur,' in *Die Freude*, Heft 11 (1925), pp. 486–95.
39. Dr Hans Graaz, *Nacktkörperkultur*. Beiträge zum Sexualproblem, Heft 10, Herausgegegen von Dr Felix A. Theilhaber, (Verlag der Syndikalist, 1927), p. 10.
40. Fuchs, 'Die Körperkultur in der Antike und Gegenwart,' p. 70.
41. No Author, 'Alt-Sparta,' in *Sonniges Land*, Heft 4 (1931), p. 69.

42. No Author, 'Alt-Sparta,' in *Sonniges Land*, pp. 70–1.
43. Georg August Grote, 'Die Lebenskraft in ihrer Beziehung zum Sonnenlicht,' in *Die Freude*, Heft 2 (1925), pp. 41–8.
44. Ruy de Fontanel, 'Die physische und geistige Entwicklung der Frau im Verlauf der Zeiten,' in Wilhelm Kästner, *Ruf an die Frauen!* (Verlag W. Kästner [1912]), p. 26.
45. Seitz, *Ein Buch*, p. 114.
46. Hans Behm, *Reigen der Keuschheit* (Robert Laurer Verlag, 1928), pp. 67–9.
47. Dr Heinrich Pudor, *Nacktkultur, Zweites Bändchen: Kleid und Geschlecht; Bein und Becken* (H. Pudor Verlag, 1906), p. 37.
48. Ibid.
49. Surén, *Mensch*, p. 18.
50. Ibid., p. 90.
51. Ibid., p. 92.
52. On the popular perception of Wilhelmine decadence see Alex Hall, *Scandal, Sensation and Social Democracy: The SPD Press and Wilhelmine Germany, 1890–1914* (Cambridge University Press, 1977), pp. 143–88.
53. Fuchs, 'Die Körperkultur in der Antike und Gegenwart,' p. 70.
54. Surén, *Mensch*, p. 181.
55. Ibid., p. 25.
56. Pudor, *Nacktkultur: erstes Bändchen*, p. 6.
57. Surén, *Der Mensch*, p. 81.
58. Richard Ungewitter, *Nackt: Eine kritische Studie* (Verlag Richard Ungewitter, 1909), p. 29.
59. Magnus Weidemann, 'Mein Meer,' and 'Meer-Nordland- und wir,' in *Wege zur Freude. Gesammelte Aufsätze und Bilder* (Robert Laurer Verlag, 1926), pp. 105–10; pp. 111–15, quotation from p. 112.
60. Surén, *Der Mensch*, p. 83.
61. Fuhrmann, 'Wege zur wirtschaftlichen Freiheit,' p. 4.
62. *Deutsch Hellas*, Serie 2, Heft 8 ([n.p.-1908]), p. 113.
63. Richard Ungewitter, *Nacktheit und Kultur: Neue Forderung* (Verlag von Richard Ungewitter, 1913), p. 49.
64. Damas, 'Ein offener Brief an alle Reformvereine,' in *Deutsch Hellas*, Serie 2, Heft 3 ([n.p.-1908]), p. 45.
65. G. Fuhrmann, 'Schönheit und Bodenrecht,' in *Hellas*, Serie 1, Heft 3 ([n.p.-1907]), p. 37.
66. Ungewitter, *Nackt*, pp. 83–4.
67. Richard Ungewitter, *Nacktheit und Aufstieg: Ziele zur Erneuerung des deutschen Volkes* (Verlag Richard Ungewitter, 1920), p. 124.
68. Surén, *Mensch*, p. 17.
69. Ibid., p. 144.

198 • Notes

70. Pudor, *Nacktkultur, Erstes Bändchen*, p. 15.
71. Dr Graaz, 'Sonnenbehandlung.' in *Lichthunger-Lichtheil: Die Lebenskrafte der Luft und Sonne, dargestellt von sechzehn Autoren* (Verlag Lebenskunst-Heilkunst, 1924), p. 28.
72. Dr Küster, 'Die Wichtigkeit der Haut im Lebenshaushalt,' in Kästner, *Kampf*, p. 44.
73. Peters, *Menschen*, p. 5.
74. Anon., 'Untitled,' in Kästner, *Kampf*, p. 20.
75. Pudor, *Nacktkultur, Drittes Bändchen: Die Probleme des Lebens und der Zeugung* (H. Pudor Verlag, 1907), p. 10.
76. Wilhelm Kästner, 'Ist der nackte Körper des Menschen unästhetisch?,' in *Kampf*, p. 72.
77. Surén, *Der Mensch*, pp. 12–13.
78. Kästner, 'Ist der nackte Körper des Menschen unästhetisch?,' p. 72.
79. Karl Bückmann, *In Natur und Sonne: Von der Sünde gegen die Natur* (Verlag Deutsche Leibeszucht, 1940), p. 31.
80. Surén, *Der Mensch*, pp. 45–7.
81. For quotation see Peters, *Menschen*, p. 5, pp. 18–19; for general sentiment see also Dr Küster, 'No title,' in Kästner, *Kampf*, p. 44; Pudor, *Nacktkultur, Erstes Bändchen*, p. 14.
82. Ungewitter, *Nacktheit und Kultur*, p. 50.
83. Bückmann, *In Natur und Sonne*, p. 17.
84. Seitz, *Ein Buch*, pp. 111–12.
85. Ibid.
86. Ibid., pp. 112–13; p. 110.
87. Ibid., p. 110.
88. Surén, *Mensch*, pp. 36–8.
89. Ibid.
90. Ibid.
91. Pudor, *Nacktkultur, Erstes Bändchen*, p. 27.
92. Vahle, *Zielskizze*, p. 13.
93. Graaz, *Nacktkörperkultur*, pp. 10–12.
94. Surén, *Der Mensch*, p. 30; Surén, *Mensch*, p. 23; Ungewitter, *Nackt*, p. 96.
95. Ungewitter, *Nackt*, p. 96.
96. Vahle, *Zielskizze*, pp. 13–14.
97. Surén, *Der Mensch*, p. 30.
98. Adolf Weide, *Verjüngung absolut*, (Selbstverlag des Verfassers, 1929), pp. 43–4.
99. Kästner, *Kampf*, p. 74.
100. Surén, *Der Mensch*, p. 18.
101. Ungewitter, *Nackt*, p. 96.

102. Ungewitter, *Nacktheit und Moral: Wege zur Rettung des deutschen Volkes* (Verlag Richard Ungewitter, 1925), p. 12.
103. Vahle, *Zielskizze*, pp. 13–14.
104. Surén, *Der Mensch*, p. 30; Surén, *Mensch*, p. 23.
105. For naked photos pick up just about any of his books. Though some feature him in a loincloth of his own design, he is still obviously slick from the oil. Surén, *Der Mensch*, p. 30.
106. On daily oiling see, Vahle, *Zielskizze*, p. 14.
107. Weide, *Verjüngung absolut*, pp. 39–40.
108. Seitz, *Ein Buch*, p. 19.
109. Peters, *Menschen*, p. 18.

Chapter 6 The Nudist Woman

1. Frau Dr Schmidt-Blankert, 'Mein erstes Luftbad,' in Wilhelm Kästner, *Kampf der Lichtfreunde gegen die Dunkelmänner* (Verlag W. Kästner [1910]), pp. 60–5.
2. Ibid., pp. 65–6.
3. Ann Taylor Allen, *Feminism and Motherhood in Germany 1800–1914* (Rutgers University Press, 1991). Emancipation through familial confines, though negatively, is what the Nazis sought and achieved; see Claudia Koonz, *Mothers in the Fatherland: Women, Family and Nazi Politics* (St Martin's Press, 1987); on the general fascist pattern see Victoria de Grazia, *How Fascism Ruled Women: Italy, 1922–1945* (University of California Press, 1992).
4. No author, 'Frauenarbeit und Volksgesundheit,' in *Das Freibad*, Heft 3 (1929), p. 33.
5. Richard Ungewitter, *Kultur und Nacktheit: Eine Forderung* (Verlag Richard Ungewitter, 1911), p. 50.
6. Ungewitter, *Kultur und Nacktheit*, pp. 91–2; see also Richard Ungewitter, *Nackt: Eine kritische Studie* (Verlag Richard Ungewitter, 1909), p. 66.
7. No author, 'Frauenarbeit,' p. 33.
8. Wilm Burghardt, *Körperbejahung und Ethik* (Dr Gerhard Isert Verlag, n.d. [1936]), p. 21.
9. Clara Rubbe, 'Die Frau,' in Wilhelm Kästner, *Ruf an die Frauen!* (Verlag W. Kästner [1912]), p. 62.
10. Renate Bridenthal, Atina Grossmann and Marion Kaplan, eds, *When Biology Became Destiny: Women in Weimar and Nazi Germany* (Monthly Review Press, 1984).
11. Thomas Laqueur, *Making Sex: Body and Gender from the Greeks to Freud* (Harvard University Press, 1990), pp. 193–243.

12. Ute Frevert, *Women in German History: From Bourgeois Emancipation to Sexual Liberation*, translated by Stuart McKinnon-Evans (Berg Publishers, 1997), pp. 131–7.
13. See Ute Planert, *Antifeminismus im Kaiserreich: Diskurs, soziale Formation und politische Mentalität* (Vandenhoek & Rupprecht, 1998).
14. Wilhelm Kästner, 'Betrachtungen über die Ehen,' in Kästner, *Ruf!*, p. 74.
15. *Das Freibad*, Heft 3 (1929).
16. Prof. Dr Rudolf Lennhoff, 'Weiblicher Körper und Leibesübungen,' in *Das Freibad*, Heft 1 (1929), pp. 4–6. Kästner, *Ruf!*, pp. 67–8.
17. Ruy de Fontanel, 'Die physische und geistige Entwicklung der Frau im Verlauf der Zeiten,' in Kästner, *Ruf!*, p. 15.
18. On anti-feminism in the Kaiserreich, the best work is clearly Planert, *Antifeminismus im Kaiserreich*.
19. On Ungewitter's thoughts, see *Kultur und Nacktheit*, pp. 97–8.
20. Ungewitter, *Kultur und Nacktheit*, pp. 97–8.
21. Kästner, 'Anatomische Grundlage zur Frauenkleidung,' in Kästner, *Ruf!*, p. 66.
22. Ibid.
23. K. Küster, 'Die Frau als Erzieherin,' in Kästner, *Ruf!*, p. 62.
24. Fritz Stube, 'Deutsche Frauen,' in *Lachendes Leben*, Heft 3 (1925), p. 17.
25. Dr Hans Fuchs, 'Die Körperkultur in der Antike und Gegenwart,' in *Das Freibad*, Heft 7 (1929), p. 71.
26. Kästner, 'Frauenkleidung,' in Kästner, *Ruf!*, pp. 67–8.
27. Richard Ungewitter, *Nacktheit und Aufstieg: Ziele zur Erneuerung des deutschen Volkes* (Verlag Richard Ungewitter, 1920), p. 30.
28. On these ideas see, Küster, 'Die Frau als Erzieherin,' in Kästner, *Ruf!*, p. 64.
29. Ibid.
30. Marianne Fleischhack, 'Frauen und Körperkultur,' in *Die Freude*, Heft 7 (1925), pp. 300–12.
31. Ernst Nickel, 'Von der Schönheit des Frauenkörpers!', in Kästner, *Ruf!*, p. 56.
32. de Fontanel, 'Entwicklung der Frau,' in Kästner, *Ruf!*, pp. 16–17.
33. Ibid.
34. Kästner, *Ruf!*, p. 6.
35. de Fontanel, 'Entwicklung der Frau,' in Kästner, *Ruf!*, p. 18.
36. Ibid., pp. 19–22.
37. Ibid.
38. Ungewitter, *Nackt*, p. 85.
39. Kästner, *Ruf!*, p. 8.
40. de Fontanel, 'Entwicklung der Frau,' in Kästner, *Ruf!*, pp. 22–4.
41. Kästner, *Ruf!*, p. 8.
42. Küster, 'Die Frau als Erzieherin,' p. 62.

43. J.M. Seitz, *Die Nacktkulturbewegung: Ein Buch für Wissende und Unwissende* (Verlag der Schönheit, 1923), pp. 83–4.
44. Dr Heinrich Pudor, *Nacktkultur, Zweites Bändchen: Kleid und Geschlecht; Bein und Becken* (H. Pudor Verlag, 1906), p. 2.
45. Siegfried Kawerau, 'Körperkultur und Familie,' in *Der Leib Urania*, Heft 1 (1924), p. 29.
46. Karl Bückmann, *In Natur und Sonne: Von der Sünde gegen die Natur* (Verlag Deutsche Leibeszucht, 1940), pp. 32–7.
47. Kawerau, 'Körperkultur und Familie,' p. 29.
48. Änne Franke, 'Die Frau und freie Lebensgestaltung,' in *Lachendes Leben*, Heft 6 (1930), p. 8.
49. Seitz, *Ein Buch*, pp. 83–4.
50. Richard Ungewitter, *Nacktheit und Kultur: Neue Forderung* (Verlag von Richard Ungewitter, 1913), p. 71.
51. Küster, 'Die Frau als Erzieherin,' p. 62.
52. Ungewitter, *Aufstieg*, p. 84
53. Küster, 'Die Frau als Erzieherin,' p. 62.
54. Ungewitter, *Nacktheit und Kultur*, p. 71.
55. Franke, 'Die Frau und freie Lebensgestaltung,' p. 8.
56. Küster, 'Die Frau als Erzieherin,' p. 64.
57. Ungewitter, *Aufstieg*, p. 25.
58. Magnus Weidemann, *Wege zur Freude. Gesammelte Aufsätze und Bilder* (Robert Laurer Verlag, 1926), pp. 89–91.
59. Dr Heinrich Pudor, *Nacktkultur, Erstes Bändchen: Allgemeines; Fußkultur*, third edition (H. Pudor Verlag, 1906), p. 5.
60. *Deutsche Fkk*, Heft 4 (1934).
61. Richard Ungewitter, *Nacktheit und Moral: Wege zur Rettung des deutschen Volkes* (Verlag Richard Ungewitter, 1925), p. 83.
62. Walter Brauns, foreword, in Emil Peters, *Menschen in der Sonne: Die Heilkraft des Luft- und Sonnenbades, rationelle Körperpflege durch Luft, Licht und Sonne,* second edition (Volkskraft Verlag, 1935), p. i.
63. Hans Surén, *Mensch und Sonne: Arisch-olympischer Geist* (Verlag Scherl, 1936), pp. 37–8.
64. Stube, 'Deutsche Frauen,' p. 17.
65. Ungewitter, *Nackt*, p. 70.
66. Ungewitter, *Moral*, p. 60; pp. 58–9.
67. Dr Thea Sutoris, 'Gesunde Mutter und gesundes Volk! Mehr Sonne – Mehr Licht! Bestrahlung werdener und stillender Mütter,' in *Figaro*, Heft 10 (1928), pp. 317–18.
68. Margarete Bink-Ischeuschler, 'Die Frau und die Nacktkultur,' in *Das Freibad*, Heft 1 (1929), p. 2.

69. Ibid.
70. Ibid.
71. On these views, he explicitly draws on the work of Richard Norhausen, especially Norhausen's work *Zwischen 14 und 18*, which concerned itself with the proper education of girls. This meant becoming wives and mothers, and called for girls to undergo a year of military style training, the *Dienstjahr*, in order to learn such skills more vigorously. See Ungewitter's *Nacktheit und Kultur* for examples and greater exposition of these ideas.
72. Ungewitter, *Nacktheit und Kultur*, p. 136; see a similar call in *Nackt*, p. 93.
73. Rubbe, 'Die Frau,' p. 71.
74. Therese Mühlhause-Vogeler, 'Die Stellung der Frau in Freikörperkultur,' in *Sonne ins Leben*, Heft 4 (1928), p. 2.
75. Küster, 'Die Frau als Erzieherin!' pp. 56–7.
76. Therese Mühlhause-Vogeler, 'Die Stellung der Frau in Freikörperkultur,' in *Sonne ins Leben*, Heft 4 (April, 1928), p. 2.
77. Elita Simon, 'Das nationale Wohl in den Händen der Frau,' in *Hellas*, Serie 1, Heft 6 ([1907]), p. 93.
78. Frau Doktor Schmidt-Blankert, 'Offener Brief,' in Kästner, *Ruf!*, pp. 76–78.
79. Küster, 'Die Frau als Erzieherin!', p. 61.
80. Rubbe, 'Die Frau,' p. 73.
81. Seitz, *Ein Buch*, pp. 111–12.
82. Küster, 'Die Frau als Erzieherin!', pp. 60–4.
83. Kästner, 'Betrachtungen über die Ehen,' in Kästner, *Ruf!*, p. 74.
84. Kästner, 'Betrachtung vom Standpunkt der Humanität,' in Kästner, *Ruf!*, p. 38.
85. Magnus Weidemann, *Deutsches Baden: Ein Führer zur Freude, Schönheit und Gesundheit* (Robert Laurer Verlag [1926]), p. 27.
86. Theo Heermann, 'Befreiung des Weibes,' in Kästner, *Ruf!*, p. 38.
87. Kästner, *Ruf!*, p. 5; p. 39.
88. Kästner, *Ruf!*, p. 6.
89. Kästner, *Ruf!*, pp. 80–2.
90. Rubbe, 'Die Frau,' p. 72.
91. Kästner, *Ruf!*, p. 56.
92. Rubbe, 'Die Frau,' p. 71; for the quotation, p. 72.
93. *Sonniges Land*, Heft 4 (1931), p. 70.
94. F. Else, 'Das Reich der Frau: "Männchen," "Weibchen" und der "neue Mensch",' in *Hellas*, Serie 1, Heft 3 ([1907]), pp. 47–8.
95. de Fontanel, 'Entwicklung der Frau,' pp. 28–30.
96. Wilhem Kästner, 'Koedukation und Nacktkultur,' in Hugo Peters, ed., *Revolution und Nacktkultur* (Verlag der Schonheit, 1919), pp. 63–4.
97. Ibid.

98. Allen, *Feminism and Motherhood*, see especially the introduction.
99. On this connection see Ulrich Linse, 'Sexualreform und Sexualberatung,' in Diethart Kerbs and Jürgen Reulcke, *Handbuch der deutschen Reformbewegungen, 1880–1933* (Peter Hammer Verlag, 1998), pp. 211–25, especially p. 215.
100. Frevert, *Women in German History*, pp. 190–2.
101. Ibid., p. 190.
102. Kästner in Peters, *Revolution*, pp. 43–4.

Chapter 7 Sex, Race and Nudism

1. Dr Bernhard Schulze, 'Rechtfertigung,' in Charly Sträßer, ed., *Jugendgelände: Ein Buch von neuen Menschen* (Der Greifenverlag zur Rudolstadt, 1926), p. 88.
2. Ursula van Zyl, 'Der sprechende Körper,' in *Das Freibad*, Heft 10 (1931), pp. 174–5.
3. Richard Ungewitter, *Nacktheit und Moral: Wege zur Rettung des deutschen Volkes* (Verlag Richard Ungewitter, 1925), p. 68.
4. Therese Mühlhause-Vogeler, 'Körperfreude,' in *Das Freibad*, Heft 6 (1925), pp. 267–9.
5. Felix Solterer, 'Die Moral und Unmoral der Nacktheit,' in *Lachendes Leben*, Heft 13 (1926), p. 12.
6. Richard Ungewitter, *Nacktheit und Aufstieg: Ziele zur Erneuerung des deutschen Volkes* (Verlag Richard Ungewitter, 1920), pp. 86–7.
7. Hans Surén, *Mensch und Sonne: Arisch-olympischer Geist* (Verlag Scherl, 1936), p. 170.
8. van Zyl, 'Der sprechende Körper,' pp. 175–6.
9. Walther Brauns, *Den Freien der Welt! Bilder aus der Lebensgestaltung neuer Menschen* (Robert Laurer Verlag, 1926), p. 6.
10. *Lachendes Leben*, Heft 2 (February: 1933), p. 17.
11. Surén, *Mensch*, p. 170; Schulze, 'Rechtfertigung,' p. 88.
12. Schulze, 'Rechtfertigung,' p. 88.
13. Margarete Bink-Ischeuschler, 'Die Frau und die Nacktkultur,' in *Das Freibad*, Heft 1 (1929), p. 2.
14. M. Seber, 'Die kulturellen Grundlagen,' in Manfred Berg, ed., *Die Wahrheit um den Körper: Ein Aufruf zur Selbstbestimmung!* (Karl Haug Verlag, 1927), p. 22.
15. Bink-Ischeuschler, 'Die Frau und die Nacktkultur,' p. 2.
16. Seber, 'Die kulturellen Grundlagen,' p. 22.
17. van Zyl, 'Der sprechende Körper,' pp. 175–6.
18. No Author, 'Zur Freiheit,' in *Hellas*, Serie 1, Heft 1 (n.p.-n.d. [1907]), p. 7.

19. Wilm Burghardt, *Körperbejahung und Ethik* (Dr Gerhard Isert Verlag, n.d. [1936]), p. 36.
20. Hans Graaz, *Nacktkörperkultur. Beiträge zum Sexualproblem*, Heft 10, Herausgegeben von Dr Felix A. Theilhaber (Verlag der Syndikalist, 1927), p. 9.
21. Frazio, 'Warum nackt?', in *Das Freibad*, Heft 11 (1930), p. 214.
22. Hermann Schmidt, 'Die Befreiung des Körpers,' in *Figaro*, Heft 7 (1928), p. 208.
23. J.M. Seitz, *Die Nacktkulturbewegung: Ein Buch für Wissende und Unwissende* (Verlag der Schönheit, 1923), pp. 16–18.
24. Walter Heitsch, *Freikörperkultur-Lebensfreude* (Robert Laurer Verlag, 1925), p. 8.
25. Wilhelm Kästner, 'Koedukation und Nacktkultur,' in Hugo Peters, ed., *Revolution und Nacktkultur* (Verlag der Schönheit, 1919), pp. 39–42.
26. Seitz, *Ein Buch*, p. 21.
27. Anon., *Freiheit dem Leibe!: Eine zeitgemäße Studie zur Förderung der Lichtbewegung Eltern und Erziehern dargeboten* (Dieck and Co. Verlag, 1927), p. 16.
28. Dr Robert Werner Schulte, *Körper-Kultur Versuch einer Philosophie der Leibesübungen* (Verlag Ernst Rheinhardt, 1928), p. 61.
29. Klara Muche, 'Luftbad und Sittlichkeit,' in Anonymous *Lichthunger-Lichtteil: Die Lebenskrafte der Luft und Sonne, dargestellt von sechszehn Autoren* (Verlag Lebenskunst-Heilkunst, 1924), p. 45 [note: this essay written in 1908].
30. Hans Surén, *Der Mensch und die Sonne* (Dieck and Co., 1924), p. 65.
31. On Surén's personal information and brush with the Kripo (Criminal Police), see BA-B NS Personal file of Hans Surén, Nr 2100 Box 0401 File 06; Nr 01663.
32. J.M. Seitz, *Soll man lachen oder weinen? Ein Spiegel der Prüderie* (Robert Laurer Verlag, 1925), pp. 48–9.
33. IFB, Nachlaß Hermann Wilkes, # 45, see also # 1937.
34. *Figaro*, 'Das Bild,' Heft 1 (1928), p. 48.
35. Surén, *Mensch*, p. 78.
36. Dr Hans Oberländer, 'Von der Bedeutung des Freiluftlebens,' in *Sonne ins Leben*, Heft 1 (1928), pp. 10–11.
37. K. Reissner, 'Die hygenische Notwendigkeit,' in Berg, *Wahrheit*, p. 33.
38. Frazio, 'Warum nackt?', p. 202.
39. Heitsch, *Lebensfreude*, p. 24.
40. Dr Hans Fuchs, 'Körperkultur und Ethik,' in *Das Freibad*, Heft 7 (1929), p. 124.
41. Burghardt, *Körperbejahung*, p. 7.

42. Adolfe Weide, *Verjüngung absolut* (Selbstverlag des Verfussers, 1929), p. 26.
43. Kästner, 'Koedukation und Nacktkultur,' p. 48.
44. K. Warnecke, 'Komm und Sieh!', in *Lachendes Leben*, Heft 5 (1932), p. 3.
45. Therese Mühlhause-Vogeler, in Berg, *Wahrheit*, p. 42.
46. Kästner, 'Koedukation und Nacktkultur,' p. 48.
47. Burghardt, *Körperbejahung*, p. 24.
48. No Author, 'Fragen aus dem Leserkreis,' in *Figaro*, Heft 15 (1927), not numbered.
49. Ibid.
50. Kästner, 'Koedukation und Nacktkultur,' in pp. 53–4.
51. Burghardt, *Körperbejahung*, p. 19.
52. No Author, *Sonnenland*, Heft 1, *Sonderausgabe: Mutter und Kind Sonniger Nacktheit* (1931).
53. Ungewitter, *Aufstieg*, pp. 82–3.
54. Ungewitter, *Moral*, pp. 23–34; see also Ungewitter, *Aufstieg*, pp. 77–82.
55. Ibid.
56. Ungewitter, *Kultur und Nacktheit: Eine Forderung* (Verlag Richard Ungewitter, 1911), pp. 77–8.
57. Ungewitter, *Moral*, pp. 23–34; see also Ungewitter, *Aufstieg*, pp. 77–82.
58. Surén, *Der Mensch*, p. 61.
59. Frazio, 'Warum nackt?', p. 214.
60. Surén, *Mensch*, p. 109.
61. Surén, *Der Mensch*, p. 61.
62. Surén, *Mensch*, p. 109.
63. Frazio, 'Warum nackt?', p. 214.
64. Therese Mühlhause-Vogeler, *Freie Lebensgestaltung: Ein Beitrag zur Neuformung des Lebens-Stiles* (Robert Laurer Verlag, 1926), p. 28.
65. Frazio, 'Warum nackt?', p. 214.
66. Kästner, 'Koedukation und Nacktkultur,' p. 50.
67. Graaz, *Nacktkörperkultur*, p. 16.
68. Dr Hans Fuchs, 'Die Körperkultur in der Antike und Gegenwart,' in *Das Freibad*, Heft 4 (1929), pp. 71–2, quote on p. 71.
69. Burghardt, *Körperbejahung*, p. 25.
70. Mühlhause-Vogeler, 'Neues Leben durch Freikörperkultur,' in *Lachendes Leben*, Heft 12 (1930), p. 3.
71. Seitz, *Ein Buch*, pp. 76–7.
72. On this see the works of George Mosse, especially, *Nationalism and Sexuality: Respectability and Abnormal Sexuality in Modern Europe* (Howard Fertig, 1985) and *The Image of Man: The Creation of Modern Masculinity* (Oxford University Press, 1996).
73. Though engenics and racial hygiene have been the focus of much

investigation, two good introductions are Robert Proctor, *Racial Hygiene: Medicine under the Nazis* (Harvard University Press, 1988) and Paul Weindling *Health, Race and German Politics Between National Unification and Nazism, 1870–1945* (Cambridge University Press, 1989).

74. The first and still valuable study on German feminism is Richard J. Evans, *The Feminist Movement in Germany, 1894–1933* (SAGE Publications, 1978), for sex, feminism and politics see especially pages 115–43. Study of the women's movement is a burgeoning field; briefly, some other valuable works on German feminism are Ute Frevert, *Women in German History: From Bourgeois Emancipation to Sexual Liberation*, translated by Stuart McKinnon-Evans (Berg Publishers, 1997); Ann Taylor Allen, *Feminism and Motherhood in Germany 1800–1914* (Rutgers University Press, 1991).

75. Kevin McAleer, *Dueling: The Cult of Honor in Fin-de-Siècle Germany* (Princeton University Press, 1994).

76. Hans Behm, *Reigen der Keuschheit* (Robert Laurer Verlag, 1928), pp. 20–1.

77. Though similar in many regards, eugenics, historians have noted, was internationalist in its scope, whereas racial hygiene focused exclusively on Germany and Germans. See Proctor, *Racial Hygiene*, pp. 10–45, but especially p. 29 for a complete discussion. Also helpful is Weindling, *Health, Race and German Politics*.

78. On Gregor Mendel's discoveries and their more important rediscovery by European biologists many years later, see Proctor, *Racial Hygiene*, pp. 29–31.

79. Hans Vahle, *Zielskisse der Freikörperkultur: Ein Leitfaden für Leibeszucht und gesundes Leben* (Polverlag, 1932), p. 25.

80. Surén, *Mensch*, pp. 171–2.

81. A good introduction is Ulrich Linse, 'Sexualreform und Sexualberatung,' in Diethart Kerbs und Jürgen Reulcke, eds, *Handbuch der deutschen Reformbewegungen, 1880–1933*, (Peter Hammer Verlag, 1998), pp. 211–25. Other works are Atina Grossmann, *Reforming Sex: The German Movement for Birth Control and Abortion Reform, 1920–1950* (Oxford University Press, 1995); Charlotte Wolff, *Magnus Hirschfeld: A Portrait of a Pioneer in Sexology* (Quartet Books, 1986); Britta McEwen, *Model City, Moral Choices: Sexuality in Red Vienna*, Ph.D. diss. University of California Los Angeles, forthcoming; and Cornelie Usbourne, *The Politics of the Body in Weimar Germany: Women's Reproductive Rights and Duties* (University of Michigan Press, 1992).

82. J.M. Seitz, *Die Ein Buch*, p. 116. On the idea of the love-match and companionate marriage as the best guarantee of marital happiness, nudists were hardly innovators, and the idea of both has a strong tradition in German thought and the German women's movements dating back some centuries. See Lynn Abrams, 'Companionship and Conflict: The Negotiation of

Marriage Relations in the Nineteenth Century,' in Lynn Abrams and Elizabeth Harvey, *Gender Relations in German History: Power, Agency and Experience from the Sixteenth Century to the Twentieth Century* (Duke University Press, 1997), pp. 101–16, especially,pp. 103–10.
83. Rudolf Koschyk, 'Wesen und Daseinsberechtigung der Freikörperkultur,' in *Deutsche FKK*, Heft 5 (1934).
84. Vahle, *Zielskisse*, p. 23.
85. *Figaro*, Heft 6 (März 1928).
86. Dr Ernst von Gaggern, 'Briefe zur ethischen Revolution,' in *Figaro*, Heft 3 (1929), pp. 86–9.
87. Dr Max Hodann, 'Die Eheform des Kapitalismus und die Prostitution,' in *Der Leib Urania*, Heft 2 (1924), pp. 59–62.
88. Therese Mühlhause-Vogeler, *Freie Lebensgestaltung*, p. 16.
89. Seitz, *Ein Buch*, p. 116.
90. Seitz, *Ein Buch*, pp. 116–17.
91. Kästner, 'Koedukation und Nacktkultur,' p. 50.
92. Karl Bückmann in Kurt Reichert, *Vom Leibeszucht und Leibesschönheit: Bilder aus dem Leben des Bundes für Leibeszucht* (Verlag Deutsche Leibeszucht, 1940), p. 9.
93. Surén, *Mensch*, p. 171.
94. Ungewitter, *Nackt: Eine kritische studie* (Verlag Richard Ungewitter, 1909), pp. 4–6, quote on p. 6.
95. Dr Hans Fuchs, 'Körperkultur und Ethik,' p. 71.
96. Burghardt, *Körperbejahung*, p. 19.
97. This and the previous quote, Walter Heitsch, pp. 25–6.
98. On this paragraph see, Herman Schmidt, 'Grundsätzliches und Erfahrungen über den Zusammenhang von Freikörperkultur und Gemeinschaftsleben,' in *Der Leib Urania*, Serie 3, Heft 10 (1927), p. 350.
99. Dr Küster, 'Die Frau als Erzieherin!,' in Kästner, *Ruf an due Frauen!* (Verlag W. Kästner [1912]), p. 62.
100. Kästner, 'Koedukation und Nacktkultur,' p. 51.
101. Richard Ungewitter, *Kultur und Nacktheit*, pp. 98–9.
102. Fuchs, 'Körperkultur und Ethik,' p. 71.
103. Koschyk, 'Wesen und Daseinsberechtigung,' p. 72.
104. Ungewitter, *Kultur und Nacktheit*, pp. 98–9.
105. Ungewitter, *Nacktheit und Kultur: Neue Forderung* (Verlag von Richard Ungewitter, 1913), pp. 130.
106. Ungewitter, *Kultur und Nacktheit*, pp. 98–9.
107. *Lachendes Leben*, 'Wir erteilen Rat und Auskunft!', Heft 1 (1933).
108. *Lachendes Leben*, 'Wir erteilen Rat und Auskunft!', Heft 2 (1933), p. 20.
109. Kästner, 'Koedukation und Nacktkultur,' p. 50.

110. Ungewitter, *Nacktheit und Kultur*, p. 130.
111. Kästner, 'Koedukation und Nacktkultur,' p. 50.
112. Fuchs, 'Körperkultur und Ethik,' p. 71.
113. Michel Foucault, *The Care of the Self*, translated by Robert Hurley (Vintage Books, 1990), pp. 147–85.
114. Ungewitter, *Nacktheit und Kultur*, p. 130.
115. Ricardo Walther Darré, quoted in Surén, *Mensch*, pp. 199–202. It should be recalled that Surén was Darré's special plenipotentiary.
116. Hans Surén, *Mensch*, p. 73.
117. Darré, quoted in Surén, *Mensch*, p. 76.
118. Bückmann in Reichert, *Vom Leibeszucht*, p. 9.
119. Ungewitter, *Moral*, pp. 22–3.
120. Vahle, *Zielskisse*, pp. 7–8.
121. Koschyk, 'Wesen und Daseinsberechtigung,' p. 72.
122. Walter Heitsch, 'Brautleute sehen sich nackt!', in *Lachendes Leben*, Heft 2 (1933), p. 6.
123. Kästner, 'Koedukation und Nacktkultur,' p. 51.
124. Seitz, *Ein Buch*, pp. 118–19.
125. Erich Frey, 'Die Erziehung zur Wahrheit – durch Nackheit,' in *Die Freude*, Heft 14 (1924), pp. 361–6.
126. Seber, 'Die kulturellen Grundlagen,' p. 21.
127. Mühlhause-Vogeler, *Freie Lebensgestaltung*, pp. 31–2.
128. Surén, *Der Mensch*, p. 108.
129. Kästner, 'Koedukation und Nacktkultur,' pp. 43–4.
130. Both quotes Mühlhause-Vogeler, *Freie Lebensgestaltung*, pp. 29–30.
131. No author, 'Nicht Vertuschen!', in *Figaro*, Heft 5 (1929), p. 167.
132. Robert Laurer, *Sonnenland*, Heft 10 (1930), p. 98.
133. Ibid., pp. 100–3.
134. Heitsch, 'Brautleute sehen sich nackt!,' p. 6.
135. Surén, *Mensch*, p. 67; see also his revised version, *Der Mensch*, p. 67.
136. Ruy de Fontanel, 'Die physische und geistige Entwicklung der Frau im Verlauf der Zeiten,' in Kästner, *Ruf!*, p. 26.
137. Dr Küster, 'Die Frau als Erzieherin!,' in Kästner, *Ruf!*, p. 62.
138. Kästner, *Ruf!*, pp. 10–11.
139. Mühlhause-Vogeler, *Freie Lebensgestaltung*, pp. 31–2.
140. Fey, 'Die Erziehung zur Wahrheit,' p. 367.
141. Anon., 'Eine neue Gemeinschaft,' in *Hellas*, Serie 1, Heft 4 (n.p. [1907]), not numbered.
142. Dr Schönenberger, 'Winke für die Benutzung des Luft- und Sonnenbades,' in *Lichthunger-Lichtheil: Die Lebenskrafte der Luft und Sonne, dargestellt von sechzehn Atoren* (Verlag Lebenskunst-Heilkunst, 1924), p. 24.

143. Fey, 'Die Erziehung zur Wahrheit,' p. 367.

Epilogue

1. StaH 136–2/81.
2. *Freies Leben: Offizielles Bundesorgan der Freikörperkulturbewegung*, Folge I (1949), not numbered. On Damm's participation see *Freies Leben: Offizielles Bundesorgan der Freikörperkulturbewegung*, Folge I (1950), not numbered.
3. Uli Linke, *German Bodies, Race and Representation After Hitler* (Routledge, 1999).
4. Again Linke, *German Bodies*, disagrees.
5. Simone Tavenrath, *So wundervoll sonnengebräunt: kleine Kulturgeschichte des Sonnenbadens*. (Jonas Verlag, 2000).
6. LaSH Abt. 260 Nr 19594.
7. Raymond H. Dominick III, *The Environmental Movement in Germany: Prophets and Pioneers, 1871–1971* (Indiana University Press, 1992).
8. See Kevin Repp's excellent study, *Reformers, Critics and the Paths of German Modernity: Anti-Politics and the Search for Alternatives, 1890–1914* (Harvard University Press, 2000).
9. Robert Proctor, *The Nazi War on Cancer* (Princeton University Press, 1999). On the Nazi reluctance to interfere see, LaSH Abt. 260 Nr 19594.
10. Rudolf Teßmann, 'Der volkswirtschaftliche Wert der Freikörperkultur,' in *Das Freibad*, Heft 12 (1929), p. 221.
11. Adolf Koch, 'Arbeitergymnastik,' in *Die Freude*, Heft 6 (June 1925), p. 261.
12. Hans Surén, *Der Mensch und die Sonne* (Dieck and Co., 1924), pp. 68–9.
13. Hans Surén, *Mensch und Sonne: Arisch-olympischer Geist* (Verlag Scherl, 1936), pp. 30–1.
14. Ibid.
15. Surén, *Der Mensch*, p. 68.
16. Surén, *Mensch*, p. 30.
17. Teßmann, 'Der volkswirtschaftliche Wert der Freikörperkultur,' p. 221.
18. Damas, 'Persönlichkeit,' in *Deutsch Hellas,* Serie 2, Heft 3 ([1908]), p. 46.
19. BA-B NS/5/VI Nr 19255 Georg Marguth, 'Maschine und Freizeit,' in *Düsseldorfer Nachrichten* Nr 181 11 April 1937, p. 5; see also Mary Nolan, *Visions of Modernity: American Business and the Modernization of Germany* (Oxford University Press, 1994) for the debate in the 1920s.
20. Therese Mühlhause-Vogeler, *Freie Lebensgestaltung: Ein Beitrag zur Neuformung des Lebens-Stiles* (Robert Laurer Verlag, 1926), p. 12.
21. This paragraph, Teßmann, 'Der volkswirtschaftliche Wert,' pp. 221–2.
22. For two rather humorously presented examples see Bill Bryson, *Neither Here Nor There: Travels in Europe* (Avon Books, 1992) and the travel guide by

Douglas Muller, *Let's GO Germany* (St Martin's Press, 1999). Travel sections of newspapers also report on nudism in Germany, with as much a tone of informing as warning the traveler about what to expect, some examples include, *The Guardian* 'Naked Ambition' (London) 23 October 1999; *Die Zeit*, 'Verkerhsamt auf Nudistenenfang' (Frankfurt) 23 August 2001.

23. Reuters, 'Nudists are set to rally' (Berlin), 13 March 2002.

Select Bibliography

Archival Sources

Bundesarchiv-Berlin (BA-B)
MfR58/4252, 4253; MfR58-774
NS/5/VI Nr 4776, 4779, 4780, 4781, 4815, 19255
NS 19 1152
NS Personal file on Hans Surén, Nr 2100 Box 0401 File 06; Nr 01663
NS Personal file on Richard Ungewitter, Nr 2101 Box 1301 File 14
R1501/109412, 109413, 110963, 110961, 110964, 126337
R 8034 Nr 462
Schneider, Zeitungsdienst reports on Tschammer and Olsen

Brandenburgisches Landeshauptarchiv- Potsdam (BLHA)
Rep 21 I Pol Nr 1207, 1232
Rep 30 Berlin C Polizeipresidium Title 121 Nrs 16945, 16990, 17001, 17040, 17042, 17050, 17130, 17165
Rep 30 Berlin C Title 148B 'Vereine' Nr 782
Evangelisches Zentral Archiv-Berlin (EZA-B)
1/A2/162, 1/A2/163, 1/A2/164, 1/A2/165, 7/3808, 7/3809, 7/3810, 7/3811, 7/3812, 7/3813, 7/3841, 7/4086, 7/4087, 14/595
Hauptstaatsarchiv Stuttgart (HSSt)
E 151/53 Bü 186
Hessisches Staatsarchiv Darmstadt (HsaD)
G 15 Groß-Gerau R 60
Internationale FKK-Bibliothek (IFB)
Nachlaß Herman Wilkes, # 45, see also # 1937
File 150-200
Kreisarchiv Eßlingen (KaE)
A2 1220
Landesarchiv Schleswig-Holstein (LaSH)
Abt. 260 Nr 19594
Niedersächsischess Hauptstaatsarchiv- Hannover (NSHaH)
Hann 180 Lün. III.XVI Nr 396; Nr 403

Sächsischesstaatsarchiv Leipzig (SSAL)
PP-V 1841, 4378, 4457, 4475, 4492, 4494
Staatsarchiv Hamburg (StaH)
#136-2/81, 614-1/1, 614-/7, 614-1/9, 614-1/10, 614-1/11, 614-1/12
Nordrhein-Westfälisches Hausptsaat archiv (Nr WHSA)
Regierung Aachen 23747. Decree from Reichs- und Prenßisches Minster des Innern from 8 July 1935
Thüringischen Staatsarchivs Greiz (TSAG):

Contemporary Periodicals

Deutsch Hellas: Erste illustrierte Reform-Zeitschrift zur Grundung des gesamten nationalen Lebens. Zugleich Organ der Buttenst'schen Empfindungsphilosophie. See also *Hellas*.
Deutsche Fkk: Zeitschrift für Rassenpflege, naturgemäße Lebensweise und Leibesübungen. Offizielles Organ des Kampfringes für völkische Freikörperkultur [n.p.-June 1933–July 1934], becomes *Gesetz und Freiheit*.
Deutsche Leibeszucht: Blätter für naturnahe und arteigene Lebensgestaltung [n.p.] 1938–43. Nr 329, fol 88.
Der Figaro: mit Bildern geschmuckte Zeitschrift für Körperkultur und freie Lebensgestaltung [n.p.-1926–1927], Becomes *Figaro*.
Figaro: Halbmonatsschrift für Geist- und Körperkultur. Publikationsorgan des Pelagianer-Bundes, Gesellschaft für Volksaufklärung über gesunde Körperpflege und hygienisches Sexualleben. Berlin: Verlag des 'Figaro.'
Fkk: Organ der deutschen Freikörperkultur, Hannover: Drückerei J. Hoffmann and Co.
Das Freibad: Monatsschrift zur Förderung des Nacktbadens, Berlin: Verlag E. Auffenberg, 1927–33.
Die Freude: Monatshefte für deutsche Innerlichkeit, Dresden: Verlag der Freude Siegfried Kuy, 1923–19.
Gesetz und Freiheit: Monatschrift der Gruppe 3 der Fachsäule im deutschen Reichsbund für Leibesübungen no publication place known. August 1934–December 1937. Becomes *Deutsche Leibeszucht*.
Hellas: Illustrierte Schriftenfolge für Natur, Kultur, Kunst und Schönheit, Wissenschaft und Sozialleben, Berlin: Verlag Hellas [1907–]. After Series 1, Heft 8 the name changes to *Deutsch Hellas*. The collection ends with Series 2, Heft 8.
Lachendes Leben, Robert Laurer, ed., Egestorff bei Hamburg: Robert Laurer Verlag, October 1925–December 1927. With January 1, 1928 issue becomes *Sonne ins Leben*, then back to L-L.
Der Leib: Beiblatt der 'Urania' für Körperkultur und gesundes Leben. Jena: Urania-Verlags G.m.b.H., 1924–32.

Licht-Land: Beilage zu den Monatsheften 'Die Freude'. Dresden: Robert Laurer Verlag [mid 1920s].
Licht-Luft-Leben supplement to *Die Schönheit*
Die Schönheit.
Sonne ins Leben see *Lachendes Leben.*
Sonnenland. Organ des Reichbundes für Freikörperkultur. In 1931 becomes *Sonniges-Land.*
Sonniges-Land [n.p.-n.d.].
Urania: Monatshefte für Naturerkenntnis und Gesellschaftslehre. Jena: Urania-Verlags Gm.b.H. 1924–29.

Published Primary Sources

Alfred-Littauer, H., 'Nacktsein und Leibesfreiheit: Gedanken zum Eheproblem,' in *Sonneland*, Heft 10 (1930).
Almenroeder, C., 'Minister Darré über die Freikörperkultur,' in *Deutsche Fkk*, Heft 3 (1933), 39.
Anon, 'Eine neue Gemeinschaft,' in *Hellas*, Serie 1, Heft 4 (n.p. [1907]).
Anon, 'Warum nackt?' in Kästner *Kampf der Lichtfreunde gegen die Dunkelmänner*, Berlin: Verlag W. Kästner [1910].
Anon. *Freiheit dem Leibe!: Eine zeitgemäße Studie zur Förderung der Lichtbewegung Eltern und Erziehern dargeboten.* Stuttgart: Dieck and Co. Verlag, 1927.
Anon, *Die Freikörperkulturbewegung über sich selbst*, a publication of the Deutscher Bund für Freikörperkultur, e.V. (DFK) ([n.p.-n.d.]).
Beck, A.E., 'Zusammenschluß is not! Ein Arbeitsausschuß deutscher FreikörperKultur-Verbände,' in *Sonnenland*, Heft 2 (1930).
Behm, H.W., *Reigen der Keuschheit*, Egestorff: Robert Laurer Verlag, 1928.
Berg, M., ed., *Die Wahrheit um den Körper: Ein Aufruf zur Selbstbesinnung!*, Stuttgart: Karl Haug Verlag, 1927.
Besser, K., 'Schamgefühl und Körperkultur,' in *Der Leib Urania*, Heft 2 (1926).
Bink-Ischeuschler, M., 'Die Frau und die Nacktkultur,' in *Das Freibad*, Heft 1 (1929).
Brauns, W., *Den Freien der Welt! Bilder aus der Lebensgestaltung neuer Menschen*, Egestorff: Robert Laurer Verlag, 1926.
Brünner, M.A., 'Nacktsport-Vereinigungen einst und jetzt,' in *Das Freibad*, Heft 4 (1931).
Buchholz, E., 'Das Luftbad für Herzkranke,' in Anonymous, *Lichthunger-Lichtheil: Die Lebenskrafte der Luft und Sonne, dargestellt von sechszehn Autoren*, Stuttgart: Verlag Lebenskunst-Heilkunst, 1924.
Bückmann, K., *In Natur und Sonne: Von der Sünde gegen die Natur,* Berlin: Verlag Deutsche Leibeszucht, 1940.

Burghardt, W., *Körperbejahung und Ethik*, Halle: Dr Gerhard Isert Verlag, n.d. [1936].
Buttenstedt, C., 'Was fehlt uns der Gesundheitpflege?', in Wilhelm Kästner, *Kampf der Lichtfreunde gegen die Dunkelmänner*, Berlin: Verlag W. Kästner [1910].
Damas, H., 'Ein offener Brief an alle Reformvereine,' in *Deutsch Hellas*, Serie 2, Heft 3 ([n.p.-1908]).
—— 'Persönlichkeit,' in *Deutsch Hellas*, Serie 2, Heft 3 ([1908]).
Damm, K., 'No Title,' in Irmgard Koch, ed., *Adolf Koch: Erinnerungen an einen Menschenfreund* [n.p.-n.d.].
—— *Fkk: Organ der deutschen Freikörperkultur* Hannover: Drückerei J. Hoffman and Co., 1972.
Deutsch Hellas, Heft 12, Serie 1 ([n.d.]).
—— Heft 8, Serie 2 ([n.p.-1908]).
Deutscher Bund für Freikörperkuttur, e.V. (DFK) ([n.p.-n.d.]).
Dittmar, F., 'Der Kernpunkt,' in *Das Freibad*, Heft 2 (1931).
—— 'Der große Tag,' in *Das Freibad*, Heft 3 (1931).
Else, F., 'Das Reich der Frau: "Männchen," "Weibchen" und der "neue Mensch",' in *Hellas*, Serie 1, Heft 3 ([1907]).
Fallada, H., *Kleiner Mann, was nun?*, Berlin: Aufbau Verlag, 1994.
Fehlhauer, 'Luftbad und Nervenleidende,' in Anonymous, *Lichthunger-Lichtheil: Die Lebenskrafte der Luft und Sonne, dargestellt von sechszehn Autoren* Stuttgart: Verlag Lebenskunst-Heilkunst, 1924.
Figaro, 'Die letzten vierzehn Tage: Ein Vorwort,' Heft 19 (1926).
—— 'Ärztliche Ratschläge für das Sonnenbad,' Heft 11 (1927).
—— 'Fragen aus dem Leserkreis,' Heft 15 (1927).
—— 'Das Bild,' Heft 1 (1928).
—— 'Ein Wort zur Aufklärung: Robert Laurer, dem 'Geistesgestörten,' zur Antwort,' Heft 3 (1929).
—— 'Freikörperkultur-Strand im Seebad Heringsdorf,' Heft 10 [1930].
—— Nicht Vertuschen!,' Heft 5 (1929).
—— 'Kritik an dem Bericht über den Internationalen Kongreß der Freikörperkultur in Dornzhausen im August Heft des *Freibad*,' Heft 11 (1930).
—— 'Tagebuch des *Figaro*: Der Zwickel im deutschen Blätterwald,' Heft 21 (1932).
—— 'Bracht gegen die Körperkulturschule Adolf Koch!,' Heft 21 (1932).
—— 'Freikörperkultur – die Hauptsorge der Polizei,' Heft 24 (1932).
Finckh, K., 'Wie ich mich abhärtete,' in Anonymous, *Lichthunger-Lichtheil: Die Lebenskrafte der Luft und Sonne, dargestellt von sechszehn Autoren* Stuttgart: Verlag Lebenskunst-Heilkunst, 1924.
Fleischhack, M., 'Frauen und Körperkultur,' in *Die Freude*, Heft 7 (1925).

de Fontanel, R., 'Die physische und geistige Entwicklung der Frau im Verlauf der Zeiten,' in Wilhelm Kästner, *Ruf an die Frauen!*, Berlin: Verlag W. Kästner [1912].

Franke, Ä., 'Die Frau und freie Lebensgestaltung,' in *Lachendes Leben*, Heft 6 (1930).

Frazio, 'Warum nackt?', in *Das Freibad*, Heft 11 (1930).

Das Freibad, 'Frauenarbeit und Volksgesundheit,' Heft 3 (1929).

—— '25 Jahre Freikörperkultur,' Heft 6 (1929).

—— 'Sieg der Freikörperkultur?' Heft 9 (1929).

—— 'Kritik am dem Berichtüber den Internationalen Kongreßder der Freikörperkultur in Dornzhausen im Aguust Heft des *Fresbad*,' Heft 11 (1930).

Freies Leben: Offizielles Bundesorgan der Freikörperkulturbewegung, Folge I (1949).

—— *Freies Leben: Offizielles Bundesorgan der Freikörperkulturbewegung*, Folge I (1950).

Frey, E., "Die Erziehung zur Wahrheit- durch Nucktheit,' in *Die Freude*, Heft 14 (1924).

Fuchs, H., 'Die Körperkultur in der Antike und Gegenwart,' in *Das Freibad*, Heft 7 (1929).

—— 'Körperkultur und Ethik,' in *Das Freibad*, Heft 4 (1929).

Fuhrmann, G., 'Wege zur· wirtschaftliche Freiheit,' in *Hellas*, Serie 1, Heft 2 ([1907]).

—— 'Schönheit und Bodenrecht,' in *Hellas*, Serie 1, Heft 3 ([n.p.-1907]).

Gay, J., *On Going Naked*, Garden City: Garden City Press, 1932.

Gemeindelexicon für den Freistaat Preußen, Band I Provinz Ostpreußen, Berlin: Verlag des Preußischen Statischen Landesamts, 1931.

Grass, G., *Die Blechtrommel*, Frankfurt: Luchterhand Verlag, 1974.

Graaz, H., 'Wesen der wichtigsten, besten, unbekannte Wirkung des Luft und Sonnenbades,' in Anonymous, *Lichthunger-Lichtheil: Die Lebenskrafte der Luft und Sonne, dargestellt von sechszehn Autoren*, Stuttgart: Verlag Lebenskunst-Heilkunst, 1924.

—— 'Der Großstädter und das Luft- und Sonnenbad,' in Anonymous, *Lichthunger-Lichtheil: Die Lebenskrafte der Luft und Sonne, dargestellt von sechszehn Autoren*, Stuttgart: Verlag Lebenskunst-Heilkunst, 1924.

—— 'Der Kulturmensch und die Körperkultur,' in *Der Leib Urania*, Heft 3 (1926).

—— *Nacktkörperkultur*. Beiträge zum Sexualproblem, Heft 10, Herausgegeben von Dr Felix A. Theilhaber, Berlin: Verlag der Syndikalist, 1927.

Grote, G.A., 'Die Lebenskraft in ihrer Beziehung zum Sonnenlicht,' in *Die Freude*, Heft 2 (1925).

Gröttrup, B., 'Ich-die Idee-und Herr Laurer: Erinnerungen-Mehr Ueberzeugungstrue zu unseren Idealen-Mehr Mißtrauen gegen die Geschaftlhuber in der Bewegung,' in *Figaro*, Heft 22 (1929).

—— 'Wiedermal: Herr Laurer,' in *Figaro*, Heft 16 (1931).

Grunewald, M., 'Hygenische Körperpflege,' in *Das Freibad*, Heft 3 (1929).

The *Guardian* 'Naked Ambition' (London) 23 October 1999.

Günther, J., 'Antike und moderne Körperkultur,' in *Die Freude*, Heft 11 (1925).

Hagedorn, B., 'Tagebuch des *Figaro*: Tagung der Körperkulturschule Adolf Koch (23 bis 25 November im Preußischen Heerenhaus),' in *Figaro*, Heft 24 (1929).

—— 'Tagebuch des *Figaro*,' Heft 1 (1930).

—— 'Tagebuch des *Figaro*,' Heft 24 (1931).

—— 'Tagebuch des *Figaro*: Polizei und Nacktkultur,' Heft 9 (1932).

Heermann, T., 'Befreiung des Weibes,' in Wilhelm Kästner, *Ruf an die Frauen!*, Berlin: Verlag W. Kästner [1912].

Heitsch, W., *Freikörperkultur-Lebensfreude*, Egestorff: Robert Laurer Verlag, 1925.

—— *Freikörperkultur Lebensfreude: Ein Führer zu Freude, Schönheit und Gesundheit*, Egestorff: Robert Laurer Verlag, 1932.

—— 'Brautleute sehen sich nackt!', in *Lachendes Leben*, Heft 2 (1933).

Hellas, 'Zur Freiheit,' Serie 1, Heft 1 (n.p.-n.d. [1907]).

Hodann, M., 'No Title,' in *Der Leib Urania*, Heft 1 (1924).

—— 'Die Eheform des Kapitalismus und die Prostitution,' in *Der Leib Urania*, Heft 2 (1924).

Holländer, F., *Wege zu Kraft und Schönheit*, film book for *Wege zu Kraft und Schönheit: Ein Film über modernen Körperkultur in sechs Teilen*, directed by Wilhelm Prager. ([n.p.-n.d.).

Isherwood, C., *Goodbye to Berlin*, London: Hogarth Press, 1940.

Ixmann, 'Die Zwickelkontrolle,' in *Lachendes Leben*, Heft 12 (1933).

Kantorowicz, 'Die allegeneinen Wirkungen des Lichtluftbades,' in Anonymous, *Lichthunger-Lichtheil: Die Lebenskrafte der Luft und Sonne, dargestellt von Sechszehn Antoren*, Stuttgart: Verlag Lebenskunst-Heilkunst, 1924.

Kästner, W., *Kampf der Lichtfreunde gegen die Dunkelmänner*, Berlin: Verlag W. Kästner [1910].

—— *Nacktsport*, Berlin: Verlag W. Kästner [1911].

—— *Ruf an die Frauen!*, Berlin: Verlag W. Kästner [1912].

—— 'Koedukation und Nacktkultur,' in Hugo Peters, ed., *Revolution und Nacktkultur*, Dresden: Verlag der Schönheit, 1919.

Kawerau, S., 'Körperkultur und Familie,' in *Der Leib Urania*, Heft 1 (1924).

Kessler, G.H., *Tagebücher 1918–1937*, edited by Wolfgang Pfeiffer-Belli, Frankfurt: Im Insel-Verlag, 1961.

Kinskofer, F., 'Das Ethos der Nacktheit,' in Manfred Berg, ed., *Die Wahrheit um den Körper: Ein Aufruf zur Selbstbesinnung!*, Stuttgart: Karl Haug Verlag, 1927.

Kirner, A., 'Der große Plan für die Münchener Freikörperkulturverbände,' in *Das Freibad*, Heft 4 (1930).
Klotz, E., 'Das Geheimnis der griechischen Schönheit,' in *Die Schönheit*, Heft 6 ([1911]).
Knobling, A., 'Fkk-Politik von Morgen,' in *Das Freibad*, Heft 11 (1931).
Koch, A., 'Arbeitergymnastik,' in *Die Freude*, Heft 6 (June, 1925).
—— 'Gymnastiksystem oder freie Körperbildung,' in *Der Leib Urania*, Heft 1 (1925).
—— 'Religion und freie Körperkultur,' in *Der Leib Urania*, Heft 1 (1926).
—— 'Schamgefühl und Körperkultur,' in *Der Leib Urania*, Serie 3, Heft 2 (1926).
—— 'Die kulturpolitischen Hintergrunde,' in *Das Freibad*, Heft 8 (1931).
—— *Die Nacktkulturparadies von Berlin*, Leipzig: Oldenburg Verlag, 1933.
Koschyk, R., 'Wesen und Daseinsberechtigung der Freikörperkultur,' in *Deutsche Fkk*, Heft 5 (1934).
Kreuzberg, 'Ein Erfolg des Luftbades,' in Anonymous, *Lichthunger-Lichtheil: Die Lebenskrafte der Luft und Sonne, dargestellt von sechszehn Autoren*, Stuttgart: Verlag Lebenskunst-Heilkunst, 1924.
Kurella, A., 'Körperseele/Drei Briefe,' in *Der Leib Urania*, Heft 1 (1924).
Küster, K., 'Nackt-Photographien,' in Wilhelm Kästner, *Kampf der Lichtfreunde gegen die Dunkelmänner*, Berlin: Verlag W. Kästner [1910].
—— 'Die Wichtigkeit der Haut,' in Wilhelm Kästner, *Kampf der Lichtfreunde gegen die Dunkelmänner*, Berlin: Verlag W. Kästner [1910].
—— 'Die Frau als Erzieherin,' in Wilhelm Kästner, *Ruf an die Frauen!* Berlin: Verlag W. Kästner [1912].
Lachendes Leben, 'Wir erteilen Rat und Auskunft!,' Heft 1 (1933).
—— 'Wir erteilen Rat und Auskunft!,' Heft 2 (1933).
Laurer, R., 'No Title,' in *Die Freude*, Heft 3 (1923).
—— in *Sonnenland*, Heft 10 (1930).
Der Leib Urania, 'Das Luftbad in der Kindererziehung,' Heft 8 (1926).
Lennhoff, R., 'Weiblicher Körper und Leibesübungen,' in *Das Freibad*, Heft 1 (1929).
Look, F., Wie denken Sie über die Nacktkultur?,' in *Figaro*, Heft 1 (1933).
Luda, G., 'Der Einfluß des Sonnenlichtes auf die Zirkulation und verschiedene Krankheiten,' in Wilhem Kästner, *Kampf der Lichtfreunde gegen die Dunkelmänner*, Berlin: Verlag W. Kästner [1910].
Lux, 'Moral and Nacktheit,' in *Deutsch Hellas*, Serie 2, Heft 1 (n.d.-[1908]).
Mann, T., *Two Stories: Unordnung und frühes Leid & Mario und der Zauberer*, edited by William Witte, New York: Rinehart & Company, 1959.
Merrill, F. and M., *Among the Nudists: The Sincere Experiences of a Young American Couple in the Nudist Centers of Europe*, New York: Garden City Press, 1931.

Muche, K., 'Luftbad und Sittlichkeit,' in Anonymous, *Lichthunger-Lichtheil: Die Lebenskrafte der Luft und Sonne, dargestellt von sechszehn Autoren*, Stuttgart: Verlag Lebenskunst-Heilkunst, 1924.

Mühlhause-Vogeler, T., 'Körperfreude,' in *Das Freibad*, Heft 6 (1925).

—— *Freie Lebensgestaltung: Ein Beitrag zur Neuformung des Lebens-Stiles*, Egestorff: Robert Laurer Verlag, 1926.

—— 'Die Stellung der Frau in Freikörperkultur,' in *Sonne ins Leben*, Heft 4 (April, 1928), p. 2.

—— 'Neues Leben durch Freikörperkultur,' in *Lachendes Leben*, Heft 12 (1930), 2.

—— 'Robert Laurer: Der Werber für die Idee der Freikörperkultur,' in *Lachendes Leben*, Heft 10 (1932).

Nickel, E., 'Von der Schönheit des Frauenkörpers!,' in Wilhelm Kästner, *Ruf an die Frauen!*, Berlin: Verlag W. Kästner [1912].

Oberländer, H., 'Von der Bedeutung des Freiluftlebens,' in *Sonne ins Leben*, Heft 1 (1928).

Pahncke, W., ed., *Geschichte der Körperkultur: Eine Auswahlbibliographie deutschsprachiger Veröffentlichungen,* Veröffentlichungen der Bibliothek der deutschen Hochschule für Körperkultur, 1967.

Parmlee, M., *Nudism in Modern Life: The New Gymnosophy*, new revised edition, New York: Alfred A. Knopf, 1931.

Peters, E., *Menschen in der Sonne: Die Heilkraft des Luft- und Sonnenbades, rationelle Körperpflege durch Luft, Licht und Sonne*, Berlin-Neuenhagen: Volkskraft Verlag [1913].

—— *Menschen in der Sonne: Die Heilkraft des Luft- und Sonnenbades, rationelle Körperpflege durch Luft, Licht und Sonne*, second edition, Stuttgart: Alfred Heyder Verlag, Volkskraft Verlag, 1935.

Peters, H., ed., *Revolution und Nacktkultur,* Dresden: Verlag der Schönheit, 1919.

Pudor, H., *Katechismus der Nackt-Kultur: Leitfaden für Sonnenbäder und Nacktpflege*, Berlin-Steglitz: H. Pudor Verlag, 1906.

—— *Nacktkultur, Erstes Bändchen: Allgemeines; Fußkultur*, third edition, Berlin-Steglitz: H. Pudor Verlag, 1906.

—— *Nacktkultur, Zweites Bändchen: Kleid und Geschlecht; Bein und Becken*, Berlin-Steglitz: H. Pudor Verlag, 1906.

—— *Nacktkultur, Drittes Bändchen: Die Probleme des Lebens und der Zeugung*, Berlin-Steglitz: H. Pudor Verlag, 1907.

—— *Mutternot!*, Langensalza: Hermann Beyer & Söhne, 1917.

—— *Mein Leben: Kampf gegen die Juda für die arische Rasse*, Leipzig: Dr. Heinrich Pudor Verlag, 1939.

Reichert, K., *Vom Leibeszucht und Leibesschönheit: Bilder aus dem Leben des Bundes für Leibeszucht*, Berlin: Verlag Deutsche Leibeszucht, 1940.

Reichstein, W., 'Freikörperkultur und Volksgemeinschaft,' in *Deutsche Fkk*, Heft 2 (1933).
Reinsch, H.H., 'Die Sonne als Heilfaktor,' in *Das Freibad*, Heft 1 (1929).
Reissner, K., 'Die hygienische Notwendigkeit,' in Manfred Berg, ed., *Die Wahrheit um den Körper: Ein Aufruf zur Selbstbesinnung!*, Stuttgart: Karl Haug Verlag, 1927.
Reith, F., 'Freikörperkulturprozeß in Danzig,' in *Das Freibad*, Heft 6 (1930).
Remarque, E.M., *Im Westen Nichts Neues*, Berlin: Propyläen-verlag, 1929.
Renatus, 'Der Kampf ums Licht,' in Wilhem Kästner, *Kampf der Lichtfreunde gegen die Dunkelmänner* Berlin: Verlag W. Kästner [1910].
—— 'Körper und Geist,' in *Die Freude*, Heft 12 (1925).
Reuters, 'Nudists are set to rally' (Berlin), 13 March 2002.
Rieck, H., 'Nacktheit als Kulturankläger,' in *Das Freibad*, Heft 6 (1931).
Rubbe, C., 'Die Frau,' in Wilhelm Kästner, *Ruf an die Frauen!* Berlin: Verlag W. Kästner [1912].
Schirrmeister, P., 'Wie legen wir Luftbader an?,' in Anonymous, *Lichthunger-Lichtheil: Die Lebenskrafte der Luft und Sonne, dargestellt von sechszehn Autoren*, Stuttgart: Verlag Lebenskunst-Heilkunst, 1924.
Schmidt, H., 'Grundsätzliches und Erfahrungen über den Zusammenhang von Freikörperkultur und Gemeinschaftsleben,' in *Der Leib Urania*, Serie 3, Heft 10 (1927).
—— 'Die Befreiung des Körpers,' in *Figaro*, Heft 7 (1928).
Dr Schmidt-Blankert, 'Mein erstes Luftbad,' in Wilhelm Kästner, *Kampf der Lichtfreunde gegen die Dunkelmänner*, Berlin: Verlag W. Kästner [1910].
Schönberger, Fr., 'Winke für die Benutzung des Luft- und Sonnenbades,' in Anonymous, *Lichthunger-Lichtheil: Die Lebenskrafte der Luft und Sonne, dargestellt von sechszehn Autoren*, Stuttgart: Verlag Lebenskunst-Heilkunst, 1924.
Schulte, R.W., *Körper-Kultur Versuch einer Philosophie der Leibesübungen*, Munich: Verlag Ernst Rheinhardt, 1928.
Schulze, B., 'Rechtfertigung,' in Charly Sträßer, ed., *Jugendgelände: Ein Buch von neuen Menschen*, Rudolstadt: Der Greifenverlag zur Rudolstadt, 1926.
Scott, G.R., *The Commonsense of Nudism: Including a Survey of Sun-Bathing and 'Light Treatments,'* London: T. Werner Laurie, LTD., 1934.
Seber, M., 'Die kulturellen Grundlagen,' in Manfred Berg, ed., *Die Wahrheit um den Körper: Ein Aufruf zur Selbstbestimmung!*, Stuttgart: Karl Haug Verlag, 1927.
Seitz, J.M., *Die Nacktkulturbewegung: Ein Buch für Wissende und Unwissende*, Dresden: Verlag der Schönheit, 1923.
—— *Die Nacktkulturbewegung: Ein Buch für Wissende und Unwissende*, Dresden: Verlag der Schönheit, 1925.

—— *Soll man lachen oder weinen? Ein Spiegel der Prüderie*, Egestorff Robert Laurer Verlag, 1925.

Selth, J., *Alternative Lifestyles: A Guide to Research Collections on Intentional Communities, Nudism and Sexual Freedom*, Westport: Greenwood Press, 1985.

Simon, E., 'Das nationale Wohl in den Händen der Frau,' in *Hellas*, Serie 1, Heft 6 ([1907]).

Solterer, F., 'Die Moral und Unmoral der Nacktheit,' in *Lachendes Leben*, Heft 13 (1926).

Sonnenland, 'Die Einheitsfront marschiert!,' Heft 2 (1931).

—— Heft 1, *Sonderausgabe: Mutter und Kind Sonniger Nacktheit* (1931).

Sonniges Land, 'Alt-Sparta,' Heft 4 (1931).

Strange, J., *Adventures in Nakedness*, New York: Alfred A. Knopf, 1934.

Sträßer, C., ed., *Jugendgelände: Ein Buch von neuen Menschen*, Rudolstadt: Der Greifenverlag zur Rudolstadt, 1926.

—— 'Der neue Kurs,' in *Das Freibad*, Heft 5 (1931), 81.

—— 'No Title,' in *Das Freibad*, Heft 7 (1931).

—— 'Ein Kardinal und acht Bischöfe,' in *Das Freibad*, Heft 10 (1931).

—— 'Neutzeitliche Freikörperkultur,' in *Sonniges-Land*, Heft 7 (1931).

Strassmann 'Der Wert des Lichtbades vom wissenschaftlichen Standpunkt,' in Wilhelm Kästner, ed., *Nacktsport*, Berlin: Verlag W. Kästner [1911].

Stube, F., 'Deutsche Frauen,' in *Lachendes Leben*, Heft 3 (1925).

Surén, H., *Der Mensch und die Sonne*, Stuttgart: Dieck and Co., 1924.

—— *Mensch und Sonne: Arisch-olympischer Geist*. Berlin: Verlag Scherl, 1936.

Sutoris, T., 'Gesunde Mutter und gesundes Volk! Mehr Sonne-Mehr Licht! Bestrahlung werdener und stillender Mütter,' in *Figaro*, Heft 10 (1928).

Teßmann, R., 'Der volkswirtschaftliche Wert der Freikörperkultur,' in *Das Freibad*, Heft 12 (1929).

Ungewitter, R,. *Die Nacktheit in entwicklungsgeschichtlicher, gesundheitlicher, moralischer und künstlicher Beleuchtung*, Stuttgart: Im Selbstverlag des Herausgebers, 1907.

—— *Nackt: Eine kritische Studie*, Stuttgart: Verlag Richard Ungewitter, 1909.

—— *Kultur und Nacktheit: Eine Forderung*, Stuttgart: Verlag Richard Ungewitter, 1911.

—— *Nacktheit und Kultur: Neue Forderung*, Stuttgart: Verlag von Richard Ungewitter, 1913.

—— *Nacktheit und Aufstieg: Ziele zur Erneuerung des deutschen Volkes*, Stuttgart: Verlag Richard Ungewitter, 1920.

—— *Nacktheit und Moral: Wege zur Rettung des deutschen Volkes*, Stuttgart: Verlag Richard Ungewitter, 1925.

Vahle, H., *Zielskisse der Freikörperkultur: Ein Leitfaden für Leibeszucht und gesundes Leben*, Wallen: Polverlag, 1932.

van Zyl, U., 'Der sprechende Körper,' in *Das Freibad*, Heft 10 (1931).
von Gaggern, E., 'Briefe zur ethischen Revolution,' in *Figaro*, Heft 3 (1929).
von Hauff, *Das Freibad*, Heft 4 (1931).
Wahr, K., 'Nacktheit und Sittlichkeit,' in *Deutsch Hellas*, Serie 2, Heft 1 ([1908]).
Warnecke, K., 'Komm und Sieh!,' in *Lachendes Leben*, Heft 5 (1932).
Warneyer, 'Ist Betätigung des Nacktsports ein Ehescheidungsgrund?,' in *Figaro*, Heft 10 (1929).
Weide, A., *Verjüngung absolut*, Freie Stadt Danzig: Selbstverlag des Verfassers, 1929.
Weidemann, M., 'Neudeutscher Idealismus,' in *Die Freude*, Heft 1 (1923).
—— 'Wichtige Mitteilungen der Schriftenleitung,' in *Die Freude*, Hefte 4-5 (1923).
—— 'Zum Geleit!,' in *Licht-Land*, Folge 1 ([n.d.]).
—— 'Körperkultur und Kultur,' in *Die Freude*, Heft 6 (1925).
—— *Deutsches Baden: Ein Führer zur Freude, Schönheit und Gesundheit*, Egestorff: Robert Laurer Verlag [1926].
—— *Wege zur Freude. Gesammelte Aufsätze und Bilder*, Egestorff: Robert Laurer Verlag, 1926.
Weschke, F., 'Erziehung zum Schönheitserkennen,' in *Licht-Luft-Leben* supplement to *Die Schönheit*, Heft 6 ([1919]).
zum Adlersthum, A.P., 'Schönheit und praktische Nacktkultur,' in *Lachendes Leben*, Heft 5 (1927), 12.
—— 'Der Weg zum Helotentum in der Freikörperkulturbewegung: Ein trubes Kapitel aus der Geschichte der Bewegung,' in *Figaro*, Heft 17 (1929).

Unpublished Dissertations and Masters' Theses

Calvo, E.-M., 'Die Nacktkultur-Bewegung- historische Entwicklung und ideologische Grundlagen,' unpublished thesis, Universität Tübingen, 1981.
Fritzen, F., 'Gesünder Leben: Die Lebensreformbewegung und deutsche Gesellschaft, 1900–2000,' Ph.D. diss. Universität Frnakfurt, Frankfurt am Main, forthcoming.
Hurley, M.C., 'A Comparative Study of the Legal Response to Public, Social Nudity in the United States and West Germany,' unpublished paper, Saint Louis School of Law, 1983.
Krüger, F., 'Die Lebensreform-Bewegung und Naturismus in Göttingen: Die wechselvolle Entwicklung der organisierten Freikörperkultur in der Weimarer Zeit und im Nationalsozialismus,' unpublished thesis, Universität Göttingen, 1999.
McEwen, B., 'Model City, Moral Choices: Sexuality in Red Vienna,' Ph.D. diss., University of California, Los Angeles, forthcoming.

Mai, A., 'Von "Sonnenanbetern" und "Lichtgläubigen": Ein Beitrag zu einer Geschichte der Freikörperkultur,' Wissenschaftliche Arbeit zur Zulassung für Staatsexamen in Frühjahr 1997, Universität Konstanz.
Oettel, G., 'Freikörperkulturbewegung und Sexualerziehung,' unpublished thesis, Universität Münster, 1972.
Ritter, D., 'Der deutsche Verband für Freikörperkultur als Anschlussorganization des deutschen Sportbundes,' unpublished thesis, Universität Tübingen, 1986.
Ross, C., 'Building a Better Body: Nudism, Society, Race and the German Nation, 1890–1950,' Ph.D. diss., University of Missouri, 2003.
Williams, J.A., 'Giving Nature a Higher Purpose: Back-To-Nature Movements in Weimar Germany, 1918–1933,' Ph.D. diss., University of Michigan, 1996.
Zinn, H., 'Die deutsche Freikörperkultur als soziale Bewegung,' unpublished thesis, Berlin, 1967.

Secondary Sources

Abrams, L., and Harvey, E., *Gender Relations in German History: Power, Agency and Experience from the Sixteenth Century to the Twentieth Century*, Durham: Duke University Press, 1997.
Albisetti, J., *Secondary School Reform in Imperial Germany*, Princeton: Princeton University Press, 1983.
Alkemeyer, T., *Körper, Kult und Politik: Von der 'Muskelreligion' Pierre de Coubertins zur Inzenierung von Macht in den Olympischen Spielen von 1936*, Frankfurt: Campus Verlag, 1996.
Allen, A.T., *Feminism and Motherhood in Germany 1800–1914*, New Brunswick: Rutgers University Press, 1991.
Andritzky, M. and Rautenberg, T., eds, *'Wir sind nackt und nennen uns "Du"....': Von Lichtfreuden und Sonnenkämpfern, eine Geschichte der Freikörperkultur*, Gießen: Annabas Verlag Günther Kämpf KG, 1989.
Ariès, P. and G. Duby, eds *A History of Private Life*, translated by Arthur Goldhammer, vol. 1, *From Pagan Rome to Byzantium* by Paul Veyne, ed. Cambridge: Belknap Press, 1987.
Bergen, D., *Twisted Cross: The German Christian Movement in the Third Reich*, Chapel Hill: University of North Carolina Press, 1996.
Bergmann, K., *Agrarromantik und Großstadtfeindschaft*, Meisenheim am Glan: Verlag Anton Hain, 1970.
Bloch, M., *The Royal Touch: Sacred Monarchy and Scrofula in England and France*, translated by J.E. Anderson, London: Routledge & Kegan Paul, 1973.
Bourke, J., *Dismembering the Male: Men's Bodies, Britain and the Great War*, Chicago: University of Chicago Press, 1996.
Bridenthal, R., Grossmann, A., and Kaplan, M., eds, *When Biology Became*

Destiny: Women in Weimar and Nazi Germany, New York: Monthly Review Press, 1984.
Browning, C., *Ordinary Men: Reserve Police Battalion 101 and the Final Solution in Poland*, HarperPerennial: New York, 1993.
Bryson, B., *Neither Here Nor There: Travels in Europe*, New York: Avon Books, 1992.
Buchholz, K., Latocha, R., Peckmann, H., Wolbert, K., eds, *Die Lebensreform: Entwürfe zur Neugestaltung von Leben und Kunst um 1900*, vol. 1, Darmstadt: Verlag Häuser, 2001.
Burleigh, M., and Wippermann, W., *The Racial State: Germany 1933–1945*, Cambridge: Cambridge University Press, 1991.
Canning, K., 'The Body as Method? Reflections on the Place of the Body in Gender History,' in *Gender & History* 11 (November 1999).
Chickering, R., *We Men Who Feel Most German: A Cultural Study of the Pan-German League, 1886–1914*, Boston: George Allen and Unwin, 1984.
Chytry, J., *The Aesthetic State: A Quest in Modern German Thought*, Berkeley: University of California Press, 1989.
de Grazia, V., *How Fascism Ruled Women: Italy, 1922–1945*, Berkeley: University of California Press, 1992.
Dominick III, R.H., *The Environmental Movement in Germany: Prophets and Pioneers, 1871–1971*, Bloomington: Indiana University Press, 1992.
Eley, G., *Reshaping the German Right: Radical Nationalism and Political Change after Bismarck*, Ann Arbor: University of Michigan Press, 1980.
Evans, R.J., *The Feminist Movement in Germany, 1894–1933*, London and Beverly Hills: SAGE Publications, 1978.
—— *Death in Hamburg: Society and Politics in the Cholera Years 1830–1910*, Oxford: Clarendon Press, 1987.
Fisher, P., *Fantasy and Politics: Visions of the Future in the Weimar Republic*, Madison: University of Wisconsin Press, 1991.
Foucault, M., *The Care of the Self*, translated by Robert Hurley, New York: Vintage Books, 1990.
—— *The History of Sexuality: An Introduction*, translated by Robert Hurley, New York: Vintage Books, 1990.
Fout, J., ed., *German Women in the Nineteenth Century: A Social History*, New York: Holmes and Meier, 1984.
Frecot, J., 'Die Lebensreformbewegung,' in Klaus Vondung, ed., *Das wilhelminische Bildungsbürgertum: Zur Sozialgeschichte seiner Ideen*, Göttingen: Vandenhoek & Rupprecht, 1976.
Frevert, U., 'The Civilizing Tendency of Hygiene: Working-Class Women under Medical Control in Imperial Germany,' in John C. Fout, ed., *German Women in the Nineteenth Century, a Social History*, New York: Holmes and Meier, 1984.

—— *Women in German History: From Bourgeois Emancipation to Sexual Liberation*, translated by Stuart McKinnon-Evans, New York: Berg Publishers, 1997.
Friederich, O., *Before the Deluge: A Portrait of Berlin in the 1920s*, New York: HarperCollins, 1995.
Fritzsche, P., *Germans Into Nazis*, Cambridge: Harvard University Press, 1998.
Gallagher, C., and Laqueur, T., eds, *The Making of the Modern Body: Sexuality and Society in the Nineteenth Century*, Berkeley: University of California Press, 1987.
Gay, P., *The Bourgeois Experience: Victoria to Freud*, vol. 1, *Education of the Senses*, New York: Oxford University Press, 1984.
—— *The Bourgeois Experience: Victoria to Freud*, vol. 2, *The Tender Passion*, New York: Oxford University Press, 1986.
Gelately, R., *The Gestapo and German Society: Enforcing Racial Policy, 1933–1945*, Oxford: Clarendon Press, 1991.
—— *Backing Hitler: Consent and Coercion in Nazi Germany*, Oxford: Oxford University Press, 2001.
Gelately, R., and Stoltzfus, N., eds, *Social Outsiders in Nazi Germany*. Princeton: Princeton University Press, 2001.
Goldberg, A., *Sex, Religion and the Making of Modern Madness: The Eberbach Asylum and German Society, 1815–1849*, New York: Oxford University Press, 1999.
Gosmann, U., 'Der reinliche Körper,' in Löneke, R., and Spieker, I., eds, *Reinliche Leiber- Schmutzige Geschäfte: Körperhygiene und Reinlichkeitsvorstellungen in zwei Jahrhunderten*, Göttingen: Wallstein Verlag, 1996.
Grisko, M., ed., *Freikörperkultur und Lebenswelt: Studien zur Vor- und Frühgeschichte der Freikörperkultur in Deutschland*, Kassel: Kassel University Press, 1999.
Grossmann, A., *Reforming Sex: The German Movement for Birth Control and Abortion Reform, 1920–1950*, Oxford: Oxford University Press, 1995.
Hall, A., *Scandal, Sensation and Social Democracy: The SPD Press and Wilhelmine Germany, 1890–1914*, Cambridge: Cambridge University Press, 1977.
Harrington, A., *Reenchanted Science: Holism in German Culture from Wilhelm II to Hitler*, Princeton: Princeton University Press, 1996.
Hau, M., *The Cult of Health and Beauty in Germany: A Social History*, Chicago: University of Chicago Press, 2003.
Herf, J., *Reactionary Modernism: Technology, Culture and Politics in Weimar and the Third Reich*, Cambridge: Cambridge University Press, 1984.
Hermand, J., *Old Dreams of a New Reich: Volkisch Utopias and National Socialism*, translated by Paul Levesque and Stefan Soldovieri, Bloomington: Indiana University Press, 1992.

Hermann, B., *Arbeiterschaft, Naturheilkunde und der Verband der Volksgesundheit, 1880–1918*, Frankfurt am Main: Peter Lang, 1990.

Hobsbawm, E., *The Age of Empire: 1875–1914*, New York: Vintage Books, 1987.

Horn, D.G., *Social Bodies: Science, Reproduction, and Italian Modernity*, Princeton: Princeton University Press, 1994.

Jelavich, P., *Berlin Cabaret*, Cambridge: Harvard University Press, 1993.

Kaplan, M., *Making of the Jewish Middle Class: Women, Family, and Identity in Imperial Germany*, Oxford: Oxford University Press, 1991.

Kelly, A., *The Descent of Darwin: The Popularization of Darwinism in Germany, 1860–1914*, Chapel Hill: University of North Carolina Press, 1981.

Kerbs, D., and Reulcke, J., eds, *Handbuch der deutschen Reformbewegungen, 1880–1933*, Wuppertal: Peter Hammer Verlag, 1998.

Kershaw, I., *Hitler: 1889–1936 Hubris*, New York: Norton, 1998.

König, O., *Nacktheit: Soziale Normierung und Moral*, Opladen: Westdeutscher Verlag, 1990.

Koerber, R., 'Freikörperkultur,' in D. Kerbs, and J. Reulcke, eds, *Handbuch der deutschen Reformbewegungen, 1880–1933*, Wuppertal: Peter Hammer Verlag, 1998.

Koonz, C., *Mothers in the Fatherland: Women, Family and Nazi Politics*, New York: St Martin's Press, 1987.

Krabbe, W., *Gesellschaftsveränderung durch Lebensreform: Strukturmerkmale einer sozialreformerischen Bewegung in Deutschland der Industrialisierungsperiode*, Göttingen: Vandenhoeck & Ruprecht, 1974.

—— 'Naturheilbewegung,' in D. Kerbs and J. Reulcke, eds, *Handbuch der deutschen Reformbewegungen, 1880–1933*, Wuppertal: Peter Hammer Verlag, 1998.

Krüger, A., 'Zwischen Sex und Zuchtwahl. Nudismus und Naturismus in Deutschland und Amerika,' in Norbert Finzsch and Hermann Wellenreuther, eds, *Liberalitas: Festschrift für Erich Angermann zum 65. Geburtstag*, Stuttgart: Franz Steiner Verlag, 1992.

Lächele, R., 'Protestantismus und *völkische* Religion im deutschen Kaiserreich' in U. Puschner, W. Sachmitz and J.H. Ulbricht, eds, *Handbuch zur völkischen Bewegung, 1871–1918* (Munich: K.G. Saur, 1996).

Laqueur, T., *Making Sex: Body and Gender from the Greeks to Freud*, Cambridge: Harvard University Press, 1990.

Linke, U., *German Bodies, Race and Representation After Hitler*, New York: Routledge, 1999.

Linse, U., 'Die Lebensreformbewegung,' in *Archiv für Sozialgeschichte*, Band XVII (1977).

—— 'Sexualreform und Sexualberatung,' in D. Kerbs, and J. Reulecke, eds, *Handbuch der deutschen Reformbewegungen, 1880–1933*, Wuppertal: Peter Hammer Verlag, 1998.

—— 'Sonnenmenschen Unter der Swastika: Die FKK-Bewegung im Dritten Reich,' in, Michael Grisko, ed., *Freikörperkultur und Lebenswelt: Studien zur Vor- und Frühgeschichte der Freikörperkultur in Deutschland*, Kassel: Kassel University Press, 1999.

McAleer, K., *Dueling: The Cult of Honor in Fin-de-Siècle Germany*, Princeton: Princeton University Press 1994.

Marchand, S., *Down From Olympus: Archeology and Philhellenism in Germany, 1750–1970*, Princeton: Princeton University Press, 1996.

Mosse, G., *Crisis of German Ideology: Intellectual Origins of the Third Reich*, New York: Grosset & Dunlap, 1964.

—— *Nationalism and Sexuality: Respectability and Abnormal Sexuality in Modern Europe*, New York: Howard Fertig, 1985.

—— *The Image of Man: The Creation of Modern Masculinity*, New York: Oxford University Press, 1996.

Muller, D., ed., *Let's GO Germany*, New York: St Martin's Press, 1999.

Naiman, E., *Sex in Public: Early Soviet Ideology: The Incarnation of Early Soviet Ideology*, Princeton: Princeton University Press, 1997.

Nolan, M., *Visions of Modernity: American Business and The Modernization of Germany*, Oxford: Oxford University Press, 1994.

Pfitzer, G., *Der Naturismus in Deutschland, Österreich und die Schweiz*, Band 1, Hamburg-Altona: Richard Danehl's Verlag, 1964.

Planert, U., *Antifeminismus im Kaiserreich: Diskurs, soziale Formation und politische Mentalität*, Göttingen: Vandenhoek & Rupprecht, 1998.

Proctor, R.N., *Racial Hygiene: Medicine Under the Nazis*, Cambridge: Harvard University Press, 1988.

—— *The Nazi War on Cancer*, Princeton: Princeton University Press, 1999.

Prost, A., 'The Family and the Individual,' in P. Ariès, and G. Duby, eds, *History of Private Life*, translated by Arthur Goldhammer, vol. 5, *Riddles of Identity in Modern Times*, A. Prost, and G. Vincent, eds, Cambridge: Belknap Press, 1991:

Puschner, U., Sachmitz, W. and Ulbricht, J.H., ed, *Handbuch zur völkischen Bewegung, 1871–1918* Munich: K.G. Saur, 1996.

Regin, C., *Selbsthilfe und Gesundheitspolitik: Die Naturheilbewegung im Kaiserreich, 1889–1914*, Stuttgart: Franz Steiner Verlag, 1995.

Reinecke, T., ' "Das heilge Feuer," eine katholische Zeitschrift, 1913–1931,' in U. Puschner, W. Sachmitz and J. H. Ulbricht, eds, *Handbuch zur völkischen Bewegung, 1871–1918*, Munich: K.G. Saur, 1996.

Repp, K., *Reformers, Critics and the Paths of German Modernity: Anti-Politics and the Search for Alternatives, 1890–1914*, Cambridge: Harvard University Press, 2000.

Rothschuh, K.E., *Naturheilbewegung, Reformbewegung, Alternativbewegung*, Stuttgart: Hippokrates Verlag, 1983.

Salmi, H., *Imagined Germany: Richard Wagner's National Utopia*, New York: Peter Lang, 1999.
Scheider, U., 'Nacktkultur im Kaiserreich,' in V. Puscher, W. Sachmitz, and J.H. Ulbricht, *Handbuch zur 'Volkischen Bewegung' 1871–1918*, Munich: K.G. Saur, 1996.
Schultz, A. and Gostomczyk, A., ' "Arbeiter gehören unter die Brause": Öffentliche Brause-und Wannenbäder in Hannover,' in Adelheid von Saldern, ed., *Wochenend und schöner Schein: Freizeit und modernes Leben in den Zwanziger Jahren, das Beispiel Hannover*, Berlin: Elefanten Press, 1991.
Spitzer, G., *Der deutsche Naturismus: Idee und Entwicklung einer volkserzieherischen Bewegung im Schnittfeld von Lebensreform, Sport und Politik*, Ahrensburg Bei Hamburg: Verlag Ingrid Czwalina, 1983.
Stern, F., *Kulturpessimismus als politische Gefahr: Eine Analyse nationaler Ideologie in Deutschland*, Bern: Alfred Scherz Verlag, 1963.
Stollberg, G., 'Die Naturheilvereine im Deutschen Kaiserreich,' *Archiv für Sozialgeschichte* 28 (1988).
Tavenrath, S., *So wundervoll sonnengebräunt: kleine Kulturgeschichte des Sonnenbadens*, Marburg: Jonas Verlag, 2000.
Toepfer, K., *Empire of Ecstasy: Nudity and Movement in Weimar German Body Culture, 1910–1935*, Berkeley: University of California Press, 1997.
Überhorst, H., *Vergangen nicht vergessen: Sportkultur im deautschen Osten und im Südentland von den Anfängen bis 1945*, Düsseldorf: Droste Verlag, 1992.
Usbourne, C., *The Politics of the Body in Weimar Germany: Women's Reproductive Rights and Duties*, Ann Arbor: University of Michigan Press, 1992.
van der Will, W., 'The Body and the Body Politic as Symptom and Metaphor in the Transition of German Culture to National Socialism,' in Taylor, B. and van der Will, W., eds, *The Nazification of Art: Art, Design, Music Architecture and Film in the Third Reich*, Winchester: Winchester Press, 1990.
van der Will, W., and Burns, R., *Arbeiterkulturbewegung in der Weimarer Republik: Eine historisch-theoretische Analyse der kulturellen Bestrebungen der sozialdemokratisch organisierten Arbeiterschaft*, Frankfurt: Ullstein Materialien, 1982.
Verhey, J., *The Spirit of 1914: Militarism, Myth and Mobilization in Germany*, Cambridge: Cambridge University Press, 2000.
von Saldern, A., ed., *Wochenend und schöner Schein: Freizeit und modernes Leben in den Zwanziger Jahren, das Beispiel Hannover*, Berlin: Elefanten Press, 1991.
Walter, F., Denecke, V., and Regin, C,. *Sozialistische Gesundheits- und Lebensreformverbände*, Bonn: Verlag J.H.W. Dietz, 1991.
Weindling, P., *Health, Race and German Politics Between National Unification and Nazism, 1870–1945*, Cambridge: Cambridge University Press, 1989.

Wolff, C., *Magnus Hirschfeld: A Portrait of a Pioneer in Sexology*, London: Quartet Books, 1986.

Ziegler, U., *Nackt unter Nackten: Utopien der Nacktkultur, 1906–1942*, Berlin: Verlag Dirk Nishen, 1990.

Index

Aachen, 18, 45
abortion, 145, 148
abstinence, 157
acclimatization, 92, 94
   see also inurement
Adler, Viktor, 23
Adlerstum, Anton Putz zum, 27
Adoa Workers Bank, 53
airbath, 80, 93–8, 119
   advice, 94, 95
   as curative, 97
   as prophylactic, 96
   facilities, 94
   nose, 116
   see also luftbad
airbathing, 81, 99, 160
airgarment, 113
alcohol, 25, 78, 93
alcoholism, 163
Allen, Ann Taylor, 133
Alltag, 130
alte Kämpfer, 25
American, 161
Americanism, 163
anarchists, 62
anemia, 75, 86, 97
Anhalt, 51
anthrax, 73
antibiotics, 73
anti-Semitism, 90, 151
Apollo, 153
Arbeitsgemeinschaft der Bünde deutscher Lichtkämpfer, 24, 43

Arbeitsgemeinschaft für Freikörperkultur und Lebensreform, 55
Arbeitsgemeinschaft für Volksgesundung, 42
Arbeitersportkartell, 52
Arheilgen, 36, 37, 39
Aristotle, 7
art, 104
   see also Europe, Greece
arteriosclerosis, 86
Artern, 22
Aryan, 110, 111, 117, 134, 157
Aryanness, 154
Asa, 48
Ascension Day, 21
Assyrians, 88
Athens, 107
Austria, 46

Babylonians, 88
baccanalia, 106
Bad Harzburg, 93
Baden, 51
Baker, Josephine, 15
Baltic Sea, 22, 56, 110
Bandmann, 40, 41
bathing, 116
Baunatal, 51
Bavaria, 51
beauty, 112
   body and, 8, 105, 112, 163
   creation of, 112–15, 126, 135

desire for, 154
feminine, 124
nature and, 112
need for, 83, 137
ugliness, 124
Bebel, August, 107
Becker, Max, 77
Berlin
  Moabit, 58, 59
  morality Leagues in, 46
  nudism in, 18, 19, 22, 42, 168
  nudist movie in, 55
  police, 41, 47
  Schund und Schmutz Commission, 47
Bescheke, H., 52
Besser, K., 4
Bink-Ischeuschler, Margarete, 130
birth control, 145, 148
birth control pill, 162
Bishop Keppler, 21
Bismarck, 2
Blätter für Volksgesundheitpflege, 77
Blanck, 45
blood
  ailments, 74, 75, 97
  'alkali blood', 97
  composition, 124
  supply, 133
  variety, 77
body,
  as historical problem, 6, 7
  as marriage criterion, 148, 149, 150
  balanced, see trinity
  concealment, 149
  conception, 67
  de-eroticization of, 135, 138–44
  denigration, 3, 5
  honesty, 154
  ideal, 115, 117
  oil, 116
  reform, 163
  sex differences in, 140
  shame, 114, 117, 126, 127, 128, 132
  women's 128

Bölsche, Wilhelm, 61
Bracht, 41
Brauns, Walter, 104
Braunschweig, 51
breasts, 114
  see also women
breeding, 1, 83, 121, 146, 153, 156
Bremen, 18
Breslau, 22, 40
British, 161
Brünner, M A,19
Bückmann, Karl, 50, 54, 55, 56, 113
Bund der Licht und Sportfreunde, 53
Bund der Lichtfreunde, 18, 22
Bund der Sonnenfreunde zu Leipzig, 28, 30
Bund für Leibeszucht
  as Nazi organization, 27, 50, 52, 146
  composition, 28, 30, 32
Bund für Mutterschutz, 134
Bund für Sonnenfreunde, 53
Burgdorf, 51
bürgertum, 32
burgfrieden, 62

calisthenics, 96, 105
Call to Women!, 122, 125
Cannstatt, 21
capitalism, 121, 163, 165
Cardinal Faulhaber, 40
Cassel, 18
  see also Kassel
catarrh, 97
Catholic Church, 40, 45, 49, 88
  campaign against nudism, 40
Catholics, 2, 62
Celle, 51
Center Party, 40, 42, 59
  politicians, 45
chauvinism, 122
Chemnitz, 55
children, 131
chlorophyll, 89

chlorosis, 86, 97
cholera, 74
Christianity
  as degenerative force, 104, 117
  campaigns against nudism, 22
  view of body, 7, 10, 104, 163
circumcision, 151, 152, 153
classical modernity, 164
clothing, 79, 149
  as concealment, 153
clothing reform, 147
communism/communists, 55, 57, 60, 63, 147
conservatives, 62
consumerism, 162
corsets, 123, 124, 158
cowpox, 74

Darmstadt, 161
Damascke, Adolf, 111
Damm, Karwilli, 51, 161
Dannenberg, 51
Danube River, 21
Danzig, 35, 36, 41, 75, 90
Darmstadt, 36, 39
Darré, Ricardo Walther, 49, 53, 56, 79, 154, 164
darwinism, 61, 126, 129, 134, 136, 145
Das Freibad, 23, 24, 84, 121
Denecke, Viola, 60
Der Leib Urania, 23
Der Lichtfreund, 19
Der Mensch und die Sonne, 23
Deutsch Hellas, 23, 59
Deutsche Gymnastik, 79
Deutsche Leibeszucht, 10, 13, 116
Deutsch Nationaler Volkspartei, 41
Deutscher Bund für Freikörperkultur, 161
Deutscher Lichtfreunde, 28, 29
Deutscher Verband für Freikörperkultur, 161
de Fontanel, Ruy, 125
de Rheidt, Celly, 45

Diaderma, 116
Die Freude, 23, 26
diphtheria, 75
district attorney, 45
dizziness, 85
Dornzhausen, 24
Dortmund, 55
Dresden, 7, 54, 78
Düsseldorf, 22

Earth, 93
East Germany, 57
education reform, 147
Egestorff, 26, 27, 52
Egyptians, 88
Elberfeld, 18
Emskanal, 22
Enlightenment, 70, 122
English, 146
English Gardens, 168
Eos, 47
epilepsy, 121
Erfurt, 18, 55
eroticism, 13, 135
Essen, 55
eugenicists, 145
eugenics, 11, 121, 145–7, 153, 155, 162
Eulau, 22
Europe, 110
  art, 104
  culture, 105
  sex and, 147
evolution, 145

factories, 121, 122
Fallada, Hans, 33
Fallingsbostal-Soltau, 51
family, 80, 131, 143, 156
fanaticism, 25
feeble-mindedness, 121
feminism, 133, 145, 147
Fichte, 41
Figaro
  campaigns against, 23, 47, 48, 49

content of, 44
  Laurer affair and, 27
  letters to, 141
  sunbathing, 92
Finckh, K., 97
Finns, 154
Finus, 36
First World War,
  end of, 46, 97, 141
  German collapse in, 10, 105
  Robert Laurer in, 26
  nudism before, 20, 25, 45, 122
  nudism after, 20, 21, 57
  soldiers, 20, 142
Fischer, Georg, 53, 54
Fleischhack, Marianne, 124
Foucault, Michel, 153
France, 111
Franke, Änne, 127
Fränzel, 51, 52, 55
free-love, 134, 157
Freiburg, 46
Freikörperkultur, 12, 13
  see also nudism
Freikörperkulturbund Leipzig, 53
Freiluftbund, 22, 52
Freiluftbund Harburg, 51
French literature, 111
Freud, Sigmund, 144
Freya Bund, 19
Frick, Wilhelm, 49, 50, 52, 53
Fuchs, A.F., 23
Fuchs, Hans, 36, 124
Fulda, 40

Galen, 7
gender, 121
genetics, 145
genitals, 90, 135, 140
gentiles, 151, 153
George, Henry, 111
Gera, 22
germ plasma, 90
germ theory, 73–7

Germans
  ancient, 88, 109–112, 154, 167, 168
  culture, 105
  degeneration and, 97, 105
  modern, 105, 109
  new, 10
German Empire, 19
  see also Kaiserreich
German Hellas, 111
German League for the Encouragement of Naked and Free Swimming, 15
German Lebensreformbewegung, 78
Gesolei, 7
Geschichte der Kunst des Alterthums, 103
Gestapo, 49, 53, 54, 55, 57
Giessen, 18
Gifhorn, 51
Gleichschaltung, 32, 50
Glogau, 18
Glüsingen, 51, 52
Goebbels, Joseph, 55
Goethe, 110, 111
Göring, Hermann, 49, 50, 52
gout, 86, 97
Graaz, Hans, 60, 61, 115
Grass, Günter, 33
Greater Germany, 55, 80
Greece
  aesthetics, 103, 128
  ancient, 100–109, 112, 117
  art, 103, 104
  body in, 103, 104, 108
  climate, 111
  collapse, 104
  culture, 105, 108, 111
  Greeks, 111, 115
  language, 103
  morality, 106
  nakedness, 103, 104, 105, 108
  nudist view of, 105
  Olympics, 104
  see also Hellas
Greeks, *see* Greece

Green Party, 165
greensickness, *see* chlorosis
Grisko, Michael, 57
Groß Gerau, 38, 39
Groß, Walther, 49, 53, 54, 56, 165
Große Anfrage, 41
Gröttrup, Bernhard, 27
Grunewald, Max, 84
gymnasium, 103

Haffstrom, 21
Hamburg
  great cholera outbreak, 73
  nudism in, 18, 22, 26, 28, 161
  nudist movie in, 55
  police, 47, 52
Hannover, 51, 52
Harburg, 51
Harz, 93
Hau, Michael, 11
Hauptamt für Volksgesundheit, 78
headaches, 85, 91
heart disease, 96, 97
Heitsch, Walter, 22, 26, 41, 104
Hellas, 103, 110, 117
Hellas Loge, 18, 19
hemmorrhoids, 97
hemoglobin, 89
Hess, Rudolf, 49, 53, 54
Hesse, 36, 39, 40, 51
Heydrich, Reinhard, 56, 57
Hildesheim, 18
Hillig, Hugo, 22, 25
Himmler, Heinrich, 56, 164
Hitler, Adolf, 13, 162
Hitler Youth, 79
Hördemann, 79
holism, 69, 70
homeopathy, 69–72, 79, 80, 163
  influence on nudism, 85, 93
homosexuality, 52, 148
  see also Hans Surén
housing reform, 147
humanism/humanists, 105

hygiene, 77, 78
  exhibition, 78
  Week of Health, 78
Hygiene Museum, 7, 78
hyperinflation, 25
hypnosis, 69

Ilsenburg, 93
immunization, 74
industrialization, 2, 11, 121
influenza, 75, 97
inurement, 96, 167

Jadeöl, 116
jewish, 153, 157
Jews, 62, 143, 151, 152, 168
Jungborn, 93
Jungmann, 38, 39
Jurke, Ida, 61
Just, Adolf, 93, 94

Kaiser, 28, 33, 46, 62
Kaiserreich, 10, 11, 45, 57, 78, 164
Kampfbund für deutsche Kultur, 50
Kampfring für völkische Körperkultur, 50, 52, 53
Kästner, Wilhelm, 19, 32, 63, 112, 115, 122
  marriage and, 153
  views on women, 123, 125, 132, 133
Kassel, 51
'Katholik', 138
Kelly, Alfred, 61
Kehrt zur Natur zurück, 94
kidneys, 97
Koch, Adolf,
  as a socialist, 58, 59, 60, 65
  as propagandist, 54
  exhibitions, 50
  schoolchildren and, 25
  setbacks, 41
König, Oliver, 11
Königsberg, 21

Index

Körperkultur, 9, 93, 105, 106, 146, 155
  Greeks and, 104
Körperpflege, 84
Kösen, 18
Krabbe, Wolfgang, 57
Kreuzberg, 97
Krüger, Arnd, 57
Kulturkampf, 2
Kulturmenschen, 84
Kürsinger, Martin, 55
Küster, Dr Konrad, 19, 86

Lachendes Leben, 23, 27, 48, 91, 129, 152
Lake Motzen, 41, 42
Lamarckian, 126
land reform, 147
Landkreis Teltow, 139
Lanz-Liebenfels, Jörg, 46
Laroche, 37
Latin, 103
Laurer, Robert
  as bourgeois, 32
  as publisher, 48
  conflict with, 26–7
  sex and, 157
Lebensrefom, 44, 56, 59, 133,
  idea of, 1
  influence on nudism, 146, 147
  milieu, 3, 25, 163
  see also Life-Reform
leib, 146
leibeszucht, 146
Leipzig, 16,
  Gestapo, 55
  morality committee, 48,
  nudist leagues in, 22, 28, 32, 53, 54
leisure time, 162, 167
Letters from Switzerland, 111
Liberal Democrats, 62
lichtbad, 115
Lichtenberg, 19
Lichtschulheim, 52
Licht Luft Gesellschaft, 22
Licht Luft Leben, 25

Licht und Sonne, 53
Liegnitz, 18
Life-Reform, 3, 5, 23, 81, 165
Life-reformers, 163, 165
Liga für freie Lebensgestaltung, 23, 28, 31, 51, 53, 161
Loge des aufsteigenden Lebens 17, 18, 19, 23
Look, Fred, 24
love match, 121, 145, 163
Ludenscheid, 18
Ludwigshafen, 41, 58
Lübeck, 28, 29, 30
Lüneburg, 51, 55
Lüneburger Heide, 22, 26
Luftbad, 23, 80, 87, 93, 113, 115
  effects, 158
  first experience, 127
  oil and, 117
  see also airbath
Lutheran Church, 42
  campaign against nudism, 42–4
Lutheranism, 40
luxury, 121
Lycurgus, 107

Magdeburg, 22
Maier, K., 80, 81
malnourishment, 97
Mann, Thomas, 33
Mannheim, 41
marriage, 146, 148–59
  arranged, 158
  companionate, 121, 156
Marxism, 53–59
Marxists, 28, 53, 67, 148
masturbation, 98, 142
mechanism, 72
Mecklenburg, 51, 56, 109
medical science, 67–70, 72, 73, 75, 77
  see also Schulmedezin
medicine, 67
  alternative, 68, 78, 80, 163
  Jewish influence, 128
Melcher, 41

Mendel, Gregor, 145
menstruation, 91
mercury, 89, 90, 93
Merseburg, 22
modernity, 2, 164
  crisis of, 11
monarchy, 64
Monboddobund, 19
morality leagues, 45, 47
  Lutheran, 45
  Protestant, 45
  Weissen Kreuz, 47
Mosse, George, 8
Möve Lodge, 53
Muche, Klara, 139
Munich, 17, 18, 22, 25, 55, 56
  nudism and, 168
Mühlhauser-Vogeler, Therese, 25, 26, 32, 144, 155, 167
Münster, 18, 22

Nackt: Eine kritische Studie, 45
Nacktbaden, 51
Nacktkultur, see nudism
Natürliche Leibeserziehung, 55
Naumburg, 22
National Socialism, 62
  see also Nazism
naturism, 70
Nazism, 166
  ban on nudism, 10, 15, 26, 27, 49, 50
  morality, 50
  Nazi State, 10, 12, 49
  Nazis 10, 12, 13, 15, 63
  nudism in, 28, 32, 53–57, 65
  party, 25, 50
  promotion of nudism in, 56, 58
  seizure of power, 32, 56
Neanderthal, 126
Neckar River, 21
nervousness, 91, 95, 97
neurasthenia, 97
Neusonnlandbund 19, 22
nicotine, 25

Nordic, 65, 111, 136, 154, 156
North Sea, 62, 110
nudism
  activity, 4
  campaigns against, 35–53
  communal, 40, 117, 155
  dance, 11
  doctors and, 69
  effects, 9, 10
  families in 29–32, 80
  goal, 1
  ideology, 3, 5, 12, 16, 18
  Marxism and, see Marxism
  marriage and, 156–9
  mixed gender, 135, 137, 139
  Nazism and, see Nazism
  politics of, 57–61
  soldiers, 20
  sports, 124, 128, 133, 153
  terms, 12, 13
Nudo-Natio, 18, 19
Nuremburg, 18

obesity, 97
Offenbach, 39
Office of Racial Policy, 53, 54
Oldenstadt, 51
Olympics,
  ancient, 104, 109
  germanic, 110
  imagery, 105
  modern, 7
  nakedness and, 104
onanism, see masturbation
Opladen, 22
Orplid, 36–9, 161

Paragraph 138, 50
Paragraph 175, 52
Paragraph 184, 45
Pasteur, Louis, 73
Pastor Küßner, 22
Peeping Toms, 38
Pelagianer Bund, 23
penal code, 45

penis, 151, 152
Persians, 116
Peters, Emil, 89, 90, 97
Pfitzer, Georg, 57
Philistinism, 2,
politics, *see* nudism
polio, 75
Pope, 49
postmodern, 164
Potsdam, 42
Prießnitzbund, 80
prostitution, 106, 157
Protestants, 62
prudery, 55
Prussia, 21, 41, 42
   East, 162
   State Parliament, 40
psychoanalysis, 144
psychology, 144
Pudor Heinrich, 16, 17, 32
   airbath and, 94, 96
   as ideologue, 110, 112
   natural elements and, 71
   on women, 128

Quedlinberg, 18
quicksilver, *see* mercury

rachitis, 85
racial hygiene, 145, 146, 151, 155, 156
racial theory, 126
racism, 11, 151
Rees, 18
reformhäuser, 163
Regin, Cornelia, 60
Rehbergen, 42
Reichsarbeitsgemeinschaft für naturgemäße Lebens- und Heilweise, 78
Reichsbahn, 55
Reichsbauernführer, *see* Darré, Ricardo Walther
Reichsbund für Körperkultur, 139
Reichssportführer von Tschammer und Osten, 54

Reichstein, Wolfgang, 62
Reichsverband für Freikörperkultur, 50
Reichsverband für Körperkultur, 36
Renaissance, 111
rheumatism, 86, 88, 97
Rhine, 47
rickets, 84, 86, 97
Rikli, Arnold, 88
Rollier, A., 77
Romans, 103, 111
Romantics, 98, 103
Rome, 103
Rothschuh, Karl, 93
Rousseau, 70, 93
Rubbe, Clara, 130, 132
Russian Civil War, 141

SA, 80
SD, 56, 57
SS, 54, 55, 56, 57, 80, 153
Saxony, 32
Scheffer, Gertrud, 31
Scheffer, Heinrich, 31
Schiller, 110
Schleswig, 28
Schmidt-Blankert, Frau Dr, 119
schulmedezin, 70, 72, 79
Schulte, Werner, 138
Schwarz, Dr, 18
Schund und Schmutz, 45, 46, 47
scrofula, 85, 86, 97
Sea of Japan, 141
Second World War, 13, 54, 58, 79
   postwar era, 13, 16, 73, 103, 161, 162
   pre-war era, 161
Seitz, J.M.
   airbath and, 95
   clothes and, 114
   nakedness and, 137
   natural elements and, 71
   nudist clubs and, 17, 24, 25
   ugliness and, 113
   women and, 127
   works by, 44
sex, 139

Senator Richter, 52
Senator von Allworden, 52
Severing, 58
sex, 122, 144, 147, 158
　as source of problems, 19, 139, 140, 144, 147
　drive, 140, 144, 154
　education, 27, 133, 155
　emancipation, 133
　excitement, 138, 139, 140
　fantasy, 140, 144
　intercourse, 49, 141, 157
　mistakes, 151
　pleasure, 138, 147, 148, 152
　pre-marital, 157
　secretions, 138
　suppression, 138
　twentieth century and, 155
sex reform, 23, 120, 121, 122, 133, 145–148
　nudism and, 155
sexism, 122
sexology, sexologists, 133, 147
sexual revolution, 162
sexuality, 11
shame, see body
Siberia, 141
Sicherheitsdienst, see SD
Silesia, 22
skin
　as breathing organ, 84, 86, 115
　as protector, 84
　color, 84, 116, 133
　healthy, 84, 115, 116
　importance of, 84–7
　symbol of health, 85
smallpox, 74
soap, 116
Social Democrats, 2, 62
socialism, 59, 163, 165, 166
Socialist Workers' Youth, 37
socialists, 59, 60, 147
soldiers, see First World War
Solon, 107

Sonnenbad, 80, 87, 98, 117, 127, 158
　see also sunbath
Sonnenkinder Sonnenmenschen, 24
Sonnenland Egestorff, 51
Spandrel Edict (Zwickerlass), 41
Sparta, 106, 107, 108, 132
Sparte für proletarische Lebensreform und Freikörperkultur, 60
spectral analysis, 76
Spöktal, 51
Spreehagen, 42
Stettin, 22
Stöcker, Helene, 134
Strassmann, 89
Sträßer, Charly, 26
Stube, Fritz, 124, 129
Stunde Null, 161
Stuttgart,
　nudism in, 16, 17, 18, 21
　nudist facility, 80
　nudist film in, 55
　Richard Ungewitter and, 76
sunbath, 80, 87, 88, 90–3
　oil and, 117
　women and, 91
sunbathing, 77, 81, 99, 160
sunburn, 91
sunlight, 85
　composition, 89
Surén, Hans, 13
　airbath and, 95
　as critic, 109
　as homosexual, 139
　as Nazi, 154
　background, 32
　bathing and, 116
　breasts and, 114
　circumcision, 153
　Greeks and, 111, 116
　marriage and, 149
　natural elements and, 71, 113
　nudist ideology and, 63, 104, 107, 110, 136, 139, 146, 154
　oil and oiling, 92
　plenipotentiary, 79

viewing nakedness and, 143
women and, 129
workers and, 166, 167
works by, 44, 54
Swabia, 162
Swedes, 154
Sylt, 62
syphilis, 74, 90, 93, 151

Tacitus, 111
Taylorism, 167
tea, 93
temperance, 3, 163
Thies, Fritz, 100
Third Reich, 28, 51, 78
Thuringia, 32, 51
tobacco, 78
Toepfer, Karl, 11
Torgau, 22
tourism, 162
Treubund für aufsteigendes Leben, 18, 26
trinity, 3, 5
tubercular, 151
tuberculosis
    consequence of clothing, 86
    creation, 75
    curing, 87
    infection, 73, 74, 84, 85, 121
    preventing, 77, 79, 86, 164
    sign of degeneration, 60
Turnvater Jahn, 79

Uelzen, 51
Ufa, 24, 43
ugliness, *see* beauty
Ungewitter, Richard, 32
    anti-Semitism and, 90
    application, 25
    bathing and, 116
    communism and, 59
    darwinism and, 61
    eroticism and, 47
    influence, 76
    Lanz-Liebenfels and, 46
    on masturbation, 142
    on women, 127, 130
    opponents of, 113
    racism and, 63
    state action against, 45, 46
    theorist, 89, 136
    works by, 44, 54, 142
United states, 163, 168
Urania, 23, 62
urbanization, 2, 121
utopianism, 11

Vahle, Hans, 5, 105, 116
Vatican, 49
vegetarianism, 69, 142, 163
venereal disease, 151, 157
Veldes, 88
Venus, 153
Venus de Milo, 43
Verband der Volksgesundheit, 60
Verband für Leibesübungen, 161
Verein Deutsche Volksheilkunde, 80
Verein für Volkshygiene, 77
Vereinigung für neuzeitliche und gesunde Lebensgestaltung, 53
Verhey, Jeffrey, 62
Verjüngung absolut!, 35, 75
Versailles, Treaty of, 35
victorianism, 164
Vienna, 55
Virchow, Robert, 73
vitalism, 69
van Zyl, Ursula, 137
Volk, 121, 128
    exhausted, 62, 121
    healthy, 124
    image of, 164
    improving, 56, 76, 80, 154, 162
    marriage and, 148
    reforming, 1, 64, 83, 106, 165
    whole, 9, 64
Volksgemeinschaft, 61–4
Volksgesundheit, 50
von Hauff, 50
von Humboldt, Alexander, 103

von Tschammer und Osten, 165
von Winterfeld, 41
voyeurs, voyeurism 11, 38, 127, 142

Wagner, Gerhard, 78, 164
Wagner, Richard, 103
Walhalla Lodge, 18, 19
Walter, Franz, 60
Wandervögel, 142
Ways to Strength and Joy, 43
  see also *Wege zur Kraft und Schönheit*
Wege zur Kraft und Schönheit, 23, 24
  see also *Ways to Strength and Joy*
Weide, Adolf, 5, 35, 36, 75, 88, 116
Weidemann, Magnus, 3, 22, 26, 32, 62, 63
Weimar Republic, 10, 11, 164
  birth of, 15, 53
  cabarets, 15, 43, 45, 46
  criticism of, 109
  fiction, 62
  freedom in, 46
  Marxism in, 56
  morality campaigns, 35
  Nazi reaction to, 49
  nudism in, 20, 22, 26, 28, 36, 57, 58, 64
  police, 36
  public health efforts, 7, 78
  struggle against nudism, 39
Wesermünde, 55

West Germany, 161, 162
Wieland, 110
Wilhelm II, 1, 46
Wilhelmine, 105, 109, 165
Wilke, Hermann, 139
Winckelmann, J.J., 103, 104
Wollin, 22
women,
  as mothers, 120, 127, 128, 129, 131, 156
  beauty, 114, 123
    see also beauty
  breasts, 114, 124
  clothing, 93
  emancipation, 121, 133
  men and, 156
  nudism and, 19, 30–2, 81, 119, 120
  physical construction, 123
  Russian, 141
  status, 132
  workers, 60, 121
working class, 137, 167
Wündrich, Hermann, 161
Württemburg, 51, 79

youth movement, 165

Zivilisationsmenschen, 84
Zucht, 146
Zumbusch, Dr, 18
Zwickerlass, see Spandrel Edict

Lightning Source UK Ltd.
Milton Keynes UK
UKHW021832121122
412014UK00014B/246